Sport, Difference and Belonging

This book combines historical and ethnographic components in examining the ideas about human variation subscribed to by coaches, commentators and sportspeople themselves. The book begins by interrogating the idea of the 'impulsive' black sportsman (and the 'impulsive' black male more generally), documenting how it came into being and gathered momentum throughout the course of British history. Drawing on the work of Paul Gilroy and Ian Hacking, the author then investigates whether such racio-logical ideas figure within the everyday behaviours of a group of young footballers.

Presenting an original ethnographic study undertaken at Oldfield United, a semi-professional football club situated in London, Rosbrook-Thompson explores how raciological ideas (and other notions of human variation) shape the self-understandings of the club's players and thereby influence the possibilities for action available to them. In conceptualising the sense of 'feeling alien' experienced by club personnel – in relation to mainstream discourses of nationhood, to politics, to the basic functioning of the nation-state and, at bottom, to the qualifications and requirements of British citizenship – *Sport, Difference and Belonging* challenges the ability of the cosmopolitan tradition to make sense of contemporary urban phenomena and seeks to develop the sociological concept of denizenship.

This book will be of interest to academics and students in the fields of sociology and social policy, 'race' and ethnic studies, urban studies, the ethnographic method and the sociology of sport. It may also appeal to politicians, policy makers and those working in the field of 'race relations'.

James Rosbrook-Thompson is currently a Lecturer in Sociology at Anglia Ruskin University. He holds a PhD in Sociology from the London School of Economics and Political Science (LSE).

Routledge Advances in Ethnography

Edited by Dick Hobbs
University of Essex and
Geoffrey Pearson
Goldsmiths College, University of London

Ethnography is a celebrated, if contested, research methodology that offers unprecedented access to people's intimate lives, their often hidden social worlds and the meanings they attach to these. The intensity of ethnographic fieldwork often makes considerable personal and emotional demands on the researcher, while the final product is a vivid human document with personal resonance impossible to recreate by the application of any other social science methodology. This series aims to highlight the best, most innovative ethnographic work available from both new and established scholars.

Sport, Difference and Belonging

Conceptions of human variation in British sport

James Rosbrook-Thompson

Routledge
Taylor & Francis Group

LONDON AND NEW YORK

First published 2013
by Routledge
2 Park Square, Milton Park, Abingdon, Oxon, OX14 4RN

Simultaneously published in the USA and Canada
by Routledge
711 Third Avenue, New York, NY 10017

Routledge is an imprint of the Taylor & Francis Group, an informa business

British Library Cataloguing in Publication Data
A catalogue record for this book is available from the British Library

Library of Congress Cataloging-in-Publication Data
Rosbrook-Thompson, James.
Sport, difference and belonging : conceptions of human variation in
British sport / James Rosbrook-Thompson.
    p. cm. – (Routledge advances in ethnography)
    1. Sports–Social aspects–Great Britain. 2. Sports and state–Great
Britain. 3. Discrimination in sports–Great Britain. 4. Racism in
sports–Great Britain. 5. Athletes, Black–Great Britain.
6. Blacks–Great Britain–Social conditions. 7. Soccer–Great Britain.
8. Great Britain–Race relations. I. Title.
    GV706.5.R67 2012
    306.4830941–dc23   2012024980

ISBN: 978-0-415-62655-2 (hbk)
ISBN: 978-0-203-10260-2 (ebk)

Typeset in Times New Roman and Gill Sans
by Cenveo Publisher Services

Printed and bound in Great Britain by the MPG Books Group

Contents

Acknowledgements

First I would like to thank Paul Gilroy and Dick Hobbs for the help and guidance that they issued so generously in supervising the study. My intellectual debt to Paul is as obvious as it is heavy – without his work this project would have been inconceivable – but I am equally grateful for the patience he has shown in light of my hapless attempts to keep pace with his thinking, in all its breadth and originality. Dick's incisive comments have been invaluable, and I owe special thanks for his help with clarity and the business of writing in general; as a novice ethnographer I couldn't have asked for a more accomplished and formidable guide. I must extend thanks to Richard Giulianotti and Chetan Bhatt, who examined the study as a doctoral thesis, for their insightful criticisms and suggestions and the kind spirit in which they were offered. I must also thank the people kind enough to have read various sections of the study and who offered such helpful commentary and constructive criticism. On this score I am grateful to Suki Ali, Claire Alexander, Doyle Hooper, Max Pettigrew, Amy Hinterberger and Gary Armstrong. I am especially appreciative of the latter whose collegiality has been unstinting and his comments both measured and astute. I offer thanks to the personnel of Oldfield United Football Club, particularly 'Geoff', 'Gianni' and 'Deborah' for giving me such a thorough apprenticeship in the world of semi-professional football. I marvel at their commitment and generosity. My partner, Caesara Gill, has withstood far more in the way of irregular hours and uneven moods than may reasonably have been expected of her. Her love and understanding are more than I deserve. Finally I must thank Ann Thompson and Ralph Feiner. To the former I owe a debt both too weighty and of too many dimensions to enumerate here – thanks Mum!

Chapter 1

Introduction

People often express their ideas about 'race' through commentary on sport. Whether stood on the touchline, perched on a bar stool or reposed on the pundits' sofa, many tend to make sense of sporting performance by appealing to racial 'truth'. Examples, therefore, aren't hard to come by.

In 1991 the Chairman of Crystal Palace Football Club, Ron Noades, described the division of labour in the current Palace side to documentary-makers. 'The black players at this club lend the side a lot of skill and flair', said Noades, 'but you also need white players in there to balance things up and give the team some brains and some common sense' (Critical Eye 1991). In the aftermath of the documentary being aired, Palace striker Ian Wright reported Noades to the Commission for Racial Equality, though subsequently admitted to feeling ambivalent about the remarks of his Chairman: 'Later, I found out that he'd said a lot that was complimentary to black players, but those comments were edited out and only the bad things left in ... In hindsight, I may have overreacted' (Wright 1997: 111).

In 1954 Roger Bannister achieved a feat many had hitherto thought impossible: he ran a mile in under four minutes. Forty-one years later, in his capacity as both former athlete and distinguished neurologist, Bannister delivered a lecture on the athletic limits of the human organism to the British Association for the Advancement of Science. 'I am prepared to risk political correctness', he ventured, 'by drawing attention to the seemingly obvious but under-stressed fact that black sprinters and black athletes in general all seem to have certain natural anatomical advantages' (quoted in Hoberman 1997: 144). He then speculated as to whether these advantages consisted in the length of the heel bone and Achilles' tendon, levels of sub-cutaneous fat, and/or the elasticity of muscle fibres. Garth Crooks, a retired footballer of Jamaican ancestry, questioned the wisdom and veracity of Bannister's controversial address: 'I don't think it matters what the bio-logical conclusions are. It forges a distinction between black and white athletes which is unhealthy, unhelpful, and untrue' (quoted in Highfield, Berry and Harnden 1995).

On 20 April 2004, former manager of Manchester United and Aston Villa, Ron Atkinson, was co-commentating for ITV on Chelsea's Champions League fixture against Monaco. While viewers watched post-match analysis, microphones that should have been switched off once the broadcast from the stadium had concluded picked up the following remark made by Atkinson with regard to the performance of Chelsea defender Marcel Desailly: 'He's what is known in some schools as a fucking lazy thick nigger' (Prior 2004). Atkinson resigned on learning that his comments had been inadvertently broadcast in several parts of the Middle East, including Egypt and the United Arab Emirates.

Raciology and historical ontology – knowledge and power ethics

Debate surrounding the relationship between human variation and sporting performance is often snagged by arguments over which statements count as 'racist' and which as benign assertions of racial difference. In an attempt to move discussion beyond these considerations, this study employs Paul Gilroy's (2000) notion of 'raciology' to interrogate the notions of racial difference which circulate within British sport. Gilroy has defined raciology as 'the lore that brings the virtual realities of "race" to dismal and destructive life' (ibid: 11).[1] His definition allows us to posit 'race', racism and raciology in some relation to one another, as the study of racial lore requires a commitment to excavating the logic which underwrites this lore rather than marking regions where raciology shades into racism and/or identifying the threshold beyond which general assertions about 'race' become unacceptable by violating one moral code or another. All raciology represents racism in more or less encoded form, and, following Gilroy, specific raciological ideas should be treated as the result of generative processes which give shape and texture to the categories of 'race'.

In an attempt to see this commitment through, here I present the findings of historical and ethnographic investigations to show how specific raciological ideas subscribed to by coaches, commentators and sportspeople themselves, within specific settings, might be analysed critically. The study's historical component (contained in Part 1) centres on the raciological idea of the 'impulsive' black sportsman (and the 'impulsive' black male more generally). More specifically, I investigate how this idea came into being and gathered momentum throughout the course of British history via the pronouncements of various 'experts' and the institutionally sanctioned discourses with which they engage. The task is then to discover whether such raciological ideas gain traction within the everyday behaviours of a group of young footballers, an inquiry which takes the form of ethnographic research. More specifically, the study's ethnographic component (contained in Part 2) focuses on Oldfield United Football Club, a semi-professional club situated in London, and the conceptions of human difference endorsed by club personnel. It should be said, though, that while both of these components use sport to access people's ideas about human variation, it is these ideas that take centre stage in the forthcoming analysis. Though sporting occasions and institutions provide a forum for the expression of such ideas, the range of institutions whose traces can be found in them exceeds the bounds of sport. I hope to show that the key to understanding conceptions of human difference, whether these rely on 'race' or more complex formulations, seldom lies within the narrow confines of one institution or another.

Before I set about examining these conceptions I should describe the concepts and methods that are employed throughout the study. As well as Gilroy's conception of raciology, these include the method of historical ontology and the attendant axes of knowledge, power and ethics.

Historical ontology (Hacking 2002a) is a programme of inquiry that implores us to consult both the historical record and ethnographic data with particular questions in mind. Put simply, it is concerned with possible ways of being at different moments in time; more specifically, it is a strain of intellectual enquiry centring on the conditions of possibility of knowledge, human subjectivity and, taken together, on the possibilities for being. It was inspired by the cues taken by Michel Foucault in his reading of the works of Immanuel Kant, while the Canadian philosopher Ian Hacking has been instrumental in developing Foucault's conception into a systematic scheme of questioning. This lineage begs elaboration.

In the early 1960s Foucault translated Kant's *Anthropology* into French and was immediately taken with the probing questions it posed, if somewhat disappointed by Kant's responses to these questions.[2] The fact that Kant looked to anthropology to establish the limits of man's potential indicated an awareness that the lot of human nature was not fixed. The challenge was to understand how our human nature may evolve to shape the destiny of the human race. Foucault detected in Kant's arguments the possibility of a shift from the transcendental subject, which serves as the condition of possibility of all experience, to the subject conditioned by the specificities of historical, social and cultural circumstance (Allen 2003). This realisation provided the impetus for Foucault's archaeological and genealogical work (1970, 2002 [1972]) in which he analysed the bases of the human sciences, their substrata, and reflected on what made them possible as modalities of thought.[3] The importance of subjectivity to Kant's conception of anthropology, along with his assertion that anthropology and geography provided 'conditions of possibility' for all knowledge, also influenced Foucault's studies of the prison (1977 [1975]), the asylum (2000 [1961]; 2001 [1963]), and his related arguments with regard to governmentality and the disciplinary society (2007, 2008a).

It was reasoning on this plane that led Foucault to the study of the 'historical ontology of ourselves', a programme outlined in his 'What is

Enlightenment?' first published in Paul Rabinow's *The Foucault Reader* (1984). Here Foucault provides critical commentary on Kant's own answer to the question 'What is Enlightenment?' (Was ist Aufkläring?) as posed by the German periodical *Berlinische Monatschrift* in 1784. In his brief response Kant characterised enlightenment as a way out of the immaturity which impels us to accept someone else's authority to lead us when the use of our own reason would serve as a better guide. It was this characterisation, Foucault noted, that made Kant's critiques so urgent and necessary; for the use of legitimate reason to be assured, critique must define the conditions under which the use of reason is legitimate in order to determine what can be known, what must be done, and how the achievement of these tasks may shape the destiny of human kind. Consonant with his views on anthropology and geography – with 'inner knowledge' (of human subjectivity) and 'outer knowledge' (of man's place in nature) – each individual was responsible for his/her role in this overall process, as Kant located humanity's passage to a state of maturity within the broader evolution of human kind. In sum, Foucault glossed Kant's response into a point of departure for a critical mode of relating to contemporary realities:

> The hypothesis I should like to propose is that this little text (Kant's 'Was ist Aufkläring?') is located in a sense at the crossroads of critical reflection and reflection on history. It is a reflection by Kant on the contemporary status of his own enterprise ... it seems to me that this is the first time that a philosopher has connected in this way, closely and from the inside, the significance with respect to knowledge, a reflection on history and a particular analysis of the specific moment at which he was writing and because of which he was writing. It is in the reflection on 'today' as difference in history and as motive for a particular philosophical task that the novelty of this text appears to lie.
>
> (Foucault 1984b: 38)

Foucault's call for a 'permanent critique of ourselves' ends with a brief formulation of historical ontology and an enumeration of its three axes of knowledge, power and ethics.[4] He asks the following questions: 'How are we constituted as subjects of our own knowledge? How are we constituted as subjects who exercise or submit to power relations? How are we constituted as moral subjects of our own actions?' (ibid: 49). It is these questions that Ian Hacking has helped to generalise, develop and clarify in investigating how 'various concepts, practices, and corresponding institutions, which we can treat as objects of knowledge, at the same time disclose new possibilities for human choice and action' (Hacking 2002a: 4).[5]

Hacking argues that 'we constitute ourselves at a place and time, using materials that have a distinctive and historically formed organization' (ibid: 3). But he is not only concerned with how 'we' constitute ourselves; he has in mind all manner of constitutings. For Hacking, the role of institutions is crucial. Concepts, practices and ideas do not come into existence through the simple process of naming. Even the dutiful repetition of a newly created name will not suffice. Names gain in authority when they are used in specific settings and circumstances; not only when people enunciate, but also when they act. When they are repeated on the plantation or the touchline, at the dispatch box or in the psychiatric evaluation room, and when they order the practices of the slave owner, the coach, the politician or the psychiatrist, they begin to take on the character of an essence. In short, 'One needs usage within institutions' (Hacking 2002b: 8).

A characteristic set of questions might include: in which sentences are names and ideas used as objects of knowledge, who speaks these sentences, with what authority, in what institutional setting, in order to influence whom, and with what consequences for the speakers and subjects? These are the kind of specific questions that I have committed to answer, but before proceeding I should emphasise that these questions are informed by particular conceptions of knowledge, power and ethics.

It comes as no surprise that, drawing heavily on the work of Michel Foucault as it does, Hacking's scheme of historical ontology is sensitive to the issues of knowledge, power and ethics. Indeed, each represents one of the three cardinal axes, so integral to Foucault's ambitions, which have been preserved by Hacking's programme of investigation. Here I examine each in turn.

When dealing with the issue of knowledge, Hacking recognises that not all epistemological objects are of the same class or magnitude; they operate at different depths. To distinguish between various items of knowledge he borrows from Foucault the distinction between 'surface' and 'depth' knowledge. Items of surface knowledge, or *connaissance*, are the labels, theories, hypotheses and prejudices of scientists, psychiatrists and all those professing institutional expertise. Their assertions and statements can be revised in light of new 'evidence', but only make sense because embedded in a deeper framework of rules that determines which count as true or false in a specific domain. These frameworks Hacking calls depth knowledge, or *savoir*, because they contain those elemental rules without which the propositions of specialists in a given area would lack meaning or credence.

The stories told in Part 1 feature both classes of knowledge. At times it is possible to glimpse and even list the elemental principles – approaching the depth of *savoir* – which frame expert pronouncements at specific stages in history. At others we have access to only these pronouncements. However, without gauging the level of each and every item of knowledge in terms of its epistemological 'depth', I hope to have struck some balance between analysing surface hypotheses and the deeper set of postulates from which they draw their sense. In Part 2 the distinction between depth and surface knowledge is understandably more difficult to draw. That said, the ethnographic data garnered at Oldfield United is interrogated according to a similar set of ontological questions relating to how club personnel conceived self and others as objects of knowledge, together with the concepts, practices and possibilities for action attached to these processes of constitution.

Employing a Foucauldian notion of power, Hacking does not see forms of power as exerted by identifiable agents or authorities in the form of measures aimed at the exclusion or repression of passive recipients. But this isn't to say that any one person or group cannot dominate another. It means that authorities rely on the other terms in a power relation – including those controlled, criminalised, etc. – for mutual support and engagement, whether witting or unwitting. Power therefore operates through unowned configurations participated in by people 'on the ground', or as Foucault called it, 'power through which we constitute ourselves as subjects acting on others' (1984b: 351).

Foucault thus disapproved of attempts to uncover the overall strategy of individual people or institutions. He was interested in the immediate, short-term, professional and political tactics of various experts, specialists and technocrats, and how the cumulative effects of their efforts create new (or reinforce existing) possibilities for being; as we have seen, Hacking generalised this ethos of questioning to include not only possibilities for people's own sense of being, but also those possibilities which see certain names, ideas, kinds of people and methods of verification emerge at parti- cular moments in history. In more concrete terms, we might discuss how certain possibilities for self-constituting can empower some (at the expense of others) or how the anonymous power of 'psychiatric' or 'criminological' discourse features in specific processes of classifying people.

Hacking's conception of ethics is necessarily related. Again it has to do with the possibilities for constituting the self, along with other ideas and concepts, as objects of knowledge. In this case he is concerned with possible ways to be (un)ethical or (im)moral; in short, with the constituting of moral agents. With the creation of new classifications and greater epistemological clarity come new or more urgent measures for treating and controlling people. This shapes how people so classified or depicted as objects of knowledge are seen in ethical terms by both themselves and others. For example, new values can spring up around certain kinds of person which promote their surveillance, detainment, disciplining, etc.

In terms of the study's basic structure, I analyse in Part 1 the emergence of the 'impulsive', 'unpredictable' black male according to the precepts of historical ontology, charting the long, unfortunate and consequential history of this raciological idea. The resulting account attempts to explain how the raciological idea of the impulsive black male came into being and gained epistemological credence throughout the course of British history, wherever possible showing how the idea has been articulated through sport.

Chapter 2 describes the fundamental oppositions laid down by Plato and shows how these were elaborated by those who followed his line of thinking. It also explores how these oppositions found their way into descriptive works such as Pliny's *Naturalis Historia* and eventually into explorers' reports, such as Richard Hakluyt's *Principal Navigations*, penned at the dawn of British capitalist expansionism. In examining responses to the African body being ascribed the status of property, I argue that Cartesian and Newtonian axioms structured British justifications for the slaving industry and, more specifically, that this epistemological setting saw notions of impulse and instinct yoked more tightly to the immediate imperatives of British colonialism. The emergence of liberalism and the cosmopolitan ethic is documented, with particular attention paid to work of Locke and Kant (regarding the respective doctrines of liberalism and cosmopolitanism) and related concessions to discrimination and exclusion; the significance of German Romanticism and the abolitionist movement is also considered. As well as examining characteristic descriptions of the black pugilists who docked on British shores in the late eighteenth and early nineteenth centuries, the chapter describes how notions of instinct and impulse featured in nineteenth-century physical anthropology. Finally, the way in which concerns over 'race', gender and class were lumped together and collapsed into the metaphor of the impulsive, unruly crowd, again in response to the pressing demands of empire, is discussed.

Chapter 3 opens by examining the impact of Darwin's *Origin of Species*. It then explores how the acceptance of evolutionary theory altered conceptions of impulse and instinct, how such conceptions were treated by the emergent psychological sciences and Britain's colonial psychiatrists, and describes the way that these were brought to bear on both Africa's burgeoning independence movements and the experiences of those immigrating to Britain from her 'New Commonwealth'. The chapter then investigates how impulsivity figured in trans-Atlantic conversations taking place within the academic discipline of criminology in the 1970s and 1980s, while also arguing that this period witnessed a reappraisal of the role of instinct and impulse within British professional sport (again under the influence of developments in the United States). Moving towards the present day, the chapter analyses government and press reports on gun/knife crime and the disturbances of August 2011, their relation to sport, and demonstrates how these reports continually summon the impulsive black male into being. Part 1 ends with a consideration of how Foucault's axes of knowledge, power and ethics figure in the history of the 'impulsive' black sportsman.

In Part 2 I turn from the assessments and assertions contained in 'expert' knowledge towards the demotic order of an inner-city football club, Oldfield United FC. The turn from historical to ethnographic inquiry is motivated by a desire to see whether the totalising claims of raciology are subscribed to by a group of young urbanites. Do figures such as the 'impulsive' black male, created and sustained by various 'expert' and 'specialist' discourses, feature within the outlook of Oldfield United's players? And, if not, how do

these players approach the issue of human variation in appraising, classifying, and explaining the strengths and weaknesses of their teammates and
opponents, i.e. in constituting self and others as objects of knowledge?

In Chapter 4 I set the ethnographic scene, describing the physical
and socio-cultural setting of the club along with the people who make
it tick. This description begins with the particular district of London
wherefrom the club takes its name, providing demographic data, a sketch of
the local landscape and a brief history of the club. Discussion then moves
to the club's personnel: first, the board, and second, the players. It is
important to provide a detailed picture of the relationships that hold the
club together because, as argued in later chapters, it is these relationships,
along with an inventory of the local landscape, that frame and modulate the
methods of human classification employed by people at the club.

Before beginning to describe and analyse these conceptions, in Chapter 5
I consider how the diversity on show at Oldfield United FC might be
understood in sociological terms. Here I suggest that, rather than the raft of
existing formulations inspired by the cosmopolitan tradition, a sociological
notion of urban denizenship is best equipped to make sense of this diversity
and the way it was approached by Oldfield United's players. As the chapter
seeks to show, the concept of denizenship centres on a sense of feeling alien
in relation to discourses of nationhood and national politics, and a subsequent refusal to meet the requirements of citizenship; it should therefore
be understood as a strategy of survival for a growing number of contemporary urbanites. Also, recovering a theme explored in Part 1, I consider
how the tradition of cosmopolitanism continues to exclude certain 'types' of
people. As illustrated throughout Part 2, this exclusion is important in
creating the possibilities for being from which the denizen chooses in forging
a life as a resident alien.

In Chapter 6 I continue to analyse the conceptions of human difference
employed by Oldfield United's players. More specifically, I describe the
processes through which players classified people and the related manner in
which they rationalised the behaviour of self and others. As detailed later
in the chapter, the local underground economy (wherein many players
operated) had important implications for the way that players conceived
of human variation, with the issues of individual personality and qualitative
uniqueness being particularly influential. The chapter concludes by
considering how the conceptions of human difference espoused by club
personnel are oriented in relation to the study's three ontological axes of
knowledge, power and ethics.

In the study's final chapter, Chapter 7, I venture some limited conclusions
on the issue of raciology and the ways in which it is nourished and reproduced by its loyal adherents. I end by considering the study's strengths and
limitations, as well as the key implications of its findings.

Part I

The history of the 'impulsive' black sportsman

Chapter 2

Plato, property and humanity

In reading biographical material, listening to commentary and overhearing numerous conversations among sports enthusiasts, the 'black' sportsman, described as given to sudden 'instinctive' or 'impulsive' outbursts, is a figure that I (and many others will) have encountered on many occasions. In 2005 Arsene Wenger was asked to comment on the career of one of his former charges, French midfielder Patrick Vieira. He had this to say: 'He was rather impulsive and once he got annoyed he would react really quickly ... He will naturally tend to stay in his comfort zone, African-style. But when he is in a situation where he has to fight, he is stimulated' (quoted in Vieira and Beckerman 2005: 214–19).

More recently, on the Saturday 21 August 2010 edition of the BBC's *Match of the Day* programme, former Liverpool and Scotland defender Alan Hansen[1] gave his verdict on the performance of Arsenal's Theo Walcott, who had scored a hat-trick against Blackpool earlier in the day:

> What you're going to judge him on is not what he does well and does instinctively, it's when he's got time to think about it. That's the big criticism. When he's got time to think about what's happening, I think he struggles a bit ... When he's got time and space to pick out the right ball, he picks out the wrong ball. People have said that he's not got a footballing brain [here Hansen referred to comments made by former England winger Chris Waddle in March 2010] and if you've not got a footballing brain, you can't acquire one ... The big problem is, that when he's got time to think about things, he never ever picks out the right ball.

Writing in *The Guardian*, journalist Martin Kelner noted comically, 'Walcott has reignited the nature vs. nurture debate, currently being conducted on *Match of the Day* by noted behavioural geneticists Alan Shearer and Alan Hansen.' Ian Wright offered his opinion to *The Sun*, condemning Hansen's criticism of Walcott:

He [Walcott] gets slaughtered by Alan Hansen. Totally and unnecessarily insulted. He's told he cannot cross. How he cannot do this, isn't very good at that – and how, when he thinks too much, there are problems. For me, that's Hansen basically saying the lad is thick.

(Wright 2010).

An anonymous respondent to Kelner's article pointed up the undertones of the exchange:

I remember when managers refused to play Black players in goal, defence or even midfield because they apparently either didn't have the guts, grit, application or intelligence. They were only good enough as wingers apparently. Spot the difference between that rubbish and the Walcott thingy.

The idea of the impulsive/instinctive, unpredictable black male has a long and significant history. The following two chapters recount this story, but do not simply review the relevant literature, sifting gently through those historical documents which happen to mention impulse or instinct. To support this claim it is important to stress that my engagement with historical and contemporary sources is both conceptually and methodologically driven. The resulting analysis attempts to explain how the raciological idea of the impulsive black male appeared and then became credible as an object of knowledge within the course of British history, wherever possible showing how the idea has been articulated through sport. In this way what follows is an excavation of academic material, press reports, government publications and biographies, along with other relevant sources, which demonstrates how a single strain of raciology, within a particular setting, might be analysed critically. However, by focusing on institutionally sanctioned forms of expertise and the role they play in creating and sustaining raciological ideas, I do not wish to resign the study to the power of such 'expert' pronouncements. As the ethnographic observations contained in Part two reveal, the notions of human variation employed within sporting institutions – 'expert' in their own characteristic way – need not always partake of racio-logic.

Following Ian Hacking's prescriptions for historical ontology, the analysis presented here seeks to answer the following questions with regard to the 'impulsive' black male: By what processes and events did he become an item of raciological 'truth', an object of knowledge? Which institutional settings hosted these events and what were their methods of verification? How did these ideas find their way into descriptions of black sportsmen, their character and performances?

This isn't the first time that questions concerning 'impulsive'/'instinctual' tendencies and sporting institutions have been addressed in the context of sociological inquiry. If the analysis relayed here relies on Hacking for philosophical and methodological guidance, in sociological terms I hope it adds detail to Norbert Elias's theory of *The Civilizing Process* (1969). In bringing his theory to life, Elias (1987: ix) linked certain historical developments to the emergence of a European habitus, or 'the self-image and social make up of individuals'. He described how in post-medieval Europe standards regarding violence, sexual behaviour, bodily functions, table manners and forms of speech were gradually transformed by advances in thresholds of shame and repugnance. Key developments were increasingly exacting standards of court etiquette and the monopoly on the legitimate use of violence possessed by centralised modern states. His theory is relevant because of its reliance on notions of impulse and instinct and its focus on sport and leisure (Elias and Dunning 1986).

Discussing the malleable child, Elias spoke of 'instinctual tendencies' being constantly formed and transformed in and through relations with others: 'Only on the basis of such an instinctual dialogue with other people do the elementary, unformed impulses of the small child take on a more definite direction, a clearer structure' (Elias 1987: 26). His basic thesis concerning instinctive and impulsive drives is that children growing up in more 'advanced' societies are socialised into large networks of interdependency. Therefore, as the child grows up he is made aware of his role within such networks and the corresponding extent of his dependency on other networked people. As networks grow, webs of action become more complex, extensive and organised – hallmarks of the Civilising Process – so to execute his role successfully the individual must attune his conduct to that of others. In doing so he becomes accustomed, from infancy, to a highly regulated and differentiated pattern of self-restraint. For Elias, these patterns of restraint were given philosophical support by the emergence and hardening of *homo clausus* – or 'enclosed man' – as a dominant mode of self-consciousness. He argues that man has been enclosed within the confines of his own subjectivity ever since Descartes introduced the distinction between subject and object at the advent of modernity. This has meant an ever-widening gap between 'I' and 'we', inside and outside, self and society. Put simply, the gap results from an entrenched epistemological view of the subject, represented by the self standing in isolation, as opposed to the object, represented by the 'outside world' of people and things. Sport and leisure also have a role to play within the Civilising Process. According to Elias, sport acts as a site for the controlled decontrolling of strong emotions in public, with sporting standards of orderliness corresponding to thresholds of acceptable violence in wider society.

These assertions tally in general outline with the history of impulse and instinct presented here, though perhaps the role of these notions within Elias's theory of the Civilising Process lacks texture in relation to certain issues. This need for specificity through deeper and more targeted historical probing emerges if Elias's theory is dissected by Foucault's three axes.

The first issue regards the names and concepts through which a human's psychical functioning has come to be understood. Elias himself records that notions such as 'mind', 'soul', 'reason' and 'instinct' are 'not simply given by nature', that the sharp differentiation of psychical functions 'is a product of a socio-historical process' (Elias 1969: 34–5), and also that the 'biological disposition for impulse-control' is 'characteristic of the evolutionary break-through from the pre-human to the human level' (ibid: 61). In examining the role of these notions and supposed thresholds within broad civilising processes, we should, without rehearsing them here, ask a set of questions centring on specific names, labels and ideas, and specific institutional sites – wherever a society's place on the 'civilising' spectrum. Furthermore, we might ask how these labels feature in discourses of exclusion, criminalisa-tion, pathologisation, and how these discourses possess a moral dimension. In sum, we should be concerned with power and its more insidious, diffuse effects, beyond issues surrounding who in a given society has a monopoly on the legitimate use of violence.

With regard to Elias's notion of *homo clausus*, it is necessary to ask how this supposedly irresistible mode of self-awareness, and the broader epistemological setting it promotes – something approaching 'depth' knowledge – has laid down the conditions of truth and falsehood within which 'surface' knowledge is formed. Furthermore, we should explore how the names and labels of this surface knowledge, in articulation with the axes of power and ethics, may provide an alibi for processes of control, subjuga-tion, etc. These terms – for our narrow purposes the constellation of terms surrounding 'impulse' and 'instinct' – are repeated within specific institut-ional sites (sporting sites included), and it is important to shed light on their diffuse effects on various groups beyond the units of 'society at large' or 'the average person' employed by Elias.[2] How are they coded in terms of 'race', gender and class?

As the chronology of the impulsive black male unfolds it becomes clear that, throughout history, references to impulse/instinct often mark points where concerns over 'race', gender and class have converged. This articula-tion of categories is no new discovery. As Anne McClintock (1995) argues so forcefully in *Imperial Leather*, 'race', gender and class come into existence in and through each other, and tend to exist in relations that are intimate, reciprocal and contradictory. However, the issue of impulse/instinct isn't a loose thread which, given a hard tug, will see the cross-stitched categories of 'race', gender and class unravel. Also, though I have ordered the forthcoming account into distinct phases, its portrayal of events along with the wider narrative that connects them are, of course, open to question. To paraphrase Donna Haraway's introduction to her own chronology of 'race', population and genome, the story presented here is not cemented by the conventions of cause and effect, but neither are its events, phases and nodal points just random free associations (1995: 336).

Myth: Plato, Pliny and *Principal Navigations*

The *Oxford English Dictionary* (Soanes 2002) defines 'impulse' as 'A sudden strong and unreflective urge to act', and 'instinct' as 'An inborn tendency or impulse to behave in a certain way'. As is reflected in these definitions, the etymological roots of the words overlap considerably. According to most authorities in etymology, the term 'instinct' dates back to 1412. It comes from the Latin word *instinctus* meaning 'instigation or impulse'. The word *instinctus* is the past participle of *instinguere* meaning to 'incite, impel'. First recorded in 1432 as 'an act of impelling, a thrust, push', the term 'impulse' originates in the Latin *impulsus* meaning 'a push against, shock', also 'incitement, instigation' (Skeat 1924). I do not mean to conflate the meaning of the two, but point to the tendency of various experts and commentators – in evidence at numerous moments throughout the chronology – to use the terms 'impulse' and 'instinct' interchangeably or in juxtaposition. In line with Hacking's prescriptions for historical ontology, it is their meaning within abstract conceptions on one hand, and their usage within institutions on the other, that are of interest rather than my own distinctions between one word and the other. I also seek to avoid the error of presentism, described by Banton (in the context of a discussion of the history of racial thought) as 'the tendency to interpret other historical periods in terms of the concepts, values and understanding of the present time' (1987: xii). This tendency can be resisted by situating the materials which feature in the constitution of the 'impulsive' black male within their historical, institutional and epistemological context. As Hacking (2002a: 3) states, these 'materials have a distinctive and historically formed organization', and it is important that we examine this organisation – and, more specifically, the formations of depth and surface knowledge within which materials relating to the 'impulsive' black male crystallise – with due rigour.

In lieu of the term 'impulse' or 'instinct', a concern with desire dominated the work of classical Greek philosophers. Plato (428–348BC) argued that higher life was ruled by reason, with reason in turn defined by a vision of order in the cosmos. Properly conceived, this vision corresponded to an ordered soul; the order of the whole, for Plato, was manifest in the Ideas of the Good. As the Good commands our love and allegiance, it provides a standard of the desirable over and above the variable appetites of bodily desire. Indeed, such desires were set in opposition to the higher life. They needed to be held in constant check as they were 'by nature insatiable' (1987 [c.380BC]: 442A), promoting excess and conflict. Plato's opposition between 'higher' and 'lower' life corresponded to a number of others which were crucial to his vision. These formed the raw materials for the family of conceptions centring on reason and desire which followed in the wake of Platonic thought (Warnek 2006).

The opposition between soul and body was very important for Plato. This posited the soul as eternal and immaterial while the body was characterised as changing and material. The legacy left by desire's connection to the body hardly needs underlining. We will see how it was picked up by Augustine, and later Descartes. Another far-reaching connection drawn by Plato was the relatedness of the body, materiality, changeability and desire with darkness within his famous allegory of the Cave. Those trapped inside the Cave faced a wall, onto which were projected the shadows of marionettes which passed in front of a fire situated behind them. Knowing no other forms of reality, the prisoners loved the sound of the marionettes and the sight of their shadows dancing on the wall (Huard 2006). Plato saw them as being focussed solely on the bodily and hence the changing. The only way wisdom could be imparted to those inside was by turning their attentions away from the darkness and illusion of the Cave – 'so much empty nonsense' (1987 [c.380BC]: 515) – to the brightness of true being. This being was represented by the Sun, whose light could only be seen by exiting the Cave.

Plato's theory and its assertions are instantly understandable to us. Even today, the idea that self-mastery consists in reason's conquering of desire and passion, and the latter's relation to the body, seems intuitive. To understand why, it is necessary to examine how Plato's basic oppositions provided the deep and self-evident basis for subsequent forms of 'surface' knowledge.

The suppositions of Plato's model remained relatively unchallenged until Descartes (according to most) ushered in the period of thought we call 'modern' in the seventeenth century (Judowitz 1988). Although Aristotle (384–322BC) did challenge the primacy of order in the cosmos and its connection with order in everyday life, the basic supremacy of reason continues to this day. The Stoics saw the process of contemplation – exalted by Plato and Aristotle before them – as worthless. However, they also saw those exercised by passions as vicious and a vision of the cosmic order as crucial to practical wisdom. As such they failed to venture outside of the bounds laid down by Plato. Indeed, to the thinker hailed as the second father of Stoicism, Plato's assertions provided the rudiments for developing an early notion of the will.

In Chrysippus (280–207BC) the idea of sensuous impulses (*hormētikai phantasiai*) emerged. Forging a crucial link which would be developed by his successors, notably Augustine, Chrysippus argued that the experience of these impulses was shared by humans and animals alike (Taylor 1989). The difference lay in the human's capacity to grant or withhold assent. That is, humans were largely (though not always) the masters of their *hormētikai phantasiai*; the experiencing of these impulses did not make a corresponding action inevitable. This capacity was not possessed by animals, for the Stoics they were mere slaves to impulse. Here Plato's idea of self-mastery was used

in an embryonic formation of the will, and a link forged between abandonment to impulse and the animal kingdom. However, by withholding from
humans the indefinite control of sensuous impulses, the Stoics left open the
issue of impulsivity's functioning within humanity.

Descriptive texts written in the ancient period are hard to come by.
However, one such text that sought to describe the universe and its natural
phenomena was compiled by the naturalist Pliny the Elder around 77AD. In
Naturalis Historia Pliny set out to index the wealth of natural phenomena
in areas such as geography, zoology, botany, mining and mineralogy.
Judged by today's standards Pliny's methods bordered on the absurd and his
assertions on the mythological. As translator and Pliny expert John Healy
has commented, Pliny's 'encyclopaedic account of the natural sciences
contains ... some 20,000 facts, from 2,000 works by 100 chosen authors.
These figures, however, represent a rather conservative estimate since no
fewer than 146 Roman and 327 foreign authors are quoted' (1991: xvii).
Given that *Naturalis Historia* (or *Natural History*) was a bricolage of
personal experience and unverified information culled from secondary
sources, it gives a good indication of the assumptions that underpinned
everyday awareness in Pliny's time. Indeed, though the text was seen as an
expert attempt to catalogue elements of the natural world, Pliny discarded
subjects like harmonics and geometry in favour of subjects that had a more
direct bearing on the everyday life of his contemporaries. As he put it, his
voluminous project was 'written for the masses, for the horde of farmers and
artisans and finally, for those who have time to devote to these pursuits'
(Pliny the Elder 1991 [77AD]: Preface, 6). Undertaken in this spirit, the
book gives us a chance to see how the assertions of his forbears entered
Pliny's descriptions and those of the authors he drew upon.

I needn't document the list of 'facts' presented by Pliny in areas such as
astronomy and mathematics. What I am interested in is his penchant for
armchair ethnography. Like those who documented the backwardness
of 'the natives' in the early years of British academic anthropology – for
whom the scribblings of travel writers and explorers were indispensable –
Pliny's assertions in this area relied on second-hand information (Murphy
2004). For encounters to be portrayed at just one remove from first-hand
experience would have been relatively rare, and this obviously had an impact
on the accuracy of the information contained in *Naturalis Historia*. Healy
is in agreement with this: 'Although Pliny has a positive contribution to
make in a number of scientific fields, the quality of his information, where
he relies on secondary sources, is inferior to that acquired through personal
experience' (1991: xxi).

In *Naturalis Historia* the set of assertions concerning impulse, passion,
desire, etc. in circulation during Pliny's time became explicitly tied to a more
or less defined geographical area, and more or less mythical groups of
people. The 'interior of Africa' was said to harbour 'the Atlas tribe in the

middle of the desert and next to them the half animal Goat-Pans, the Blemmyae, Gamphasantes, Satyrs and Strapfeet' (Book 5: 44). According to Pliny, the Atlas tribe were 'primitive and subhuman', the Cave-dwellers

> hollow out caves which are their home; their food is snake meat. They have no voice but make a shrill noise, thus lacking any communication by speech. The Garamantes do not marry but live promiscuously with their women. The Augilae worship only the gods of the lower world. The Blemmyae are reported as being without heads; their mouth and eyes are attached to their chest. They have no human characteristics except their shape ... I cannot think of any more to record about Africa.
>
> (1991: 45–6)

Even within this short passage a number of the ancient thinkers' assertions about 'lower' orders of life were connected with Africa and its inhabitants.

In Platonic thought, as we know, the higher life was ruled by reason. According to Pliny's description of the African interior, no indications of higher life – anything of the soul and therefore immaterial in nature – were to be found. The only group listed as having spiritual pretensions directed them towards 'the gods of the lower world'. For Plato, another feature of the lower life was abandonment to passion and desire; Pliny had the Garamantes living 'promiscuously with their women'. Plato also characterised the body as material and changing. Living in the interior Pliny described 'half animal' beings and those with 'their mouth and eyes attached to their chest ... with no human characteristics except their shape'. Like the Atlas tribe these were 'primitive and sub-human', the material of their bodies existed in a kind of grotesque, proto-evolutionary flux. The darkness allegorized by Plato was also exemplified by the Cave-dwellers who, as their name suggested, led a benighted existence. Some of the Stoics' assertions were also exemplified by this mythical group. The connection between animals and enslavement to impulse was present in the animal-like, shrill outbursts they emitted in lieu of any considered communication by speech.

Religious thought also made an important contribution around this time. Two years before the release of Pliny's *Naturalis Historia*, the Jewish general and historian Falvius Josephus (37–c.100AD) published *Contra Apion*. The book was a retort to various attacks on Judaism that followed the release of Josephus' earlier work *Antiquities of the Jews*. The passages of the book important for our purposes contained biblical stories used to substantiate Josephus' argument: the Creation, Cain and Abel, the Tower of Babel, Moses' exhortation, and the tripartite division of the world along with the curse on Ham and his posterity. Though all would feature prominently throughout the history of race-thinking in Western Europe, the last would be most important in terms of the emergence of the 'impulsive' black male.

Following the biblical flood, Josephus described a world divided into three parts, each being the respective domain for one of Noah's three sons: Japhet was consigned to Europe, Shem to the region of the Indian Ocean, Persia, Chaldea and Armenia, and Ham to Africa, Egypt and Libya. But Ham became subject to a curse after happening upon his naked and drunken father:

> Being drunk, he (Noah) fell asleep and lay naked in an unseemly manner. When his youngest son saw this, he came laughing, and showed him to his brethren; but they covered their father's nakedness ... when Noah was made sensible of what had been done, he prayed for posterity to his other sons; but for Ham, he did not curse him, by reason of his nearness in blood, but cursed his posterity.
>
> (Josephus 1851 [75AD]: 1.6.3)

As Hannaford has claimed, 'From Josephus through Jean Bodin in the sixteenth century, this account remained the orthodox interpretation of the division of mankind' (1996: 91). Our next protagonist would embroider this story with important value judgements as well as build upon Plato's oppositions. He would also lay the ground for Descartes by offering up what might be called a proto-cogito (Taylor 1989).

Through his teacher Plotinus, the theologian and philosopher Augustine (354–430AD) imbibed the thought of Plato and brought it to bear on his spiritual beliefs. Indeed, in many ways Augustine's gloss on the biblical division of the world was an attempt to synthesise his scriptural and Platonic loyalties (Chadwick 2008). Augustine's version had Shem as a circumcised Jew and the flesh of Christ; Japhet as an uncircumcised Greek and representative of the Church; and Ham as estranged from his brothers, being heated, restless and representative of heresy: 'The tribe of heretics, not with spirit, not of patience, but of impatience' (Genesis 16.2).

In learning Plato's teachings Augustine came to see the soul (along with God) as immaterial in nature, accepting the duality of the bodily and the non-bodily. This entailed taking on the whole raft of Platonic oppositions. Augustine adopted Plato's duality of the body (as bodily in essence) and soul (as non-bodily in essence) by mapping onto it the Christian distinction between the spirit and the flesh. Plato's Ideas of the Good were similarly translated into a theological lexicon. Not surprisingly, in Augustine these became the Ideas of God; all created things were given their form by these Ideas, and every entity existed insomuch as it participated in them (Stump and Kretzmann 2001). According to Augustinian doctrine, mortal individuals should read these entities as signs. They were the external manifestation of God's thoughts and were by extension inherently good. Taken together these signs formed a rational order in the universe that partook of God's Ideas and which humans should therefore know and respect.

So, while Plato used the image of the Sun as the source of enlightened consciousness – towards which we should turn after escaping the intellectual shackles of the Cave – the ultimate object of enlightened being for Augustine was God. In terms of the influence these continuities had on the oppositions he took from Plato, those which remained intact and were embellished by Augustine were the oppositions of soul vs. body, spirit vs. matter, higher vs. lower, eternal vs. temporal, immutable vs. changing. But one that was not prominent in Platonic thought, and which became a master trope in Augustine, was the opposition between inner and outer man.

For Augustine the inner man was represented by the soul, and the outer man by those things considered 'bodily'. These latter included the senses, and here Augustine built on a connection drawn by both Plato and the Stoics. As detailed earlier in the chapter, Plato associated desire, passion, and hence insatiability, with the body. This association was animated by those trapped inside the Cave, a preoccupation with sights and sounds drawing their attention to the shadows that flitted across its walls; captivated by the senses, they were detained by their own limited understanding. Chrysippus went further, viewing sensuous impulses as phenomena experienced by man and animal alike. The difference lay in the issue of control. Similarly, for Augustine the bodily senses and the objects they carried in train such as desire, passion, etc. were connected with beastly existence. Following the Stoics, Augustine viewed this outer realm of sensuous experience and desire as something that man and beast had in common.

The legacy left by Augustine for Cartesian thought should also be mentioned.[3] As already noted, the distinction between inner and outer man drawn by Augustine corresponded to that between higher and lower life. For him, the way to go about finding God was not by exploring the external domain but through a radical inward turn. In order to contemplate the domain of objects man relied on God for a kind of perceptual support. In this way God illuminated man's inner being, and this was crucial in coming to know one's surroundings in the world: 'Do not go outward; return within yourself. In the inward man dwells truth' (Saint Augustine of Hippo 1991 [c.390AD]: 72).

The inward turn enjoined by Augustine would have people focus on the sensation of awareness, on the first-hand experience of contemplation. This was crucial to the manner in which Augustine answered the sceptic, who charged that in reality, man could know nothing. In response Augustine showed that it was impossible for one to doubt his own existence, for he must exist in the first instance in order to be deceived. Unlike Descartes', the remainder of Augustine's assertions did not rest on this argument. The mind–body dualism for him was something more implicit, which required less logical explanation. But the centrality of self-awareness established by Augustine – what would later be called subjective experience – was crucial to the argument put forward by Descartes at the birth of the modern period. As Taylor states, 'Augustine was the inventor of the argument we know as the "cogito", because Augustine was the first to make the first-person standpoint fundamental to our search for the truth' (1989: 133). While not absolutely crucial to the story told here, these continuities in Western thought are important in outlining the intellectual horizons of respective time periods.

Conventional accounts of history tell us that the Middle Ages cast a shadow conducive to dim understanding; that the period fostered little innovation within the fields of natural science and moral theory (Toulmin 1990). Our next departure from the world of ideas does little to challenge these accounts. This concerns the mid-sixteenth century – the late Middle Ages – 100 years before Descartes set about constructing his great edifice of verifiable knowledge. At this time the myths and stories of traders and explorers were beginning to circulate, and reports of British emissaries' formative contact with the African continent rested on the body of assumptions we have already examined. These assumptions were weaved into the mythological canon that existed in Britain. Such store was set by these assumptions because their raciological content was now crucial to Britain's imperial project.

Though travel writing compendia emerged earlier, such as Mandeville's *Travels* (completed shortly after 1360), the most influential of these was Richard Hakluyt's *Principal Navigations*, published in 1589 (Hakluyt 1914 [1589]). This was a collation of reports written by adventurers such as Richard Eden. In comparing its descriptions of Africa with those compiled by Pliny 1500 years earlier, it is evident that myth remained the principal mode of narration. As James Walvin has averred, throughout the 250 years which followed the publication of *Principal Navigations*, this part-factual, part-fictional response to Africa would characterise English understanding of the black continent. As he put it, 'the myths of Africa were to prove more resilient than its truths' (Walvin 1973: 28).

The mythological character of *Principal Navigations* (a work cannibalised by other authors in the years following its publication) is in evidence throughout the work. The second volume includes a description of a fight between an elephant and a dragon, while also depicting

[a] region called Troglodytica, whose inhabitants dwell in caves and dens: for these are their houses, and the flesh of serpents their meat, as writes Plinie, and Diodorus Siculus. They have no speech, but rather a grinning and chattering. There are also people without heads, called Blemines, having their eyes and mouth in their breast.

(Hakluyt 1914: 169)

The similarities with Pliny's *Natural History* are noteworthy.

One passage describes 'a people of beastly living, without a God, love, religion, or common wealth' (Hakluyt 1914 [1589]: Volume 4, 57) dwelling in the African interior. Here again are connections between a lower life bereft of spiritual integrity or love and the animal kingdom. The laziness of black Africans irked Hakluyt: 'the Negros in a long time would not come to us, but at the last by ... perswasion' (ibid: 99–100), and passion and impulse ruled in the absence of reason or any relationship with a (legitimate) higher being. Crucially, these early imperial reconnoitres linked such passion and impulse to violence. The fourth volume described the 'so unreasonable' Negros prone to sudden bouts of violence. The fifth volume reinforced this view. It reported 'Negros consent about forty Englishmen cruelly slain and captivated' (ibid: 45). The centrality of the body was again present, as Hakluyt reported of 'tall and strong' (ibid: 65) people ruled by the 'law of nature' (ibid: 38).

After his incisive consideration of *Principal Navigations* and its influence on Elizabethan England, Walvin asserts that 'the African came to be seen as a dramatic inversion of their (Elizabethan Englishmen's) most deeply cherished social and cultural values' (1973: 19). I would go further and argue that this inversion was inevitable. Rather than being a product of the (proto)colonial encounter itself, the mythology cum travel writing of *Principal Navigations* was a matter of moral and intellectual architecture. The oppositions through which explorers made sense of Africa and its peoples were conceived in the abstract by Plato 2000 years before Hakluyt's volumes were published. Explorers identified with one side of these oppositions, not surprisingly with the characteristics of 'higher' life. This justified their setting out on various expeditions. Inasmuch as, before and after their (more or less imaginary) encounters with Africans, these Africans were ascribed the characteristics of 'lower' life – abandonment to impulse included – the explorers' actions were somewhat of a formality.

At the turn of the seventeenth century, abstract conceptions of lower life were being applied to produce effects which were anything but mythical. The period from 1600 to 1640 witnessed the growth of capitalism and an attendant orgy of expropriation – of common land parcelled up and common people herded up (Linebaugh and Rediker 2000). Tracts of land in England were enclosed while 'commoners' in Africa, Ireland, England, Barbados and Virginia were seized. Hakluyt himself wanted these 'swarmes of idle persons' – who, like those he spied in the African interior, were 'of beastly living without ... a common wealth' (Hakluyt 1914 [1589]: 57) – set to work in the plantations of Virginia, England's newly acquired colony. It wasn't laziness alone that justified this strategy. In *An Advertisement Touching an Holy War*, Francis Bacon described those he identified as fair game for *jihad*:

> If there shall be a congregation and consent of people that shall hold all things to be lawful, not according to any certain laws or rules,

but according to the secret and variable motions and *instincts* of the spirit; this is indeed no nation, no people; any nation that is civil and policed may cut them off the face of the earth.

(1868 [1622]: 33)

Central to the founding rites of capitalism, idleness and impulse/instinct had been pulled into the orbit of economic necessity, and here they would ossify. The next necessity was enslavement.

Slaves to impulse: property and the creation of outsiders

The work of French philosopher Rene Descartes (1596–1650) marked a decisive break with the Middle Ages. On one hand Descartes mapped out the tenets of scientific procedure. On the other, following Augustine, he revolutionised the world of general philosophy by stripping down experience to its bare bones (Schlutz 2009). This made philosophy a more democratic affair; accessible and doable for all those disposed to reflective thought.

Debate still rages as to whether Descartes did indeed throw open the doors to the 'modern' period. This need not concern us here.[4] What is important are the influences of Descartes' work on British society and, more specifically, on the emergence and justification of the slaving industry. Most important was the manner in which Descartes took on Plato's oppositions (refracted through Augustine) and used them in his own distinction between mind and body.

I have already discussed the influence of Augustine on Descartes and his method, often boiled down to his cogito (*cogito ergo sum* – I think, therefore I am). The centrality of Augustine's first-person perspective to Descartes' intellectual dictum is obvious. However, through his mind and body distinction Descartes effected an internalisation which differed from Augustine's in crucial ways. This internalisation became hugely influential in the modern age. Instead of turning towards something external to realise their potential beyond the bounds of sensible experience (like Plato's Ideas), Descartes encouraged people to turn inwards, to the ideas located in the mind. By following this procedure, people could build an order of ideas whose truth was undeniable. This would represent an edifice of certain knowledge, the veracity of which was not guaranteed by any substantive, external authority but by generating certainty 'through a chain of clear and distinct perceptions' (Taylor 1989: 144). Thus the authority of reason no longer rested on something external and substantive, it was now supported by something internal and procedural, and this had a bearing on the distinction between mind and body.

Descartes saw Plato's scheme as flawed. He recognised no external Ideas which we should turn towards (as Plato had encouraged), and thought

Plato's confusion resulted from a misunderstanding of the immaterial and the material. He emphasised the ontological break between the soul and body, imploring readers to see the former as immaterial and the latter as part of the material world. This much didn't represent any radical breach with previous lines of thought. The new twist was to objectify the human body in order to disengage completely from the experience senses (e.g. seeing colour or feeling heat). For Descartes this could only be achieved by seeing the body as a mechanism, from the view of a disengaged, uninvolved observer (Garber 2000). Recognising the split between mind and body was therefore crucial for Descartes' shift from substantive to procedural reason.

As did Plato's conception of higher and lower life, Descartes' mind–body dichotomy brought a series of related oppositions in its train. Most fundamental was the opposition between the rational freedom of moral and intellectual reason and the causal necessity of mechanical processes that function in the material world. Reduced to a distinction between rationality and causality, this also meant a dichotomy between human awareness and the realm of natural phenomena. As Toulmin has argued, this set of dichotomies was given further impetus throughout the modern period:

> After 1660, there developed an overall framework of ideas about humanity and nature, rational mind and causal matter, that gained the standing of 'common sense': for the next 100, 150, or 200 years, the main timbers of this framework of ideas and beliefs were rarely called into question.
>
> (1990: 107–8).

Though the broad strokes of Descartes' distinction would become profoundly influential, some of its more nuanced implications were important for the development of impulse/instinct as a raciological idea.

Unlike previous theorists, Descartes did not see all 'passions' as being inherently reckless or 'lower'. He saw them as emotions in the soul caused by the movement of animal spirits which functioned to sustain the life of the organism. These survival impulses were often violent. What the mind–body distinction allowed us to do was remain in control of these passions, giving them licence when it served our well-being to do so and refusing to grant such licence when it did not: 'great souls ... whose reasoning powers are so strong ... that although they have passions, and often even more violent than is common, nonetheless their reason remains sovereign' (Descartes 1645, quoted in Taylor 1989: 150). This link to animal spirits and the faculty of great men (but not all men) to resist the mechanism of passions became important, influencing Newton later in the century. The second crucial point was the issue of control itself. By viewing the world – and human bodies – mechanistically, it became possible to control this domain. People could intervene within the functional, material world and in doing so make this domain subject to instrumental mastery. Indeed, the idea of instrumental mastery and the alibi of scientific knowledge it provided would become crucial in various attempts to defend the slaving industry.

During the British annexation of the West Indies in the seventeenth century, the status of Africans remained relatively tacit. In the previous century the pioneering slave-trader John Hawkins had referred to black 'merchandise' (Walvin 1973: 38) but this didn't indicate any widely accepted categorisation. It was only in 1672, when the Royal African Company was granted its charter, that the reality of life for Africans came to be reflected in official terminology. The charter declared that emissaries of the Company could 'import any redwood, elephants' teeth, negroes, slaves, hides, wax, guinea grains, or other commodities' (Calendar of State Papers 1669–74, cited in Walvin 1973: 39). Thereafter the race was on to match the realities of the slave trade with the terms of the various Navigation Acts (the first of which was released in 1651).[5] This meant that ambiguity surrounding the status of African slaves could no longer be skirted around. An imprimatur was sought from the Solicitor-General, who duly obliged: 'negroes ought to be considered esteemed goods and commodities within the Acts of Trade and Navigation' (ibid). So, in a move which combined the axioms of Cartesian orthodoxy with the spread of private property rights, and while Descartes' ideas were beginning to enjoy currency within exalted circles of British society, the Navigation Acts decreed that African bodies should be treated as material commodities. These bodies were items of property at the mercy of instrumental control. The British government had commanded as much. Planters and investors now had to rationalise the form that this control would take, with the work-rate of the African becoming a crucial issue. As in the past, this reasoning would lean on the intellectual architecture of the day.

Newton's three-volume work *Philosophiæ Naturalis Principia Mathematica* (published in 1687) contained his laws of motion and would prove to be one of the most important scientific works ever written (Chandrasekhar 1995). His method followed the programme prescribed by Descartes and his findings built on the dichotomies present in Cartesian thinking.[6] Newton endorsed and developed Descartes' respective distinctions between mind and matter and humanity and nature. But most crucial for our purposes was the assertion (contained in his first law of motion) that matter is fundamentally inert until acted upon by an external body. Added to Descartes' oppositions, this meant seeing the passive, material body as distinct from the active, rational mind.

As they became so influential it is necessary to list the assumptions, ratified by Cartesian and Newtonian orthodoxy by the end of the seventeenth century, that are relevant to the story unfolding here:

1. Reason is connected with intellect/spirit and emotion with the body/ carnal influences;
2. The material substance of nature is essentially inert until acted upon by an external force;
3. Physical objects and processes cannot think or reason;
4. The essence of humanity is the capacity for rational thought and action;
5. Reason can be distorted by the causal imperatives of the body – the emotions frustrate/distort reason.

(Toulmin 1990)

Together these axioms represented a system of regularities on the basis of which subsequent theorising about the world would be accorded value or acceptability.

The theoretical distinction between reason and the emotions contained in Newtonian-Cartesian orthodoxy was pervasive from the seventeenth to the mid-twentieth century and helped to cement the practical contrast between rationality and impulsiveness. As Toulmin has contended: 'What began as a theoretical distinction in Descartes, between the intellectual power of human "reason" and the physiological "causes" of the emotions, turned into a practical contrast between (good) rationality and (bad) sentiment or impulsiveness' (ibid: 134–5).

For Britain this period witnessed the expansion of empire in lockstep with mercantile (and then industrial) capitalism. Of course, both of these developments rested on the trade in, and labour of, African slaves. Conventional wisdom described African slaves as inherently lazy: 'generally idle and ignorant' (Seller 1685: 90); 'Nothing but the utmost Necessity can force them to Labour: They are besides ... incredibly lazy and stupid' (Bosman 1704 quoted in Fryer 1984: 141).[7] But though this stereotype would be used to defend plantation slavery, in the years before Descartes' and Newton's ideas formed the intellectual backdrop there remained a school which argued along different – in fact, diametrically opposite – lines. For example, Hugh Jones opined that 'They (slaves) are by nature cut out for hard Labour and Fatigue' (quoted in Fryer 1984: 142).

A justificatory hymn sheet would yet emerge, as the oppositions consonant with Platonic thought were given further intellectual warrant throughout the Enlightenment period. Writers would draw upon them and link their conceptions of lower life with the African more stridently as the eighteenth century wore on. This was music to the ears of those who identified with the economic imperatives of the plantations. Indeed, in some cases the writers and investors were one and the same.

It is perhaps little known that English Enlightenment philosopher John Locke had £600 invested in the Royal Africa Company. He was prescient in using the innocence of the child to question the status of the 'Negro' within the human family:

The child can demonstrate to you, that a Negro is not a Man, because White-colour was one of the constant simple Ideas of the complex Idea he calls Man: And therefore he can demonstrate by the Principle, It is impossible for the same Thing to be, and not to be, that a Negro is not a Man.

(Locke 1975 [1690]: 62)[8]

His work – which posited the mind as a *tabula rasa* that received information from the senses and used its mental faculties to process and manipulate these sensations – would inadvertently contribute to debates over the standing of the African mind (in relation to that of the white man). But he also provided the founding texts of the liberal tradition[9] – and perhaps most importantly, economic liberalism – which, together with Kant's cosmopolitan ethic, had important implications for those compelled to occupy the margins of Britain's imperial order. Central to these implications were the conceptions of time and space employed by Locke and Kant.

As already noted, the implications of Locke's philosophy were developed into the basic tenets of liberalism (Laski 1997 [1936]; Waldron 2002). In his writings Locke presupposed an isolated and deracinated individual subject only to the ideals of liberty and freedom. Through the Euclidean lens through which he viewed land (and 'nature' more generally), space is seen as uniform and continuous – what David Harvey has described as 'absolute space'.[10] One plot of land is thus an exact analogue of another unit of comparable size, with distinctive geographical and topographical features being glossed over; no concessions were granted to the influence of a given spatial or temporal context or to any related sentiments of allegiance or belonging. As Mehta (1999: 29) argues, 'By rendering nature and the encounter with it sentimentally inert, Locke denies locational attachments as having any individual significance in relation to political identity.'

This view is made explicit in Locke's description (in the *Second Treatise*) of the origins of private property.[11] Here Locke casts nature as inert and valueless: 'Nature and Earth furnished only the most worthless materials, as in themselves' (1960 [1662]: 43). Nature, 'The common mother', remains inert and infertile until she is 'subdued' for the 'benefit of life' through labour (ibid: 28). The only way to generate worth out of this continuous, passive space, bequeathed by God and therefore held in common by all men, was to mix what was by definition held in private, *my* labour, with what was held in common, nature. As Locke put it, 'every man has a *Property* in his own *Person*' and given that this property is held exclusive of others, 'mixing' it with a portion of (commonly held) nature made that portion 'properly his' (ibid: 6).

The alchemy described by Locke not only imbued the land with value, it also made that portion of land the rightful property of the labourer. All of this boiled down to a couple of basic assumptions: 1) private property originated from the mixing of human labour with nature held in common; 2) human labour is the principal source of value (Mehta 1999). These assumptions pointed towards a conflation of property rights and political power. Within Locke's vision of the nation-state, the boundaries of this political unit corresponded to an aggregate of private property belonging to those individuals contracted to form a distinctive political society or government. (Importantly, Locke and those that followed in the tradition of the liberal social contract came to attach certain conditions to legitimate forms of consent.) There was no place within this vision of absolute, bounded space for land held in common or much of a political existence for those without private property of their own. As Laski put it, 'A state has been made in which property is the effective title to citizenship' (1997 [1936]: 153). For Locke, the possibility of political unity rested on the parcelling up of land held in common, a prospect which in turn relied on the exclusionary potentialities of absolute space. Along with its stringent denial of geographical and historical factors in the emergence of distinct polities, Lockean liberalism repudiated any connection between notions of territorial belonging and nationhood. This was a view which, as Mehta (1999) underlines, provided the intellectual and normative grounds for the liberal justification of the British empire.

The claims made by Locke in his *Two Treatises of Government* are trans-historical, trans-cultural and trans-racial. Here Locke identifies a set of characteristics common to all human beings, central to which is the assertion, foundational to liberal theory and its universalistic bent, that everyone is naturally free:

> To understand political power right, and derive it from its Original, we must consider what State *all* Men are naturally in, and that is, a *State of perfect Freedom* to order their Actions, and dispose of their Possessions, and Persons as they think fit, within the bounds of the Law of Nature, without asking leave, or depending on the Will of any other Man.
>
> (1960 [1662]: 2:4)

However, away from Locke's pronouncements on universal humankind lurked a concession to discrimination and exclusion. This is found in his *Thoughts Concerning Education* (1880), a treatise released in 1693 following the collation and adaptation of a number of letters Locke had sent to an aristocratic friend on the subject of child tutelage. His views on the appropriate place of children in society must be considered in light of the arguments he put forward in *Two Treatises*, and, more specifically, his argument with respect to consent.

In the second treatise Locke claimed that consent should be the fundamental ground for the legitimacy of political authority. Among other things, consent required acting in view of the constraints designated by the laws of nature. These laws are fundamental moral principles, legislated for individuals and collectives by God, to which we must abide despite our natural proclivity for freedom. For Locke, these natural laws are accessed through the exercising of natural human reason (Laski 2007 [1920]). Those unable to exercise reason, whether permanently (i.e. 'lunaticks' or 'ideots') or temporarily (i.e. children), cannot rightfully provide any expression of consent. These groups can, by implication, be excluded from the bounds of political constituency and governed without consent.

In *Thoughts Concerning Education* we see Locke abandon the universal anthropological guarantees granted to all humankind in favour of a precise and detailed description of the processes through which the faculties of reason are inculcated: 'the principle of all virtue and excellency lies in the power of denying ourselves the satisfaction of desires … and this power is to be got and improved by custom, made easy and familiar by an early practice' (Locke 1880 [1693]: 103). He also underlines the importance of good breeding and the correct observation of social distinctions; the former showing in the 'Measures of Civility' that structure 'good company', the latter being 'the only fence against the world'. As Mehta concludes:

> From even the most casual reading of the *Thoughts*, one sees that education and, more specifically, reasoning involve understanding a world replete with social and hierarchical distinctions. Far from giving expression to capacities that are universal because they presume on so little, education is an initiation into the enormously significant specifications of time, place, and social status.
>
> (1999: 62)

Here an abstract and universal conception of humankind is lost in the scramble to assert the importance of hierarchies that inscribe time and space and thereby exclude certain groups from a given political constituency on the basis of their 'immaturity'. Mehta (1999) calls those liberal strategies of exclusion that focus on the issue of maturity 'civilizational infantilism', arguing that, rather than issuing from the practical considerations and restraints of empire, such strategies were legislated for by the theoretical underpinnings of the liberal tradition. Locke's argument regarding maturity, rationality and consent would later be extrapolated when liberal theory was faced with calls for self-governance from Britain's colonial subjects (Pitts 2006).

The work of another Enlightenment thinker, Immanuel Kant, was also important in this connection. Given the foundational role he accorded to geographical and anthropological knowledge as 'conditions of possibility' for all knowledge, it is unsurprising that Kant's cosmopolitan ethic is underpinned by particular notions of space and human nature. It was these notions that allowed Kantian cosmopolitanism to follow Lockean liberalism in smuggling a number of concessions to prejudice and discrimination under the veil of universalism.

Kant saw space as fixed and immovable, concerning himself with spatial structure and clearly demarcated boundaries. The issue of boundaries was crucial, as Kant introduced a federal structure to the global cosmopolitan order; the absolute, bounded spaces he envisaged corresponded to national territories. Like Locke, Kant viewed humanity in the abstract, seeing humankind as subject to the universal laws of reason. As such all those human beings residing permanently within the territory of a given sovereign state were defined as its citizens. However, Kant distinguished his cosmopolitan vision from the purely ethical cosmopolitanism of the Stoics by employing the idea of 'maturity' as a normative measure of rational behaviour – and on this basis not all residents of a sovereign state qualified as citizens.

In his *Geography* the issue of maturity and its geographical causes is explored freely:

> In hot countries men mature more quickly in every respect but they do not attain the perfection of the temperate zones. Humanity achieves its greatest perfection with the White race. The yellow Indians have somewhat less talent. The Negroes are much inferior and some of the peoples of the Americas are well below them.
>
> (Kant 1999 [c.1756]: 21)

Equally important were his musings on how and why natural endowments (which he called 'temperaments') are transformed by human practices into 'character': 'what nature makes of man belongs to temperament (wherein the subject is for the most part passive) and only what man makes of himself reveals whether he has character' (Kant 1974 [1772]: 203). Here Kant reflected on how far human kind had progressed in moulding temperaments into character through the fashioning and development of culture. This introduced the dichotomy between 'animal' and 'civilised' being, and led Kant to contemplate the different rates at which men (nested within various populations) developed character out of temperament. He did so by analysing differentials in the character and culture of national populations. Sadly the works relied on a crude environmental determinism that often shaded into outright racism.[12]

The issue of progress is pertinent because within the cosmopolitan federation envisioned by Kant, not only could a sovereign state deny the privileges of citizenship on the grounds of immaturity, it could refuse access to visitors from other states (provided it did not result in the visitor's destruction)[13] on the same premise. Despite the seeming attachment to universalism, it appears that Kant had certain types of citizen and stranger in mind when peopling his cosmopolitan order – not all members of a 'cosmopolitan' nation qualified as citizens:

> Those inhabitants, or even a part of them, which recognize themselves as being united into a civil society through common descent, are called a nation (gens); the part which segregates itself from these laws (the unruly group among these people) is called rabble (vulgus), and their illegal union is called a mob (agree per turbas), a behavior which excludes them from the privileges of citizenship.
>
> (1974 [c.1772]: 96)

Those failing to live up to normative standards of maturity (rationality) in the eyes of state representatives were expelled to the interstices of Kant's federated structure.

So, despite high-minded talk of freedom and liberty as universal values in Kantian cosmopolitanism and the tradition of liberalism, both formulations undercut the scope of universalism by appealing to the geographical and anthropological specificities they so vigorously deny in order to exclude certain 'types' of people.

As figureheads of the Enlightenment were consigning Africans to lower life, questioning their status as humans, and writing an exclusionary potential into the doctrines of liberalism and the cosmopolitan ethic, Newton's laws were being popularised throughout Europe. After a visit to London, Voltaire returned to France and spread the word of Newtonian orthodoxy. Newton's ideas also featured in that compendium of Enlightenment wisdom, the *Encyclopédie*, published by Diderot, d'Alembert and Holbach from 1751.

Meanwhile the abolitionist movement was gathering speed. In 1748 Montesquieu's *De l'esprit des Lois* unleashed an attack on the slave trade that was incisive, if couched in irony. (Because of this irony some planters took Montesquieu's comments literally as being supportive of slavery.) In mounting this attack he was the first philosopher of world renown to throw his weight behind the cause of abolition:

> Were I to vindicate our right to make slaves of the Negroes, these should be my arguments. The Europeans having extirpated the Americans, were obliged to make slaves of the Africans for clearing such vast tracts of land. Sugar would be too dear if the plants which produce it were cultivated by other than slaves. These creatures are all over black, and with such a flat nose, that they can scarcely be pitied. It is hardly to be believed that God, who is a wise Being, should place a soul, especially a good soul, in such a black and ugly body.
>
> (Montesquieu 1959 [1748]: 238)

Montesquieu was joined in his cry for common humanity by Rousseau. In *La Nouvelle Héloise*, we hear the hero, St Preux, state:

> I saw Europe transported to the extremes of Africa ... I saw these vast and unfortunate countries which seemed destined only to cover the face of the globe with slaves. At their vile appearance, I turned away my eyes, out of disdain, horror and pity; and on beholding one-fourth part of my fellow creatures transformed into beasts for the service of the rest, I grieved to think that I was a man.
>
> (Rousseau 1761: 234)

As Walvin has noted, 'Rousseau's impact on European thought was seismic' (1973: 179). He saw human nature as characterised by benevolence, and nature as an inner source giving rise to certain spontaneous impulses. For Rousseau, these impulses represented the voice of nature, and to live in conformity with nature was to attain ultimate happiness: 'I long for the time when, freed from the fetters of the body, I shall be myself, at one with myself, no longer torn in two, when I myself shall suffice for my own happiness' (1964 [1762]: 257). In this way he radicalised the inward turn of Augustine, overlooking the disengagement exhorted by Descartes and paving the way for a philosophy of self-exploration. However, Rousseau didn't dispense with the vision of a providential order; the inner voice he affirmed ran in tandem with a notion of the universal good discovered partly through a turning within (Taylor 1989). It was only with a new ethic of nature that the inner voice of true sentiment came to define what the good consisted in. This ethic was formulated in Romantic expressivism, and many of its relevant strands emerged from a group of intellectuals situated in late eighteenth-century Germany.

Periodising the era of the German Romantics – sketching the internal divisions of 'early' and 'late' as well as broader historical outlines separating the 'Classical' from the 'Romantic' – has proved a frustrating task for tidy-minded chronologists (Schmidt 2009; Seyhan 2009). However, there is some consensus in seeing the French Revolution as laying down the key historical conditions for the movement's emergence.[14] Rousseauian language – of trust in the goodness of nature latent in virtuous men – came to the fore at the height of the Revolution. And in Germany, where the Revolution arrived on the heels of invading French soldiers, the sense of crisis and possibility it generated was a catalyst for an intellectual movement which had important implications for the way that impulses came to be understood. This movement was a German brand of Romanticism.

The group – though its membership is contested – included the Schlegel brothers (August Wilhelm and Carl Friedrich), G. P. F. von Hardenberg (Novalis), J. G. Fichte, F. W. J. Schelling, Friedrich Hölderlin, E. T. A. Hoffmann, Heinrich von Kleist and Ludwig Tieck, while also important for our purposes are the 'pre-Romantic' J. F. Herder and the Romantic scientist F. A. Mesmer. Though differences in outlook can be discerned in their works, the shared philosophical assumptions of the group have been identified by Paul Kluckhohn (1941) as: a preference for dialectical and cyclical over linear thinking and ideas of infinite unity and infinite multiplicity of the sublime and yearning for the infinite; a determination to hover above unresolved contradictions; a merging of the sacred and profane together with the sublime and the trivial; expression through irony; an awareness of the contrast between ideal and reality as emergent through self-reflection; an empathetic understanding of nature (versus a dissecting of nature via reason)[15] and participation in its creativity; an emphasis on the unity of body, soul and spirit; an interest in the unconscious forces of the soul; and a central role for fantasy and emotion in forming Romantic individuality. These assumptions may appear to oppose fundamentally the set of values enshrined by Enlightenment science and philosophy. However, it is important to recognise in the philosophical, literary and artistic efforts of the German Romantics a rejection of some, but not all, Enlightenment principles; the movement advocated a turn against the overly mechanistic and reductive tendencies of Enlightenment thinking, rather than a wholesale dismissal of its theoretical credentials.

Pre-Romantic theoretician J. G. Herder provided a picture of nature as a great current of sympathy running through all entities: 'See the whole of nature, behold the great analogy of creation. Everything feels itself and its like, life reverberates to life' (1912: 50). For Herder, man was the only creature capable of awareness of this unity and was thus charged with bringing it to expression.[16] This picture of nature was adopted by Hölderlin, Schelling and Novalis (Furst 1979) who saw the inner voice – the impulse of nature – as a privileged mode of access to the natural order and the providential significance of things. But access to this mode could be barred by the uncompromising stance of disengaged, calculating reason, that is, a view external to nature (which is seen as a merely observed order). It was therefore through feelings that humans were admitted to the deepest moral and cosmic truths. As Novalis (1953: 379) put it, 'The heart is key to world and life', while for Herder, all passions and emotions 'can and must be operative, precisely in the highest knowledge, for this grew out of them all and can only live within them' (1912: 199).

Expressivism, the key to harnessing these passions and emotions, allowed for a new and more comprehensive individuation. Central to expressivism was the idea that each individual is different and original and that this influences how people are called upon to live. The subsequent obligation was to explore, give rein and do justice to our originality as individuals. As Herder argued: 'Each human being has his own measure, as it were an accord peculiar to him of all his feelings to each other' (ibid: 291). In expressing his originality each individual gave specific shape to the inchoate feelings and impulses which constituted his inner voice. In this way expression was not simply an unveiling or a making manifest but a bringing into being, affording a fuller definition to imperfectly formed feelings and sensations (Taylor 1989).[17]

Herder extended the idea of expressive individuation to the realm of national culture and character, asserting that different *Völker* have their own way of expressing their humanity, and should not waste time imitating others; cultures develop in their own geographical and climactic contexts, and this principle needed to be protected. Here he followed the anthropologist J. F. Blumenbach in seeing customs as rooted in geography and climate, using this view to argue that different cultures develop divergent principles of rationality and accommodating it to the idea of a common origin of all human life. In this way Herder combined notions of universalism and cultural relativism, identity and difference (Niekerk 2009).[18]

As well as (and in relation to) its preoccupation with expressivism, the Romantic period in Germany also witnessed the emergence of a current of science and psychology which sought to counter some of the founding principles of the seventeenth-century Scientific Revolution and eighteenth-century Enlightenment. More specifically, Romantic science offered alternatives to three central trends: secularisation, the differentiation in spheres of knowledge associated with empirical inquiry (principally the divide between the humanities and the natural sciences), and the Cartesian dualism of subject and object, mind and matter (Barkhoff 2009). Romantic scientists took their cue from the speculative philosophy of nature formulated by Schelling in his *On the World Soul* (2011) [1798] and *First Outline of a System of a Philosophy of Nature* (2004) [1799]. Schelling's fundamental assumption in these works was the existence of a monistic, spiritual 'world soul' encompassing the physical and metaphysical, the object world and the human spirit, body and mind. The movement's preoccupation with forces which confounded calibration and measurement but could only be observed in their effects, such as magnetism, electricity and galvanism, signalled its debt to Schelling.

Foremost among the variants of Romantic medicine and psychology was animal magnetism, or mesmerism, a movement which challenged the ultimate superiority of reason over the unconscious as affirmed by the enlightened worldview. Romantics were emboldened by the evidence it seemingly proffered for Schelling's world soul. Its originator was the late Enlightenment medical doctor Franz Anton Mesmer, who claimed that running 'magnetic' passes along the body had cathartic and calming effects.[19] One of Mesmer's French followers, the Marquis de Puységur, caused a stir after inducing a somnambulist trance in one of his patients, and in directing the manipulations of the magnetiser towards the psyche (rather than the body, as Mesmer had taught) the magnetic trance pointed towards the darkness of the unconscious realm. Indeed, Mesmer is acknowledged as one of Freud's important forerunners, with his theory occupying a central place in the discovery of the unconscious. His movement incited Romantic authors to weave the notion of unconscious impulses into tales concerning the psychological formation of modern subjectivity. Here we see authors like Hoffmann, Tieck and von Kleist 'show sympathy and fascination with the abnormal and the pathological, put the terrifying powers of our unconscious impulses on display and explore the conditions under which inspiration can turn into madness and enthusiasm into disaster' (Barkhoff 2009: 219). However, just as later conceptions of the unconscious were amenable to raciological assertions about 'savage' populations (see Chapter 3), for Romantic theologian and aesthetician Jean Paul the theory of mesmerism afforded the chance to explore 'the enormous realm of the unconscious, this true inner Africa' (Richter 1970: 1182).

The German Romantics thus widened and radicalised the possibility of a post-expressivist subject with 'inner depths', while – despite its universalism – admitting the influence of geographical differences in the formation of national character and culture. In terms of impulse and instinct as raciological ideas, the notion of inner depths – where the impulses of nature are felt and articulated by those possessing expressive power (particularly in music and art) – would be crucial to later psychological (and criminological) assertions about the 'impulsive' black male. As detailed in the following chapter, Nietzsche detached these natural impulses from any notion of intrinsic benevolence; a move which cleared the ground for later psychological explanations of 'impulsivity', their relationship to violent criminality and psychopathology, as well as contemporary ideas concerning 'good instincts'. But, as noted above, the German Romantic preoccupation with inner depths was also conducive to nascent formulations of the unconscious. As Böhme (1981: 136) has put it, notions of the unconscious present in Romantic science and literature created a 'proto-psychoanalytical structural field' wherein the characteristic tensions and traumas of the bourgeois family unit could be explored. This field was drawn upon by Freud,[20] who, in extrapolating the Romantic association of the unconscious with darkness, looked to 'savage' populations for well-preserved specimens of the unconscious.

Back in England, the abolitionist movement continued to apply pressure. British writer Thomas Day attempted to further the cause by dedicating his epic poem *The Dying Negro* to Rousseau. In the teeth of this mounting criticism, colonial administrator Edward Long took it upon himself to respond on behalf of the planters. His voluminous *History of Jamaica* (published in 1774) showed clear shades of Enlightenment racism and Cartesian-Newtonian orthodoxy. One of the *History*'s disquisitions ended by hinting that the Hottentots belonged to a distinct species: ' ... a people very stupid, and very brutal ... In many respects more like beasts than men ... they are very nimble, and run with a speed that is almost incredible. Has the

Hottentot, from this portrait, a more manly figure than the orang-outang?' (Long 2002 [1774] VII: 357). Echoing Hume, Long delivered his verdict on the Negro's lack of achievement:

> In general, they are void of genius, and seem almost incapable of making progress in civility or science. They have no plan or system of morality among them. Their barbarity to their children debases their nature even below that of brutes. They have no moral sensations, no wish but to be idle. They are represented by all authors as the vilest of the human kind, to which they have little more pretention of resemblance than what arises from their exterior form.
>
> (Ibid: 353)

And in labouring the point, he put forward a rhetorical question that could scarcely be more characteristic of Newtonian–Cartesian doctrine: 'how vast is the distance between inert matter, and matter endowed with thought and reason?' (ibid: 372).

For the more narrow purposes of the chapter, Long saw the Negro as sensuous and impulsively violent: 'Their hearing is remarkably quick; their faculties of smell and taste are truelly bestial; where the passions rage without any control ... A blind anger, and brutal rage stand in place of manly valour' (ibid: 391–401). Even their meagre talents were down to instinct, not reason: 'Brutes are botanists by instinct', they apply 'chief medicaments at random, without any regard to the particular symptoms of the disease ... they have formed no theory' (ibid: 383). Most of the passages contained in Long's *History* could have been culled from Pliny's *Natural History*.[21]

Long had shown how abstract theory could be mapped onto social reality. He saw in Newton's work – in the identification of nature's material bodies which remained passive and inert until acted upon by an external force (Descartes' active, rational mind) – a scientific rendering of the plantation's division of labour. Following Long's example, other planters and interested parties posited Africans as part of nature: material, inert, bereft of rationality, abandoned to natural impulse. For example, in 1796 British historian Bryan Edwards wrote that the maroons of Jamaica were 'savages more ferocious and blood-thirsty than the animals that track them' (1796: xviii), and had 'no inclination to sober industry ... their thoughts and attentions seemed engrossed by their present pursuits, and the objects immediately around them, without any reflection on the past or solicitude for the future' (ibid: xxix–xxxi). Three years earlier he had described the inhabitants of the Windward Islands as acting on 'the effect only of sudden impulse ... (the) predominance of passion awakens the instincts of nature' (Edwards 1793: 30–33).

As documented above, by the twilight years of the eighteenth century the ideas of laziness and instinct/impulse had become closely aligned with the ongoing imperatives of empire, in both outpost and metropole. Politicians and reformers, having begun to identify England's urban areas as places where wealth accumulated and men decayed, called upon theories of degeneracy to argue that urban dwellers were a class apart (Nordau and Mosse 1993). These theories were also used to comprehend threats to order that cut along lines of 'race', class and gender – again, both at home and further afield. As McClintock so deftly observes, what followed can be characterised as processes of abjection:

> Under imperialism certain groups are expelled and obliged to inhabit the impossible edges of modernity: the slum, the ghetto ... the colonial Bantustan and so on. Abject peoples are those whom industrial imperialism rejects but cannot do without: slaves ... the colonized, domestic workers ... the unemployed, and so on.
>
> (1995: 72)

Humanity: two's company, three's a crowd – articulated categories in imperial modernity

For Britain's ruling classes the last few years of the eighteenth century were tumultuous. Spectres of change were all around; the protests of the anti-slavery movement were reaching fever pitch, the French Revolution was rumbling on, and the French colony of St. Domingo – despite the various interventions of France, Britain and Spain – was on the way to becoming the Free Republic of Haiti (Porter 2001). Reports of this latter upheaval were a particular cause for frustration and concern. After their expulsion from St. Domingo in 1798, the British armed forces reflected on the victorious black rebels' 'barbarity ... not their bravery, or determination' (Geggus 1982: 287). Peter Jackson, a man posted away from the revolution's theatres of battle as a hospital inspector, was equally grudging: 'they (the blacks) are by disposition so indolent, so unenergetic in action ... that it is ... more than probable that ... the conquest of Saint Domingue might have been effected' (quoted in Geggus 1982: 288). In the aftermath of independence, a white bishop spared by the uprising sent a memorandum to Napoleon which underlined the importance of his ministry: 'with the difference of colour, and with the warm climate, religion was necessary to restrain the effervescence of the passions. Without it the blacks would again abandon themselves to their brutal instincts and would indulge in new excesses' (quoted in James 2001 [1938]: 302).

For the West Indian plantocracy and its investors, all this was a frightening portent of the horrors that would follow emancipation. They railed against the 'radical' abolitionists with renewed vigour, haunted by the levelling of the 'proper' social order. Here are the protestations of one earl, speaking in 1793:

The idea of abolishing the slave trade is connected with the levelling system and the rights of man ... What does the abolition of the slave trade mean more or less in effect, than liberty and equality? What more or less than the rights of man? And what is liberty and equality, and what the rights of man, but the foolish fundamental principles of this new philosophy. If proofs are wanting, look at the colony of St Domingo and see what the rights of man have done there.

(*Annual Register* 1793: 90, quoted in Fryer 1984: 211)

This sentiment continued to take cues from the leading lights of natural science.

In 1792 a book penned by leading Swedish taxonomist Carl Linnaeus, *Systema naturae*, was translated into English. It described the African in the following terms: 'H. *Afri*. Of black complexion, phlegmatic temperament, and relaxed fibre ... Of crafty, indolent, and careless disposition, and are governed in their actions by caprice ... ' Mindful of Platonic, Cartesian and Newtonian oppositions, consider Linnaeus' thumbnail sketch of the European: 'H. *Europaei*. Of fair complexion, sanguine temperament, and brawny form ... Of gentle manners, acute in judgement, of quick invention and governed by fixed laws ... ' (Linnaeus 1792: 45).

The issue of predictability had also become important. The Age of Reason had identified unpredictability with 'chance, superstition, vulgarity, and unreason' (Hacking 1990: 1). As a result, the oppositions attached to impulse and reason entered the nineteenth century with new bedfellows: (vulgar) chance and (rational) law. While Europeans were subject to 'fixed laws', Africans were 'governed in their actions by caprice'. Impulsivity – which spelt unpredictability, chance and vulgarity – must be brought to the heel of these rational laws, meaning the African must be kept under the stewardship of the white man.

Even the movement for abolition couched its arguments in terms of the 'conditions of possibility' for knowledge which prevailed in late eighteenth- and early nineteenth-century Britain. The rise of the movement was linked to the emergence of a new middle-class consciousness in Britain's urban centres (Oldfield 1998). Here the bewildering variety of choice made available by urban life to the middle-class consumer combined with new fears over indebtedness and contempt for the excesses of the 'Fashionable Great' (some of whose manners and vices were imitated by the 'embroidered rabble') (England 2009 [1772]). This contempt was animated by appeals to nature which often pitted artificial city values against a romanticised bucolic idyll in which simpler, more wholesome values were cherished.

Corresponding with the valorising of nature was a more benevolent stance towards the poor and dispossessed, with charity and almsgiving encouraged and miserliness condemned. Understandably, these concerns offered the prospect of a more enlightened attitude towards black people – though this was by no means universally realised.[22] The American Revolution had unleashed a wave of heated discussion regarding political representation, which saw radicals liken their situation to that of slaves. Disenfranchisement, argued the reformer and former naval officer John Cartwright, 'is the very definition of slavery' (quoted in Oldfield 1998: 33). In many ways it was this connecting of slavery to the political condition of thousands of native-born Britons which gave the struggle for abolition more immediate significance.

Four years after American victory in the Revolutionary War, the Society for the Abolition of the Slave Trade was founded. Its founding members included Samuel Hoare, George Harrison, William Dillwyn, John Lloyd, Joseph Woods, Philip Sansom, Granville Sharp and Thomas Clarkson. They were soon joined by Member of Parliament for Hull, William Wilberforce, who would lead the parliamentary campaign for abolition. Nine of the twelve founding members of the Society were Quakers, while the vast majority hailed from middle-class backgrounds rooted in commerce and business (Gibson Wilson 1996). Their tactics showed a keen awareness of the power of the market and consumer choice. Members of the Society devoted a great deal of time and energy to its subscription lists, and were sure to record as much information as they could about the subscribers, including their status, place of residence, etc. In the context of an emergent consumer society, these details were important as a means of self-advertisement; seeing the names of local people whom one recognised and respected helped the lists to grow. Social emulation was thus a key factor in the Society's mobilisation of public opinion.

Aside from the importance of consumer imperatives, the abolitionists relied on humanitarian and economic arguments.[23] These arguments were informed by the ideas of rationalism, progress and liberty. Society member Granville Sharp thus argued in 1789 that:

> there is no reason for any description of his Majesty's subjects to be alarmed at the proposed abolition of the slave trade under the delusive fear that a decline in the cultivation of the sugar colonies will be the consequence.
>
> (Quoted in Jordan 2005: 96).

The petitioners of Halifax averred that 'by wholesome Laws and humane Treatment of the Negroes already in the islands, the Cultivation of the West India Estates would be effected as a less Expense' (quoted in *Leeds Intelligencer* 1792) (Editorial 1792a). Meanwhile, those identified with the old landed interests in the West Indies slowly began to desert the anti-abolitionist ranks because of fear relating to the likely effects of Caribbean over-production, rather than any humanitarian issues (Anstey 1975; Pollock 2007; Williams 1964).

The American Revolution, as well as inflaming debate over representation, saw the cause of anti-slavery become linked with the character and destiny of the British nation. After British defeat in America, abolition came to be seen as a redemptive act (Colley 2003). A notion of general, indefinite progress had taken hold in Britain after 1760 (Spadafora 1990), manifested by material advance as well as population growth, the cause of liberty and shifting attitudes towards animals, children, women, the sick and the insane. After the Revolution people began to question whether the slave trade was compatible with this vision of progress and, furthermore, whether it was an impediment to future progress. Petitioners in Birmingham dubbed the trade a 'National Disgrace' (quoted in *Aris's Birmingham Gazette* 1792) (Editorial 1792b) while a Halifax meeting in 1788 deemed it 'unworthy of the Character of Britons' as citizens of 'the most liberal Nation on Earth ... to support Commerce by Slavery' (quoted in *Leeds Intelligencer*, Editorial 1788a). The people of Plymouth thought the slave trade was 'directly opposite to that inherent love of freedom which characterises this nation' (quoted in *Sherborne Mercury* 1788) (Editorial 1788b), a nation described throughout the 1792 petition campaign as 'free and enlightened' (Oldfield 1998).

Many petitioners followed Society stalwart Thomas Clarkson in focusing on the ruinous effect of the trade on the health of British seamen. As Michael Jordan (2005: 90) has documented, 'He (Clarkson) and others in the committee discerned, accurately, that blue-stocking readers were likely to be more sympathetic to the welfare of British sailors aboard slave ships than their African cargoes.'

Slaves were described in terms consistent with the picture of progress, change, sensitivity and compassion which enjoyed wide currency among Britain's middle-classes. Literary representations of slaves such as Sancho in Priscilla Wakefield's *Excursions in North America* or the 'Negro beggar' in Thomas Day's *The History of Sanford and Merton* were 'children of nature', 'helpless innocents dragged away from their "happy homes" by fraud and violence' (Oldfield 1998: 144). Olaudah Equiano, perhaps the most prominent African involved in the abolitionist movement, saw abolition as 'the next link in the chain by which (blacks) could haul themselves out of degradation' (quoted in Fryer 1984: 111). In arguing the cause of abolition in the House of Commons in 1805 – two years before the passing of the Slave Trade Act which outlawed British involvement in the trade – Wilberforce intoned that Africa's 'negro' inhabitants represented 'a degraded race of beings, actuated only by a brutal impulse' whose lot was 'capable of much improvement' (Hansard 1805: 672).

The infantilising of 'the negro' was deeply ingrained. As Fryer has stated: 'Virtually every science and intellectual in nineteenth-century Britain took it for granted that only people with white skin were capable of thinking and governing' (1984: 169). By the time of the Emancipation Act in 1833, although 'The Negro was legally freed ... in the British mind he was still mentally, morally and physically a slave' (Stepan 1982: 1). But why was this so? The social and political context of Britain was an important factor. Industrial capitalism was being handed the baton from its mercantile forerunner, and this stretched the distance between colonial metropole and satellite, the industrial and non-industrial, white Britons and non-white colonial subjects and, of course, between the governors and those governed. Like the economic necessities of the plantocracy, the material conditions of the metropole affected the race-thinking of British intellectual life.

The early stages of the nineteenth century saw the emergence of physical anthropology, whose proponents were largely enabled by the return to vogue of the Great Chain of Being (Stocking 1996). This idea can be traced back to Aristotle's *Scala Naturae* which had nature arrayed along a great continuous ladder; indeed, to distinguish between each rung required a sensitivity to almost imperceptible graded differences (Lovejoy 1976). The Chain spanned the breadth of nature from simple organisms to Man, implying that even complex, 'higher' beings shared some nature of the 'lower' animals. This fuelled speculation over the link between man and the animals, a link strengthened by research involving primates. Another task was to map the races of man onto this graded scheme, and back up widely held assumptions about racial hierarchy with hard physical evidence. At the beginning of the nineteenth century the fledging discipline of phrenology was first to take up the cudgels. It would dominate the landscape of racial science for the first 50 years of the century (Stepan 1982).

The science of phrenology took shape within the distinctive social and intellectual environment of post-revolutionary France (Tomlinson 2005). This environment, as Frank Manuel argues, hosted 'one of the crucial developments in modern intellectual history ... the reversal from the eighteenth century view of man as more or less equal ... to the early nineteenth century emphasis upon human uniqueness, diversity, and dissimilarity' (1971: 221). Names synonymous with this influential but short-lived endeavour include Franz-Joseph Gall, Johan Gasper Spurzheim, George Combe, Horace Mann and Samuel Howe. The method was first formulated by Gall, who envisioned a practice that involved reading the character and abilities of a man from the size of his mental organs (as revealed by the contours of the cranium). Spurzheim oversaw the transformation of phrenology from a practice to a fully developed social and moral philosophy: a prescriptive system defined around middle-class values such as balance, order and conscientiousness. Combe popularised the science in Britain, targeting the working classes with a programme of reform based upon the values of self-help and practical Christianity (Tomlinson 2005).

Grasping the skull in hand and giving its contours a learned grope told people little they didn't already know. In 1819 the British surgeon Sir William Lawrence decided to enter the world of phrenology to tie his beliefs about 'race' and culture to the structure of the 'Negro' skull. He opined that black people

> indulge, almost universally, in disgusting debauchery and sensuality ... insensibility to beauty of form, order, and harmony, and almost entire want of ... elevated sentiments, manly virtues, and moral feeling ... The inferiority of the dark to the white races is much more general and strongly marked in the powers of knowledge and reflection, the intellectual faculties ... than in moral feelings and dispositions.
>
> (Lawrence 1819: 363)

As such, black people were controlled by bodily urges, consigned to lower life, and incapable of reflective, intellectual enterprise. In 1825 Combe spoke in the same vein: Africa was 'an unbroken scene of moral and intellectual desolation' (1825: 563), while the higher forehead and moral organs of the African indicated deficiencies in 'Conscientiousness, Cautiousness, Ideality, and Reflection' (ibid: 582).

The influence of these ideas was also being felt in the world of sport. In the late eighteenth and early nineteenth centuries a handful of black pugilists – predominantly African Americans – made a name for themselves in Britain. Some arrived under servitude; others came in search of the best fighters that Britain had to offer. Chief amongst them were Bill Richmond and Tom Molineaux, though a host of others are worthy of honourable mention, as Massa Kendrick receives here. The son of Georgia-born slaves, Richmond travelled to Britain at the age of 14 as servant to a British General. After a spell in Yorkshire he moved to London, becoming a prize-fighter in the early 1800s. In Pierce Egan's 1823 book *Boxiana*, Richmond is described as calm, yet prone to outbursts of violence: 'placid, even to the degree that could not be expected ... In instances of unmerited reproach, his indignation would no longer let him remain quiet' (1823: 448). Indeed, according to Nat Fleischer, 'when provoked, he was a real terror' who wore 'an excited and somewhat nervous look upon his ebony countenance' (1938: 24–27). In the art of boxing, his abilities were innate rather than studied or considered: 'his knowledge of the science is completely intuitive' (Egan 1823: 447).

In 1803 Richmond welcomed another young African–American fighter, who had arrived in Britain after working his passage as a deckhand. This was Tom Molineaux, described by Dowling as 'a rude, unsophisticated being', who, 'resting upon his pugilistic pretensions to excellence, offered himself to the notice of the public' (Egan 1823: 361). He was taken under the wing of Richmond and went on to enjoy an illustrious career, his most iconic moment being a narrow defeat to Tom Cribb that lasted 39 rounds. His last fight occurred in 1815.

According to reports, Molineaux trained little: 'It would be absurd to remark, that MOLINEAUX underwent any thing like regular training'

(Egan 1823: 368). His first trainer complained that the young fighter was 'too docile and didn't take his training too seriously' (quoted in Fleischer 1938: 44). In the ring he relied on uncontrollable outbursts of ferocity rather than well-honed skill: 'Rimmer's spirited conduct made Molineaux quite ferocious, who went in desperately, and was intemperate enough to make play' (Egan 1823: 365); 'upon the appearance of blood, (Molineaux) became rather impetuous. He attacked Fuller ferociously' (Ward 1814, cited in Fleischer 1938: 44). In 1997 George MacDonald Fraser's *Black Ajax*, a historical novel about the life of Molineaux, was published. Into the mouth of Lucien de la Guise, the cousin of Molineaux's slave owner Richard Molineaux, Fraser put the following appraisal:

> Obedient to the commands of Spicer (Molineaux's trainer), Tom delivers his blows and at once retires, back or to the side as seems best, in ungainly fashion. But as Spicer continues to cry: 'Circle, circle!' his gait changes, as though by some instinct in his primitive brain.
>
> (1997: 31)

Another black fighter to dock on British shores was Massa Kendrick. Originally from St. Kitts in the British West Indies, Kendrick came to London in 1811, announcing his arrival by goading Bill Richmond into a street fight. Most of his activity in the ring occurred between 1819 and 1826, with Kendrick enjoying mixed success. Fleischer described Kendrick as 'a pugnacious chap ... an unruly fellow and his refusal to train properly, cost him dearly' (1938: 66). The roughly sketched portrait of the black pugilist thus contained many well-rehearsed characterisations. Outside the boxing ring, these characterisations continued to be developed by physical anthropologists.

By the middle of the nineteenth century physical anthropology still offered little in the way of sophistication. Robert Knox, a Scottish anatomist and zoologist whose likeness was burned in effigy for his role in the Burke–Hare body snatching saga of 1828, exemplified many of its tendencies. He took it upon himself to cobble together the most virulent scraps of racist anthropology in circulation at the time. In the resulting *The Races of Men*, published in 1850, Knox made himself clear: 'respecting the size of some African skulls ... I feel disposed to think that there must be a physical and, consequently, a physiological inferiority in the dark races generally' (1850: 226). The 'eternal, unalterable qualities of race' polarised Saxons and Africans and engendered a mutual hatred that was equally immutable: 'Furthest removed from the Saxon race, the antipathy between these races is greater than between any other: in each other they perceive their direct antagonists' (ibid: 449). Saxons possessed 'acquisitive and applicative genius' (ibid: 10), while Africans were 'lazier than an Irishman' (ibid: 235–36) and 'merely feel the instinct' (ibid: 449). The raciological ideas of laziness and impulse/instinct had survived the birth of physical anthropology.

Indeed, the 1850s saw Henry Mayhew make dilettantish references to physical anthropology in the introduction to his *London Labour and the London Poor*. Citing a Dr Pritchard, Mayhew distinguished between skulls that wander, skulls that settle, and those of a mediate variety. Among 'hunters and savage inhabitants of forests ... a form of head is prevalent which is mostly distinguished by the term "prognathous", indicating a prolongation or extension forward of the jaws' (1851: 1). The wanderers had 'broad lozenge-shaped faces and pryamidal skulls'. The civilised – 'those who live by the arts of cultivated life' – 'have a shape that differs from both of the above mentioned', theirs were 'oval or elliptical' (ibid).

Subsequent references to impulse and instinct were inevitable. Mayhew's gravest fears about the lower orders of London were embodied by those crafty hawkers of fruit and vegetables, the costermongers. His portrayal of this group entrenched their place within Victorian iconography. But in the spirit of this era, descriptions of the costermonger relied on references to other undesirables. Costermongers were

> men whom, for the most part, are allowed to remain in nearly the same primitive and brutish state as the savage – creatures with nothing but their appetites, instincts, and passions to guide them ... and the same utter ignorance as marks either the Bosjesman, Carib, or Thug.
>
> (Mayhew 1851: 213)

'We have witnessed how', he commented of the costermonger elsewhere in the first volume, 'instinct with all the elements of manhood and beasthood, the qualities of the beast are principally developed in him, while those of the man are stunted in their growth' (ibid: 25). Mayhew afforded a brief but telling glimpse at the motivations behind this damning portrayal. Here his concerns were laid bare: 'The politics of these people are detailed in a few words – they are nearly all Chartists ... Their ignorance and their being impulsive, makes them a very dangerous class' (ibid: 20).

Over the course of the 1840s and 1850s the appeal of phrenology began to ebb. However, its positivistic tenor and commitment to investigating 'racial' differences – within a continuous natural domain – would be grasped again later in the century, when physical anthropology gained its second wind (Stocking 1968).

The next two important developments, as well as forcing us to backtrack 15 years or so, occurred in the realm of ideas but had huge material implications. The first took place in 1835 with the emergence of Quetelet's *homme type*, or Average Man (Cooper 2007). The *homme type* tied a statistical average to a delimited group of people, rather than to the human species in its known entirety. This meant taking stock of national characteristics and using these averages to pronounce upon racial type. It was seen as a huge development. *Athenaeum* in England lauded the publication of Quetelet's *A Treatise on Man*, in which 'the average man' was propounded, as 'forming an epoch in the literary history of civilization' (1835: 661). The scramble for concrete national and racial statistics was now on.

The idea of the normal and the pathological occupying a single continuum was also crucial. This second development occurred around mid-century and saw the norm come to replace the standard as the most efficient way to diagnose a society's ills (literally, in one sense, as a continuous deviation from the 'normal' was borrowed from pathology.) August Comte, the father of positivism, enshrined this continuum in the world of social science (Giddens 1974). He drew on the work of Broussais who had introduced the continuum to biomedical science a little before 1800. According to Comte, social science should not be based on standards, either met or not met, but should adopt a continuous scale that ranged from the normal to the pathological. This continuum – together with Quetelet's Average Man – proved indispensible to physical anthropology and sociology, and also provided the ideological point of departure for the eugenics movement (Bashford and Levine 2010; Gillam 2002). But it was some time before these disciplines, both steeped in positivism, picked up the ideas of Quetelet and Comte with renewed zeal. For the time being it was the relationship between 'racial' characteristics and political–economic concerns which detained the attentions of the British.

Mid-nineteenth-century Britain was preoccupied with the declining productivity of its colonial plantations. This was quickly linked to the new free status of black plantation workers. As Douglas Lorimer reports, 'By the mid-century, sugar exports had fallen to about 75 per cent of the pre-1833 totals', with planters rationalising that 'African religious practices had survived in contravention of Christian teaching; the sexual norms of a slave past had not adapted to Victorian ideas of rectitude; and, most importantly, blacks had not responded satisfactorily to the capitalist work-ethic' (1978: 125).

For abolitionists, philanthropists and missionaries in Britain, freedom offered the Negro a chance to hoist himself onto a plane of equality with whites. This equality would be indicated by work ethic, which could be measured most accurately in terms of economic output. By 1850, however, overseers reasoned that no such elevation had occurred. The plantocratic machine was beginning to splutter, and the alleged explanation was black indolence. As the newspaper *John Bull* suggested, 'the negro is disinclined to labour, and has not the disposition towards self-improvement manifested by the white man' (Editorial 1859: 825).

But the most bilious description of black indolence was written by Thomas Carlyle. Described by *The Cambridge History of English Literature* as 'The strongest moral force in the literature of his time', in his *Occasional*

Discourse on the Nigger Question (1853) Carlyle averred that Africans had been created inferior and as such should serve their European masters. In the face of economic downturn and social upheaval, Carlyle's invective throbbed with desperation and made his most urgent concerns very clear:

> How pleased, in the universal bankruptcy abroad, and dim stagnancy at home, as if for England too there remained nothing but to suppress Chartist riots, banish united Irishmen ... and wait with arms crossed till black anarchy and Social Death devoured us also; how pleasant to have always this fact to fall upon: Our beautiful black darlings are at last happy, with little labour except to the teeth, which surely, in those excellent horse jaws of theirs, will not fail!
>
> (Carlyle 1853: 4)

He drew parallels between freed African slaves, the British working classes, and the Irish: 'To have "emancipated" the West Indies into a Black Ireland; "free" indeed, but an Ireland, and Black! ... At home too, the British Whites are rather badly off, several millions of them hanging on the verge of continual famine' (ibid: 4). Carlyle was also troubled by women, whom he saw as rebellious: 'We have thirty thousand Distressed Needle-women, – the most of whom cannot sew a reasonable stitch; for they are, in fact, Mutinous Serving-maids, who, instead of learning to work and obey, learned to give warning' (ibid). And for the freed black of the West Indies, Carlyle sounded this cautionary note:

> Alas, let him (the freed black) look across to Haiti, and trace a far sterner prophecy! Let him, by his idleness, rebellion, banish all White men from the West Indies, and make it all one Haiti ... nothing but a dog-kernel and a pestiferous jungle – does he think that will for ever continue to gods and men?
>
> (Ibid: 38)

For Carlyle, the freed black slave needed delivering from his impulsive out-bursts of violence lest he 'die of sullen irreconcilable rage, of brutish laziness and darkness' (ibid: 15).

By this time the basic anthropological universalism present in Locke's *Two Treatises* was echoed only faintly in the work of figures such as J. S. Mill (Rosen 2003). Like Carlyle, though in less colourful prose, Mill argued that independence for Britain's 'black' colonies was undesirable for all parties. In his essay *On Liberty*, a defence of the principle of liberty as necessary for the mental development of human beings, Mill followed Locke in applying the principle to mature adults only. Crucially, he extended this line of argument in refusing to apply the principle of liberty to 'backward societies', and in doing so introduced the idea of historical progress into the canon of liberalism bequeathed to him by Locke:

> Liberty, as a principle, has no application to any state of things anterior to the time when mankind have become capable of being improved by free and equal discussion. Until then, there is nothing for them but obedience to an Akbar or a Charlemagne, if they are so fortunate as to find one.
>
> (Mill 1859: 16)

Countries occupying a lowly position on Mill's imaginary civilisational scale, and hence located at a 'great distance' from Britain, should be ruled by 'advanced' nations. They were not yet civilised enough to cope with the demands of self-rule, and some period of development and civilisation – more specifically, of colonial rule and education – must elapse before they were fit for such demands (Sullivan 1983). However, because Britain would always progress more quickly, backward nations forever lagged behind and this way the realisation of their independence could be deferred indefinitely.

Mill put forward this historicist argument in refusing to sanction the self-governance of African and Indian populations. Like other nineteenth-century liberals, he drew upon and valorised the 'cosmopolitan right' propounded by Kant. Indeed, the liberal framework was now wedded to notions of cosmopolitanism and progress, a union achieved by combining putative grades of schooling with stages of historical development using the structure of Kant's federated system. As we have seen, the dependence on notions of education and maturity issued from Locke's characterisation of tutelage as a necessary stage through which children must be guided in order that they acquire the reason necessary for expressing contractual consent, an argument eventually distilled into the 'white man's burden' in the early twentieth century.

The view of the African as immature in civilisational terms wasn't confined to the West Indian plantocracy and the architects of liberalism. Governor G. D'arcy of Gambia wrote in 1862 that, 'Viewing the African as a labourer ... being without education, he acts from impulse, and has no control over his emotions and passions' (quoted in Lorimer 1978: 124). That same year, speech therapist and hobby anthropologist James Hunt delivered his now infamous paper 'Negro's Place in Nature' to members of the London Anthropological Society in London. Hunt adduced a number of 'facts we now have at hand' in explaining 'the physical and mental characteristics of the Negro, with a view of determining ... the station he should occupy in the genus Homo' (1864: 5). Among these 'facts' was the testimony of Count Gorz, who wrote of the Negro in Cuba: 'Their character is very degraded; the moral feeling entirely undeveloped; all their actions proceed from animal impulse' (quoted in Hunt 1864: 19). The following year saw *Blackwood's Edinburgh Magazine* begin to serialise the diary of explorer John Hanning Speke. According to an article published in January 1864, two factors hindered the captain in his efforts to discover the source of the Nile: 'the haughty rigidness of the court etiquette, and the impulsive African natures ever bounding against its restraints' (Speke 1864: 12).

Anthropological interest in the Irish had also intensified (Stepan 1982); this at a time when, in the aftermath of the Chartist movement, workers in Britain were squaring up to the political and economic clout of the ruling classes. Further comparisons between blacks, the Irish and the working classes were not long in coming. As Bernard Semmel contended:

> The English governing classes in the 1860's regarded the Irish and the non-European 'native' peoples just as they had, quite openly, regarded their own labouring classes for many centuries: as thoroughly undisciplined, with a tendency to revert to bestial behaviour, consequently requiring to be kept in order by force, and by occasional but severe flashes of violence; naturally lazy and unwilling to work unless under compulsion.
>
> (1962: 134–35)

Victor Kiernan has argued along similar lines, asserting that:

> discontented native in the colonies, labour agitator in the mills, were the same serpent in alternate disguises. Much of the talk about the barbarism or darkness of the outer world, which it was Europe's mission to rout, was a transmuted fear of the masses at home.
>
> (1969: 316)

These masses were conjured through colonial tropes. The slums of the East End – deprived areas straddling that lifeblood of empire, the River Thames – were 'a wilderness wherein they, who live like wild beasts upon their fellow creatures, find prey and cover' (Southey 1829: 108). They were 'swamps' peopled by 'shadows' that could only be meliorated by an urgent and rigorous subjection to 'progress' (Godwin 1972 [1859]: 1).

Carlyle also proved to be a trailblazer in his castigation of women. They wouldn't be spared the discourses of idleness current at the time. As Anne McClintock has argued, 'A commonplace story depicts the middle-class Victorian woman's life as a debauch of idleness' (1995: 160). The manufactories had stolen the labours of tailoring, millinery, wool-sorting, etc. traditionally performed by women. Industrial modernity saw to it that they were no longer seen as productive by eliding their domestic labour and peddling the myth of their uselessness. Though sat idle in the drawing room rather than the plantation or the slum, women were likewise given to indolence and impulse: 'Her dreamy torpor was ruffled only by hysterical ailments ... given to irrationality and hysteria' (ibid: 160). The idle yet periodically hysterical woman became 'domestic woman' defined, along with her lazy yet impulsive counterparts in imperial discourse, against 'economic man'.[24]

By the 1860s British eyes were fastened on events taking place across the Atlantic and, more specifically, on the practices of American slavery. Lancashire depended on the importation of cotton from the southern states, and British interest in West Africa had waned. Furthermore, economic downturn had seen class distinctions become more salient. People's opinions about 'race' fell back on assumptions about class difference, and mid-Victorian attitudes to events taking place in the American south reflected this preoccupation. With the American Civil War underway, many Britons lent their voices to concerns over prospective emancipation in the US, with the fall in sugar production along with the violence of St. Domingo and the Indian Mutiny of 1857 weighing heavily on their minds. But in 1865, with the dust of the Civil War settling and emancipation realised, Britain received a jolt from the Caribbean. A rebellion was fomenting within its own sphere of imperial control, and the fallout would hold up a mirror to British society by stoking debate over 'race', class and, to a lesser extent, gender (Walvin 1973).

On 11 October 1865 the court house in Morant Bay, Jamaica, became engulfed by a crowd of black settlers. It had gathered to express frustration at the skewed notion of justice promoted by local magistrates. These magistrates, who were also local planters, had a tendency to mete out harsh sentences to settlers accused of occupying land which they did not rightfully own. The crowd was promptly read the Riot Act – but to no avail. They edged towards the house and began to hurl stones. A militia, a group of volunteers called the 'Custos', retaliated by firing rounds into the group of settlers, killing seven and wounding numerous others. The crowd responded angrily, forcing the Custos back into the courthouse, after which the two groups exchanged shots for several hours. Settlers eventually set the house alight, forcing the Custos and court officials to flee, with the rioters in close pursuit. The Custos along with 15 other officials were murdered, and the rebels went on to raid a number of estates, killing two more local white planters (Higman 2010; Thomson 2009).

The Governor of Jamaica, Edward John Eyre, was in Kingston receiving garbled reports from Morant Bay; he wasted no time in declaring martial law. This lasted for 30 days during which troops executed 439 black settlers and flogged 600 others, burning over 1,000 huts and other homesteads along the way. The troops encountered no resistance. Eyre suspected that local mulatto landowner – and vocal critic of the Governor – George William Gordon – had masterminded the uprising. He ensured that Gordon was hunted down, tried before a summary court martial, and executed. But Eyre hadn't anticipated the groundswell of opinion brewing at home. Surprised by mixed reactions to his handling of the affair, he tried to head off further criticism by appealing to African caricature:

> The negro is a creature of impulse and imitation, easily misled, very excitable, and a perfect fiend when under the influence of excitement which stirs up all the evil passions of a race little removed in many respects from absolute savagery.
>
> (Communication with the Colonial Office 1866)

But opposition was beginning to mount. Political reformers in Britain were quick to draw parallels between events in Jamaica and their own struggles to bring about parliamentary reform.[25] Piqued by the winds of change blowing through Britain and its overseas territories, the government took action. Eyre was suspended and a Royal Inquiry commissioned. The subsequent report, presented to parliament in April 1866, failed to placate philanthropists and political activists, who by then had formed the Jamaica Committee. The Committee responded by initiating its own legal proceedings against the former Governor, charging him with the murder of Gordon (Evans 2005). Sympathizers with Eyre, in no short supply at the time, responded by forming the Governor Eyre Defence and Aid Committee. The battle lines had been drawn in a struggle that would captivate Victorian England, pulling various luminaries and intellectuals within its orbit. In Eyre's corner – as official members of his Aid Committee – were the Earl of Shrewsbury and Thomas Carlyle. Other Eyre supporters included John Ruskin and Charles Dickens. Serving on the executive of the Jamaica Committee were John Stuart Mill, Thomas Huxley and Herbert Spencer among others, while the Committee was also supported by Sir Charles Lyell and Charles Darwin. Amid the hue and cry of the subsequent court case and its portrayal in the public arena, a well-worn set of raciological ideas were recited. As Douglas Lorimer has pointed out, 'the difference between the two opinions in the Eyre controversy demonstrated that the mid-Victorians' differences in racial attitudes were closely related to differences in political outlook' (1978: 181).

The *Morning Herald* issued its approval to the authorities in Jamaica: 'The original nature of the African betokened itself in acts of horrible mutilation ... after all, the executions were important as examples, and the rabble of this rebellion were in all likelihood drunken and worthless savages responsible for their misdeeds' (cited in Lorimer 1973: 184). According to a legal reporter for *The Times*, this 'original nature' saw blacks carry out the most flagrant atrocities *on both sides*. W. F. Finlason claimed that, aside from the bloodthirsty acts of violence perpetrated by rebels, responsibility for excessive military violence lay with the Maroon and Negro soldiers of the West India Regiment (1869: 361). Reacting to the uprising, Professor

John Tyndall wrote a letter to his scientific colleague, Joseph Hooker, opining that 'the Negro is ... as a rule eminently fickle, impulsive and cruel', and that he considered 'the Negro far below the level of the Englishmen'. However, he conceded that 'there are many Englishmen worse than the Negro, because the worst classes of the best races are worse than the worst of any and all the inferior races' (1867: 340). Indeed, the *Saturday Review* drew a direct comparison between the impulsive, unthinking nature of black settlers and that of the English working class mob. According to an article published in an 1866 edition of the *Review*, the Negro 'is neither ferociously cruel nor habitually malignant. He often does cruel and barbarous things; but so do our draymen and hackney-coachmen and grooms and farm-servants through want of either power or thinking' (Editorial 1866).

Women also lent certain characteristics to the portrait of the mob. The latter decades of the nineteenth century – as well as witnessing the upheaval of Morant Bay, anarchist attacks, and the Trafalgar Square revolts – saw demands by female insurgents for access to education and suffrage (Pugh 1986). This brushed the mob with the image of femininity. For Gabriel Tarde, the mob's 'fickleness' and 'docility' were characteristically female: 'The crowd is feminine, even when it is composed, as is usually the case, of males' (quoted in Barrows 1981: 47).[26]

Legal proceedings against Eyre foundered in 1868. But the domestic crisis brought about by the Morant Bay affair ensured that debates over black indolence were dredged up and resumed against the backdrop of rebellion. As the African explorer Sir Samuel Baker remarked in 1870:

A creature of impulse, seldom actuated by reflection, the black man astounds by his complete obtuseness ... He is acted upon by the bad passions inherent in human nature ... And these natural instincts being a love of idleness and savagedom, he will assuredly relapse into an idle and savage state, unless specially governed and forced to industry.

(1870: 269)

Faced by economic hardship and concerted protests for reform, and rather than drag individual threats along in single file, the Victorian ruling classes recognised an opportunity to conflate both domestic and colonial threats to the socio-economic order. The most potentially disastrous were those posed by idleness and impulsiveness; they spelt decreased productivity and paroxysms of rebellion. The rationalisation of these threats drew on an image that became the articulating metaphor *par excellence* – the degenerate crowd: 'As the embodiment of deviant agency, the crowd became the metonymic symbol of the unemployed and unruly poor; who were in turn associated with women; who were associated with "primitives" and the realm of empire' (McClintock 1995: 119). It was peopled by various forms of lower life – lazy, impulsive, and unpredictable – and required subjection to rational, economical control. In the meantime the ruling classes, headed up by economic man, had been furnished with a new theory to explain their social and economic supremacy. This would see rituals of abjection, so central to the management of empire, don the graded stripes of evolutionism. The following chapter recounts this story, describing how evolutionary biology, then evolutionary psychology, cast the idea of the 'impulsive' black male in a new light.

Chapter 3

Darwin, Freud and 'good instincts'

Another bout of intense research in physical anthropology took place during the last few decades of the nineteenth century. Researchers were buoyed by the positivism of Comte and the continuing digestion of Darwin's *Origin of Species*, published in 1859. Darwin's work had placed man firmly within nature's overarching scheme. But as is the case with so many groundbreaking ideas, the decade following the release of *Origin* was witness to intense controversy and resistance (Dennett 1996). Its publication did not represent a threshold, 'before and after' moment in intellectual history (Desmond and Moore 1992). So rather than billing this moment as a scientific revolution or epistemic rupture, we can borrow a useful metaphor from the French philosopher of science, Pierre Duhem. He used the motion of a mounting tide to conceptualise scientific progress:

> Whoever casts a brief glance at the waves striking a beach does not see the tide mount; he sees a wave rise, run, uncurl itself, and cover a narrow strip of sand, then withdraw by leaving dry a terrain which it had seemed to conquer, a new wave follows, sometimes going a little further than the preceding one.
>
> (Duhem 1956 [1906]: 38)

Perhaps Darwin's mammoth contribution is best conceived in this way. His work certainly raked all the intellectual and scientific shingle of preceding years to develop a theory that ventured further than any existing doctrine.[1] The view of progressive time consummated during the Enlightenment clearly influenced Darwin's theory of evolution; it also helped to shape the eugenics movement pioneered by his half-cousin, Francis Galton.

Humanity after Darwin: savagery, the child and the 'criminal man'

Eventual assent to Darwin's work showed in a profusion of evolutionary metaphors. In many instances these were used to denigrate members of the lower orders and throne the white, middle-class European (male) at the top of the evolutionary tree (Wolpoff and Caspari 2007). Acceptance of evolutionary theory also meant a change in the way that impulse and instinct were understood. Drawing on the work of naturalist Jean-Baptiste Lamarck, anthropologists came to see habitual impulses organised as instinct. As the historian of anthropology George Stocking has put it, 'a Lamarckian view of mental evolution ... [meant] a gradual incorporation of habitual experience into the instinctual structure of the brain' (1987: 226). This was demonstrated by philosopher and political theorist Herbert Spencer, whose work remained loyal to Lamarck's conception of instinct (Francis 2007).

Thinkers in the late nineteenth century tried to assimilate both their intellectual biases and racial prejudices to Darwin's theory. In his attempt at a systematic evolutionary theory, Spencer argued that 'Nearly everyone' testifies to the 'quick perceptions of the uncivilized' whose predominating trait was 'impulsiveness' (Spencer 1876: 84–5). He described the ultimate criterion of 'fitness' in evolutionary struggle (within the intellectual and moral spheres) as the repression of immediate impulsive responses. Reminiscent of Chrysippus and the Stoics 2000 years before, this mastery 'marked off those who were intellectually capable of conceiving the future consequences of their behaviour, and who were morally capable of bringing instinctive impulse within the control of this rational conception' (Stocking 1987: 228). Even those who rejected Lamarckian principles gave instinct and impulse a central role in marking off lower rungs of the evolutionary ladder. In *Hereditary Genius*, a preliminary text of the eugenics movement, Francis Galton depicted the impulsive savage without indulging his well-known fondness for statistics:

> Much more alien to the genius of an enlightened civilization than the nomadic habit, is the impulsive and uncontrolled nature of the savage ... The instinct of a savage is admirably consonant with the needs of savage life; every day he is in danger through transient causes; he lives from hand to mouth, in the hour for the hour, without care for the past or forethought for the future: but such an instinct is utterly at fault in civilized life ... The conscience of the Negro is aghast at his own wild, impulsive nature, and is easily stirred by the preacher, but it is scarcely possible to ruffle the self-complacency of a steady-going Chinaman.
>
> (1869: 348–50)

Popular evolutionism had become a veritable cosmology for the Victorian middle-classes. By comparison with the savage, and by direct appeal to impulse, it could neutralise any perceived threats from members of the lower orders. Just as the metaphor of the crowd had served to relieve ruling class tensions, those who made up the unruly crowd (both at home and abroad) were recast in an evolutionary mould. The line-up was the same: Negros, women, peasants, Irishmen. 'What they shared, with each other and with savages, were certain mental characteristics: governed more by impulse, deficient in foresight, they were in varying degrees unable to subordinate instinctual need to human rational control' (Stocking 1987: 229). As in the past, these groups had something else in common besides their impulsiveness: they were all exploited by British imperial rule. In revisiting McClintock's terminology, (pop) evolutionism furthered the process of their abjection.

It did this in a number of ways. With the gradations of evolution scaled between more or less developed, higher and lower forms of life, subordinate positions in the social and evolutionary hierarchy were seen to correspond. Those 'immature' in evolutionary terms were not fit to participate in civil society on equal terms with white, middle-class males. The concession was that their progress and eventual 'fitness' for equal participation was inevitable; however, the notion of evolutionary gradualism made this progress painstakingly slow. As Plato's oppositions and Cartesian–Newtonian orthodoxy had been before, evolutionary metaphors were flogged at the altar of professional, political and economic expedience: 'The law that nature makes no jumps can be taught by the history of mechanical contrivances, in such a way as at least to make men cautious how they listen to scatter-brained revolutionary suggestions' (Pitt Rivers 1891: 116). All this hastened the emergence of certain paradigmatic figures. These represented the twin faces of savagery: the child and the criminal. Both were impulsive, instinctive and emphatically male[2] – while the characterisations imputed to these figures also featured in commentary on the black sportsmen of the day.

The child

As Cynthia Russett (1989) has detailed, a revaluation of childhood took place among scientists and political commentators in the latter decades of the nineteenth century. Images of the fresh-faced, innocent child gave way to those of the nefarious newborn. The views of sexologist and social reformer Havelock Ellis pointed towards the political utility of these images: 'The child is naturally, by his organization, nearer to the animal, to the savage, to the criminal, than the adult' (1860: 212).

The international political climate of the 1870s meant that Darwinian theory was interpreted and used in distinctive ways. European leaders were steeling themselves in preparation for the Scramble for Africa, and aware that the 'dark continent' would soon become a crucible of imperial competition, nationalisms were being ratcheted up at home. It was this environment which shaped notions of the 'unfit' and invested social

Darwinism with such force, and in many ways the physical anthropology of the day amounted to the major European powers sizing each other up in Darwinian terms. This meant reinterpreting European history in terms of race struggle, with the victors winning out by virtue of their biological fitness.

As well as following from a politically charged reading of Darwin's theory, the intensification of research in physical anthropology was fuelled by the invention of new-fangled devices and formulas for measuring the skull and the body's various other extremities. In 1844 Swedish anatomist Anders Retzius had introduced the cephalic index for charting the skull's dimensions (as a refinement of Camper's eighteenth-century facial angle), and after 1870 Frenchmen Broca and Topinard continued to develop instruments for similar purposes. Broca, widely considered the father of physical anthropology, founded the Société d'Anthropologie de Paris in 1859. In the following 35 years over 25 million Europeans had their anthropometric measurements recorded (Stocking 1968). This European narcissism directed attention away from Africa and its inhabitants, but the process was so smooth because assumptions regarding Negro inferiority were widely accepted by the time anthropometrics came to vogue. The data provided by such measurements permitted the levelling of an individual down to the generalised attributes of a given 'race'.

Much like the evolutionary bravado of Europe's major powers, justification for the impending Scramble and conquest of African peoples did not rest on any accurate reading of Darwin. Existing prejudices about the inferiority of Africans (along with other members of 'the lower orders') were simply translated into the vocabulary of evolutionism. As such, the 'lower' races were laggards within evolution's 'survival of the fittest'; they represented the underdeveloped stages of the white European in his days as an evolutionary fledgling. Within such a framework the emergence of the child savage as an evolutionary motif did not require any intellectual contortion on the part of anthropologists. Cast in the role of evolutionary child, the Negro was fused in an underdeveloped state where maturity meant being middle-class, European and male. The logic was simple. Echoing the conceptions of lower life first outlined by Plato, 'in savage life ... Darwin believed man was governed by instinct' (Stepan 1982: 64). It followed that if 'periods of maturity ... differ among races as they do among plants', the Negro was a 'child race' (Browne 1901: 15 cited in Stocking 1968: 66).

Thus, after measuring 152 skulls belonging to Negros and Europeans, American physical anthropologist Robert Bennett Bean concluded the following:

> The Caucasian is dominant and domineering, and possessed primarily with determination, will power, self-control, self-government, and all the attributes of the subjective self ... The Negro is in direct contrast by

reason of a certain lack of these powers ... there is instability of character incident to lack of self-control ... and there is lack of orientation, or recognition of position and condition of self and environment, evidenced by a peculiar bumptiousness.

(1906: 379)

The view by the turn of the twentieth century was encapsulated by Charles Ellwood:

The negro child, even when reared in a white family under the most favourable conditions, fails to take on the mental and moral characteristics of the Caucasian race. His natural instincts, it is true, may be modified by training, and perhaps indefinitely in the course of generations; but the race habit of a thousand generations or more is not lightly set aside by the voluntary or enforced imitation of visible models, and there is always a strong tendency to reversion.

(Cited in Stocking 1968: 246–7)

The child savage, immature in evolutionary terms because of his slavish adherence to instinct, lacked the menace of the impulsive mob. But when aligned with the political imperatives of the Scramble he became part of the vocabulary of imperialism. In Kipling's *White Man's Burden* (first published in 1899)[3] were found 'new-caught, sullen peoples, half-devil, half-child'. This view of the 'savage' was the centrepiece in the civilising mission's iconography of benevolence. It occluded the violence and barbarity of colonial conquest. But the memory of savage rebellion – in St. Domingo, India and more recently Morant Bay – wasn't erased by the acceptance of Darwinian theory. Fears about the impulsive violence of the savage, now partially subsumed under the Darwinian term 'instinct', still needed to be articulated. These fears were expressed through commentary on the instinctive violence of the psychopathic criminal.

The criminal

In the early 1870s, Jewish–Italian physician Cesare Lombroso had a vision while examining the corpse of a notorious criminal:

At the sight of the skull, I seemed to see all of a sudden lighted up as a vast plain under a flaming sky, the problem of the nature of the criminal – an atavistic being who reproduces in his person the ferocious instincts of primitive humanity and the inferior animals.

(Lombroso and Lombroso-Ferrero 1911: xxv)

As this passage hinted, Lombroso's subsequent work incorporated many of Darwin's theoretical principles (Gibson 2002). In *Criminal Man*, released in 1876, Lombroso concluded that criminals were born, not made. Anthropometric measurement indicated that criminals represented a throwback to the dark days of man's evolutionary past. In their evolutionary immaturity they were like savages or children: 'Savages and criminals are alike in the impetuosity and instability of their passions. Savages ... have quick and violent emotions; while their strength and passions are those of adults, in character they are like children' (Lombroso 2006 [1876]: 69). We need not read between the lines to trace a link between Lombroso's conception of savage, lower life, and the Negro. As Lombroso experts Mary Gibson and Nicole Hahn Rafter state in an introduction to their translation of *Criminal Man*:

> In order to reproduce the flavour and intent of Lombroso's language, we have retained his original terms, including *savages* and *primitives* for non-white peoples ... while these terms prove inappropriate for current academic analysis, they were ... typical of nineteenth-century scientific discourse and provide valuable insight into Lombroso's worldview.
>
> (Ibid: 36)

Lombroso was also influenced by the proximity of the savage and the animal in the evolutionary chain, with the idea of instinct being central to their shared brutality:

> In the animal world, over population results in the abandonment and killing of those unable to work. Savage tribes have inherited this instinct, so that children and wise men continue to murder the infirm with the full consent of those sacrificed.
>
> (Ibid: 178).

In asserting that the African skull was savage and an archetype of the atavistic, born criminal (ibid: 179), Lombroso appealed to anthropometrics:

> Among criminals the jaw is more developed than in normal men. The average weight of the jaw is 84 grams in criminals, 80 g among normal men, and 78 g among the insane. A similar pattern emerges when we examine the diameter of the jaw ... In his study of twenty-four French murderers, Orchanski confirmed that offenders exhibit large jaws similar to those of savage men.
>
> (Ibid: 303)

The implications of Lombroso's criminal anthropology were clear. The savage, in childlike character, instinct and physical form, resembled the paradigmatic criminal. Unsurprisingly, some of these characteristics were applied to black athletes.

'Savage' sportsmen?

Arthur Wharton was Britain's first 'black' footballer. Wharton's father was Grenadian with mixed Scottish and African–Grenadian parents; his mother was the daughter of a Scottish trader and a Fante royal. His father Henry, a reverend, was the first African–Caribbean man to be named General Superintendent of the Gold Coast District of the Wesleyan Missionary Society (Vasili 1998; 2000). Arthur was born here, in Accra, the capital of what is now Ghana. A goalkeeper, Wharton first appeared for Cannock and Cannock White Cross in the season 1883–4 and over the next 20 years would turn out for Darlington (1885–8), Rotherham Town (1889–94 and 1895–6), Sheffield United (1894–5), Stalybridge Rovers (1896–7 and 1899–1900), Ashton North End (1897–9) and Stockport County (1902–4).

During this time Wharton's performances were understood and reported through the idioms of the day. As his biographer Phil Vasili noted after combing through numerous match reports and eye-witness reports, Wharton and other black athletes at this time were repeatedly described in terms of 'agility ... instinctive endurance, insentient durability ... deriving from their animalism' (1998: 186). According to reports, Wharton's performances were animated by impulsive outbursts of activity: '"Darkie" Wharton ... became famous for crouching in the corner of the goal until the last minute when he would literally spring into action, diving across the goal to make fantastic saves' (Burgin, cited in Vasili 1998: 3). Not all were so enamoured of his carefree demeanour: 'Is the darkie's pate too thick for it to dawn upon him that between the posts is no place for a skylark?' (Griffiths, 1887, cited in Vasili 1998: 69); 'Mr Suddell is making a great mistake in trusting so important a task to so fickle a performer' (ibid: 70).

As Wharton's career entered its twilight years, other black sportsmen were having their performances interpreted in similar ways. In 1908 Jack Johnson became the first black heavyweight champion of the world by knocking out Tommy Burns. (Unable to find a venue in the United States, Johnson was forced to stage the title bout in Australia.) In the course of his triumph Johnson's somewhat brash and ostentatious conduct – both inside and outside the ring – had worried Reverend Meyer of the National Free Church Council, who campaigned against Johnson's upcoming fight with 'Bombardier Billy' Wells due to take place in London in 1911:

> The present contest is not wholly one of skill, because on the one side there is added the instinctive passion of the Negro race, which is so differently constituted to our own, and in the present instance will be aroused to do the utmost that animal development can do to retain the championship.

> (Cited in Green 1988)

The 'instinctive passion' of figures such as Johnson – lamented by the Reverend – would soon be cast in new terms.

Humanity after Freud: impulse and instinct under the sign of psy

After the precepts of Darwinian theory had been accepted, biological evolutionism became a wellspring for understandings of historical and contemporary events. But as the nineteenth century drew to a close, biological explanations of the world began to recede and psychology became ever more discrete and legitimate as an avenue of evolutionary investigation. Indeed, psychoanalysis would become the twentieth century's chief model of causality (Gilman 1985). Following the turn to psychology as a source of explanation for various happenings and behaviours, so too the category of 'race' strayed from its biological heartland into the psychological realm (Gilman 1993). This recasting of the evolutionary scale in psychological terms meant a flurry of interest in the primitive mentality, with examinations of the primitive mind relying on analogies between the savage, the child and the criminal. Here I will examine the work of Lucien Levy Bruhl and Carl Jung, but as befitted the high priest of psychoanalysis, Sigmund Freud provided the definitive account of the 'savage' mentality in his *Totem and Taboo* (1918). However, Freud's whole project of psychoanalysis would not have been possible without the intellectual legacy left by Friedrich Nietzsche. So before exploring what psychoanalysis had to say about impulse and instinct, we should pause to consider Nietzsche's contribution to our story.

Nietzsche's philosophy was important in its prefiguring of Freud's work as well as its opposition to Darwinism and unquestioned conceptions of progress 'for the good' (along with the dualisms which they endorsed). In short, Nietzsche began to shed light on the blind spots of modern hubris, his sharp-witted analyses and literary flair providing an inspiration for postmodernist philosophers of the twentieth century. Of the various strains of dissension and penetrating insight contained in Nietzsche's oeuvre, many were addressed to what he called the 'will to power' (Williams 2000). And though Nietzsche's monism had a composite quality which makes it difficult to pull out single strands of his philosophy for the narrow purposes I have in mind here, I shall nevertheless attempt to describe the will to power in terms of its relevance to impulse and instinct without underselling its singular thrust.

Nietzsche noted that since ancient Greece man had been issued with moral prescriptions to control impulses for the sake of his happiness and well-being. This usually meant harnessing them to some 'higher' spiritual end; conduct which accorded to 'higher' forms of life. In doing so man was not only behaving rationally, but was acting as a moral agent.

Recognising this, Nietzsche saw notions of 'rationality' and 'morality' as conjoined; they were both defined by the unyielding repression of impulses. As his biographer Walter Kaufmann has commented: 'moral codes are systems of injunctions against submission to various impulses, and positive moral commandments always enjoin a victory over animal instincts' (1974: 214). But Nietzsche was not given to dualistic thinking. He echoed the German Romantics in rejecting the entrenched opposition between rationality and nature, reason and impulse, and refused to sanction the idea that impulse had no rightful place as a motive for action.[4]

For Nietzsche, impulse and reason were two manifestations of one ba force – the will to power. This latter was a drive to self-overcoming and did not mean the victory of one force over its antithesis. Standing aloft was the Nietzschean 'overman', triumphant in his battle for self-overcoming because his ascetic lifestyle had itself become instinctual: 'asceticism becomes in them second nature ... an instinct' (Nietzsche 1973 [1895]: 57). Impulses were not to be quelled or extirpated. To achieve greatness required the mastery and harnessing of strong impulses to appropriate ends (*sublimieren*):

> Instead of employing the great sources of strength, those impetuous torrents of the soul that are so often dangerous and overwhelming, and economizing them, this most shortsighted and pernicious mode of thought, the moral mode of thought, wants to make them dry up ... Overcoming of the affects? – No, if what is implied is their weakening and extirpation. But employing them: which may also mean subjecting to protracted tyranny (not only as an individual, but as a community, race, etc.). At last they are confidently granted freedom again: they love us as good servants and go voluntarily wherever our best interests lie.
>
> (Ibid: 383–4)

It was not he whose impulses were weak or few in number that represented the 'overman', for nothing stood before him to be overcome. Nietzsche summed it up characteristically in one of his aphorisms: 'one must yet have chaos in oneself to be able to give birth to a dancing star' (1969 [1887]: 5). The project of sublimation was a solitary one; it was for the man set apart from the crowd which gathered under the auspices of nationalism, 'race', organised religion or the state. Nietzsche deplored these solidarities because they hindered the individual's ability to realise himself, and to do so for himself alone. He saw those unable to escape the laws and commands of others as weak, conjuring them through familiar analogues:

> All men obey certain laws, and most of them obey laws that others command them to obey. Children do this, and so do primitive men who submit to medicine men, totems, and taboos; and Nietzsche believed

that most of his contemporaries were, in the respect, in the same class
with children and primitives.

(Kaufmann 1974: 250)

Nietzsche's monism also sought to deny any complete separation of soul
from body, and spirit from flesh. The following passage is illustrative:

Suppose we note one day that somebody in the market place laughs
at us as we pass: depending on whether this or that drive is just then at
its height in us ... and depending on the kind of man we are, it will
be an entirely different experience ... one seeks to start a fight about
it; ... another thinks as a consequence how ridiculous he is; and
still another one is gratified that he has contributed to the gaiety
and sunshine of the world.

(Nietzsche, quoted in Kaufmann 1974: 268)

Opposing the simple equation of advancement with the passing of time
which had become popular since the publication of Darwin's *Origin
of Species*, Nietzsche also rejected the image of modern man cutting
an inexorable swathe through history in the name of 'progress'. This conception of absolute, linear, progressive time was challenged by Nietzsche:
'"Progress" is merely a modern idea, that is, a false idea' (1973 [1901]: 4).
Furthermore, by surveying the historical record, Nietzsche came to repudi-
ate his contemporaries and exalt those artists and philosophers whose work
was of a longer vintage: 'The goal of humanity cannot lie in the end but
only in its highest specimens' (1983 [1874]: 9).

These strains of Nietzsche's thinking had a direct bearing on Freud, yet it
was only after Freud's death that Ernest Jones, Freud's former colleague
and confidant, revealed the high esteem in which Nietzsche was held
by the father of psychoanalysis (in his *The Life and Work of Sigmund
Freud* 1953). Most fundamentally, Freud followed Nietzsche in taking a
monistic approach and questioning modern hubris. For Nietzsche's will to
power was substituted Freud's notion of the unconscious, which likewise
threatened the sovereignty of the modern subject. He also drew on notions
of the unconscious which emerged in the science and literature of German
Romanticism.

Rather than bringing his impulses under control, the rational actor was
himself acted upon by irresistible impulses which had their seat in
the unconscious (Muckenhoupt 1997). And this storehouse of suppressed
memories and desires should be understood in a particular way. In 1911
Freud addressed the Weimar Congress of the International Psycho-
Analytical Association. Jones marked the event as momentous because for
the first time Freud 'uttered the dictum that the unconscious contains
not only infantile material but also relics from primitive man' (1953: 363).

As did Nietzsche's, Freud's monism spoke of human universals; all men at all times were subject to the content of their unconscious. Freud's monism – like the implications of Nietzsche's philosophy and the 'proto-psychoanalytical field' of German Romanic science – brought with it an uncomfortable truth: unbeknown to their rational, conscious sides, all men had something of the evolutionary laggard about them (Ornstein 1992).

Having marked the co-ordinates of the unconscious zone – for x and y read infantile and primitive – Freud began a detailed charting of its land-scape.[5] He turned to anthropological descriptions of 'savage' societies to discover which elements of the primitive psyche lived on in the modern unconscious as atavistic throwbacks. On examining these reports he began to draw parallels between the primitive psyche and that of the neurotic.

Freud was harvesting the work of James Frazer, and more specifically his *Golden Bough*, first published in two volumes in 1890.[6] Frazer had explained the customs and conventions of Australian savages, but Freud was not overly concerned with plotting their whereabouts in geographical terms. The scale he had in mind was temporal, and the primitives he read about had yet to rack up any mileage. This gave Freud an opportunity to trace relics of the modern unconscious to the minds of men who muddled around as people might have done during 'pre-historic' times: 'There are men still living who, as we believe, stand very near to primitive man ... and their mental life must have a peculiar interest for us if we are right in seeing in it a well-preserved picture of an early stage of our own development' (1918: 1). In this way Frazer's Australian primitives stood for primitives the world over; however dispersed over the surfaces of the globe, they each stood in the same relation to history.

Totem and Taboo's respective analyses of primitives and neurotics made many appeals to impulse and instinct, and for the most part these notions were used interchangeably:

> The instinctual desire is constantly shifting in order to escape from the impasse and endeavours to find substitutes ... for the prohibited ones. In consequence of this, the prohibition itself shifts about as well, and extends to any new aims which the forbidden impulse may adopt.
>
> (Freud 1918: 30)

Both were called upon as Freud added texture to the primitive, infantile unconscious and drew comparisons between the savage and the neurotic. On the primitive mind: 'in a primitive mind the awakening of the memory of a forbidden action in naturally linked with the awakening of an impulse to put that action into effect' (ibid: 34). The child faced a similar one-sided battle: 'In consequence ... of the child's primitive psychical constitution, the prohibition does not succeed in abolishing the instinct ... and everything else follows from the continuing conflict between the prohibition and the instinct' (ibid: 29). And though the neurotic experienced comparable urges, Freud drew an important distinction. While 'impulses have the full value of facts for the primitive', and though neurotics 'in their childhood ... had these evil impulses ... and turned them into acts so far as the impotence of childhood allowed ... neurotics are above all inhibited in their actions ... Primitive men, on the other hand, are uninhibited: thought passes directly into action' (ibid: 160–1).

But these extracts alone do not do justice to the nuances of *Totem and Taboo*. Though he underlined the impulsive nature of the primitive psyche, Freud set his argument against the backdrop of universality, and some of his contentions can be read as measures toward the redemption of the 'savage' mentality. While savages experienced strong urges to kill their enemies and were wont to act upon them, 'the impulses which they express towards an enemy are not solely hostile ones. They are also manifestations of remorse, of admiration for the enemy, and of a bad conscience for having killed him' (Freud 1918: 39). Freud undertook a similar project for the issue of primitive superstition:

> If we take instinctual repression as a measure of the level of civilization that has been reached, we shall have to admit that even under the animistic system advances and developments took place which are unjustly despised on account of their superstitious basis.
>
> (Ibid: 97)

His argument relied on an analogy with children:

> I am laying myself open to the charge of endowing modern savages with a subtlety in their mental activities which exceeds all probability. It seems to me quite possible, however, that the same may be true of our attitude towards the psychology of those races that have remained at the animistic level as is true of our attitude towards the mental life of children, which we adults no longer understand and whose fullness and delicacy of feeling we have in consequence so greatly underestimated.
>
> (Ibid: 99)

With echoes of Nietzsche's 'overman', Freud also argued that a life dominated by powerful impulses wasn't the sole preserve of the savage. He did so by evoking the figure of the artist:

> Only in art does it still happen that a man who is consumed by desires performs something resembling the accomplishment of those desires ... There can be no doubt that art did not begin as art for art's sake. It worked originally in the service of impulses which are for the most part extinct to-day.
>
> (Ibid: 90)

So, though one reading of *Totem* would ruffle the poise of modern man, seeing civilization as a veneer for a more savage existence, another might strengthen the link between impulsiveness and the primitive mind.

Around the time that Freud was poring over Frazer's anthropological materials and mapping out his argument for *Totem and Taboo*, the French scholar Lucien Levy-Bruhl was writing his *Primitive Mentality* and *How Natives Think* (although both would be released in Britain some time after *Totem*, in 1923 and 1926 respectively). Levy-Bruhl's works were more extensive than *Totem*, but mirrored it in many ways. He likewise drew on the anthropological work of others to bring his argument to life, and followed similar lines when ascribing characteristics to the primitive mind. Thus primitives displayed a marked lack of thought and reflection, with Levy-Bruhl identifying a lack of abstract reasoning as the primitive mentality's essential trait. In the absence of any such reasoning, passions and the senses were given free rein: 'the impressions which the individual has of himself whether living or dead ... have only a far-off resemblance to ideas or concepts. They are felt and lived, rather than thought' (Levy-Bruhl 1923: 447). And while 'emotional and passionate elements scarcely allow thought, as thought, to obtain any mastery' (Levy-Bruhl 1926: 109), instinct also played a role in halting any abstract reasoning: 'Judgements would involve intellectual processes which are quite simple and familiar to us, but for which the primitive has neither taste nor aptitude. He instinctively shuns them' (1923: 403). Likewise, for the primitive 'emotions (are) experienced ... almost instinctively at the sight of a certain object' (1926: 106).

Like Freud, Levy-Bruhl undertook a redemptive project for the primitive mind, though he refused to venture as far. Although Jung would later label Levy-Bruhl 'an authority in the field of primitive psychology' (1970: 106), Levy-Bruhl never argued that primitive thinking had a psychological source. He borrowed the idea of collective representations[7] from Durkheim in contending that group beliefs, similarly inculcated in all primitives, shaped perceptions which matched the structure and function of primitive societies – and that the value of group beliefs should be judged in this context. In this way, though he was directly concerned with the primitive mind, Levy-Bruhl's explanation for its functioning was sociological or socio-cultural rather than psychological. Though primitives 'have the same senses as ours ... and their cerebral structure is like our own ... we have to bear in mind that which their collective representation instil into all their perceptions' (1926: 43). However, there was no universality where collective representations were concerned. For Levy-Bruhl, no traces of the primitive mentality could be found in the mind of modern man, and so much the better. So while Freud and Levy-Bruhl both shunned biological explanations of primitive thinking, their redemptive accounts gestured in different directions.

The next relevant inquiries into the primitive mind followed a reading of Levy-Bruhl's lengthy works in terms of the unconscious. These were carried out by Carl Jung, the father of analytical psychology. Jung relied heavily on Levy-Bruhl's work but embarked on a radical project to psychologise the primitive mind (Lawson 2007). This meant scrapping sociological explanations in favour of psychological ones, seeing the primitive as situated not within the particular configurations of his society but in a psychological state of unconsciousness. Both instinct and impulse figured in his argument:

> Our psychic processes are made up to a large extent of reflections, doubts and experiments, all of which are almost completely foreign to the unconscious, instinctive mind of primitive man ... It is just man's turning away from instinct – his opposing himself to instinct – that creates consciousness ... Until this stage is reached the psychic life of the individual is essentially governed by impulse.
>
> (Jung 1930: 16)

Following Freud, Jung saw this unconscious state as something that every human being passed through; viewing the unconscious as characteristically infantile and primitive, but also universal. In this way Jung did not appraise the primitive mind in terms of how closely its concepts approximated to 'reality'. Instead, the operations of the primitive mentality were valuable as objects of study insomuch as they gave upon the workings of the unconscious. For Jung, not only did the primitive mind offer salutary lessons about modern man's own unconscious, but moderns should actively reconnect with their unconscious sides – instinct, impulse and all.

Meanwhile, the red of British territorial mandate swilled around maps of the African continent. With the Scramble over, Britain could count the Gambia, Sierra Leone, the Gold Coast, Nigeria, the Sudan, Uganda, British Somaliland, Kenya, Tanganyika, Rhodesia, and the regions which made up South Africa and South West Africa among its territories. Information about each territory and its inhabitants was valuable for the ongoing management of empire, and in 1924 Sir Godfrey Lagden surveyed the British Empire's 'native races' for just this purpose. His *Native Races of the Empire* was part of a 12-volume collection which aimed to 'provide the ordinary reader with a bird's-eye view of the manifold activities of the Empire as a whole' (1924: iv). The occasion for the publication was the Management of the British Empire exhibition which took place in London and where

> the vast material resources and industries of the Empire would be brought vividly before the public ... there should be a record and survey of the growth and development of this far-flung congeries and peoples that are called the British Commonwealth of Nations.
>
> (Ibid)

Lagden dedicated the first 170 pages of his survey to the native races of Africa, whose childlike, instinctive character was conducive to impulsive, unpredictable behaviour. Unsurprisingly this called for paternalistic modes of surveillance and control. The natives were 'savage, cruel and treacherous ... of a turbulent temper', their indigenous tribal systems 'bred in the people treacherous and brutal instincts and left no room for the growth of intellect or improvement in the conditions of living' (Lagden 1924: 18). The bushmen were 'almost without intelligence but had strong animal instincts ... imitative rather than inventive' (ibid: 7), while the Bantu race 'had all the traditional love for their chiefs which children have for their parents' (ibid: 16). All this necessitated comprehensive systems of governance: 'The change has been great, and there can be no doubt that there is need of education and of the white man's continuous control ... to prevent them slipping back into the state in which he found them' (ibid: 85).

The study of the native mind had become a discipline in itself, and this meant that political questions could be posed in psychological terms: Was the African mind fit to govern and withstand the demands of industrial modernity? Was African subjectivity of sufficient depth for the granting of independence? What about levels of African intelligence? Thus impulse and instinct were further codified in the terminology of psychology and its cognate disciplines. Put bluntly, if the terms had become mentality, temperament and intelligence, the stakes were freedom and autonomy.

Levy-Bruhl's concern with the relationship between the primitive mind and collective representations (borrowed from Durkheim) had opened up the possibility that socio-cultural factors could explain the workings of the primitive mind. This was reflected in the chief concern of colonial administrators and their superiors back in Britain: 'culture contact'. As industrial modernity lurched into Africa, concerns were raised over the ability of African minds to cope with its 'civilised' demands. The fact that the issue was figured in terms of culture had much to do with the movement of psychology, sociology and anthropology away from the aegis of biology. We have seen authors like Levy-Bruhl make sense of the primitive mentality by employing Durkheim's notion of collective representations. This made the issue cultural rather than biological. Detailing the clash between respective bundles of (individual) psychology and (group) culture – native (pre-modern) versus imperial (modern) – was therefore the mandate of colonial anthropology and psychiatry. Jock McCulloch (1995) has called this joint enterprise 'ethno-psychiatry'.

With its concentration of psychiatrists and anthropologists, Britain's East African colonies became a testing ground for theories of culture contact. The story of colonial psychiatry in these territories is best told through the work of two key figures: H. L. Gordon and J. C. Carothers. At different times these two men stood in the vanguard of ethno-psychiatry in Britain's

East African colonies, presiding over its development into one of the British empire's most innovative yet politically conservative institutions.

African 'backwardness' had long aroused the professional interest of anthropologists and other colonial attachés. Lodged in a remote Kenyan farm, H. L. Gordon – a physician cum self-titled 'medical farmer' – began to ruminate on the issue himself. Were efforts to educate the African being expended in vain due to the innate limitations of the African mind? Even worse, were programmes designed in the corridors of civilisation likely to corrupt the inchoate mind of the Kenyan native, with disastrous effects? Gordon could give his ideas a more professional gloss after being offered a position at Mathari Mental Hospital in Nairobi. Here he assisted the Kenya government by examining the mental disorders prevalent among the native population, drawing conclusions about the 'natural limits' of the African mind.[8]

As Mahone and Vaughan (2007) have claimed, rather than being representative of psychiatry as we know it today, the work of Gordon, his colleagues and successors was the product of an *ad hoc* profession concerning any explanation of behaviour in psychological terms. Few, if any, of these practitioners spoke with certified authority; most possessed no formal qualification in psychiatry. And the insular world of settler society – awash with reports, records and amateur ethnographies as it was – meant that the opinion of a physician and the whimsical psychologising of a colonial administrator were given comparable licence as 'psychiatric' discourse. Of the discipline's earliest practitioners, Gordon was the most eager to see his work give rise to practical applications.

Reading a paper entitled 'The Mental Capacity of the African' to members of the 'African Circle' in 1935, Gordon could draw on over a decade of experience at Mathari Mental Hospital. If the paper was a good indication of how far colonial psychiatry had travelled as a 'scientific' discipline, it also demonstrated that not everyone was willing to give up on biology just yet. It was littered with citations of 'microscopic measurements', 'cells' and 'cortexes'. This technical language served to ennoble Gordon's hunches; despite his quoting scientific measurements of the brain recorded by colleague F. W. Vint, his appeals to technical expertise were largely specious. 'The microscopic measurements showed a 15 per cent quantitative deficiency of the native cortex as compared with the European cortex', said Gordon. 'The net result points ... to the cortex or grey matter as the site of a biological deficiency which would account for the biological actions on a lower level; and this we think opens the way to study of racial backwardness by the biological approach' (Gordon 1935: 239).

Though he felt that 'he need not go further into these intricate technical matters', one of his 'most distinguished friends, Dr. J. H. Sequeira' had previously described them in greater detail. His results, published in the *British Medical Journal* three years earlier, showed that no matter how 'intricate' matters had become, assumptions about the African mind were regrettably familiar. Sequeira elaborated on Vint's observations of the frontal cortex – after acknowledging Gordon and his pioneering role in colonial psychiatry – the foremost being differences in the respective sizes of the infragranular, granular and supragranular layers; the native was abundant in the former layer, but deficient in the two latter. Sequeira explained the significance of these differences:

> The infragranular layer is held to be the seat of the representation – the physical basis – of the animal instincts, reproduction, self-preservation, etc.; the granular layer that of the perception of sensations; while the supra-granular layer is concerned with the will, intellect, control, etc. The two latter may be looked upon as the physical basis of the mind. In the East African therefore, animal instincts are provided with 6 per cent more physical basis than in the European, but the physical basis of 'mind' shows a preponderance in favour of the European of 9.3 per cent.[9]
>
> (1932: 581)

Discourses of psychopathology would soon be used to criminalise colonial subjects. Here Britain's colonial psychiatrists followed the lead of Antoine Porot, the dominant force in Algerian psychiatry and an employee of the University of Algiers. In 1932 Porot and his colleague, D. C. Arrii, released a study which described the impulsiveness of Algerian Muslims. As McCulloch reported, 'According to Porot and Arrii, Algerians were violent by heredity, congenital compulsives who could not channel their aggression to socially constructive ends. Their impulses were such that they frequently led to homicide' (1995: 107). Four years later, Horace Shelley and W. H. Watson, who practised psychiatry at the Zomba Asylum in Nyasaland (modern day Malawi), decided to classify every one of the asylum's inmates. They deemed over half to be 'criminal lunatics', and sought to explain the high incidence of homicide among native psychotics by the fight-or-flight mechanism of primitive man: 'It cannot be expected that the native can exercise complete control over such powerful instincts after such a comparatively short period of contact with civilising influences' (Shelley and Watson 1936: 729).

Following Gordon's retirement, the discipline of colonial psychiatry continued to professionalise and widen its remit. More terms and concepts emerged with a view to characterising the African mind as more researchers around Africa were sold on the importance of 'psychological' research. Within this setting the influence of Freud and Levy-Bruhl's respective descriptions of the primitive mind became more dominant. Chief among the newly coined concepts were notions of African temperament, intelligence and personality. Stanley Porteus provided an account of *Temperament and Race* as early as 1926, though as McCulloch has asserted, Porteus's notion of temperament was simply a synonym for 'human nature' or for the elements of 'human nature' somehow coded in terms of 'race'. The concept was picked up by University of Edinburgh graduate Simon Biesheuvel, who gave a fuller explanation of temperament in his book *African Intelligence* (1943). Biesheuvel saw the African temperament as shaped by 'primary functioning'. Those whose behaviour was characteristic of primary functioning 'tended to be more impulsive, restless, lively; distractible, inconsistent and variable, particularly in mood, than the average' (1943: 183). Secondary functioning was precisely the opposite: 'more cautious, calm, and quiet, regular in attention and way of working, even of mood and consistency than the average ... It is this temperament factor which determines stimulability, variability, and constancy of response' (ibid).

South African psychiatrist B. J. F. Laubscher's *Sex, Custom and Psychopathology* (1937) was woven through with Freudian orthodoxy; this obviously resulted from a close reading of *Totem and Taboo*. He used Freudian theory to explore the relationship between the 'pagan' culture of his African patients and their susceptibility to mental illness. His work echoed *Totem* in portraying pagan African culture as corresponding to time immemorial and similarly relied on the analogy between the mind of the African and that of the European child; the African, like the child, had no means of differentiating between words and actions because of his homologous unconscious: 'The native in his setting reacts to his unconscious images and fears as does the child to his dreams, and these unconscious impulses, where they fall within the category of forbidden impulses, are transformed into living objects' (Laubscher 1937: 49).

By the time *The African as Suckling and as Adult* was released in 1943, its author, J. F. Ritchie, had amassed 21 years of experience with the Northern Rhodesia Education Department. Much like his confrères elsewhere in Africa, his clinical experience wasn't underpinned by any formal training in psychiatry. Ritchie was interested in the African (male) personality, shifting the locus of investigation and explanation to the African family unit, and more specifically to methods of child rearing. He advocated the same polarities as Biesheuvel, seeing the African personality as lacking all balance and initiative, living in the moment and abandoned to passions. By contrast, Western man was capable of clear and objective thought, basing his decisions on the cogency of rational argument.

Ritchie, 'a convinced Freudian', explained the dysfunctional African personality by identifying developmental thresholds within the suckling period of a child (1943: 4). He deemed that the African mother's breast-feeding regime was too generous. Indeed, as a regime it lacked any real temporal structure; the mother would simply present the child with her breast whenever it cried or motioned towards hunger. For Ritchie, this regime of feeding on demand also went on for too long, sometimes until the child was three years old. Such indulgence meant the baby never learned to sublimate its anger, hatred and hostile impulses. To make matters worse, the period of abstinence practised by parents during suckling expired exactly as the child was weaned. Thus, 'the infant is perfectly correct in seeing a close association between deprivation of his mother's breast by day and the fact that he is deposed and replaced by his father as her bed fellow at night' (ibid: 12). The consequences were serious: 'The father, then, becomes the object of the child's murderous hatred ... Thus: the child hates his father and has an impulse to kill him. In similar circumstances, you and I would have just the same impulses' (ibid: 13). In later life this hatred for the father (and to a lesser extent the mother) was projected onto all figures vested with authority, as African modes of education failed to repress the child's murderous instincts:

> Now early educative influences usually teach the child of civilization that aggressiveness is bad in itself ... in time the child does tend to repress or control the aim of the instinct ... It is otherwise with the African infant ... the aim of the aggressive instinct is destruction, annihilation ... the haphazardly nursed African lives almost entirely in the present ... in this way they are like very young children, in whom thinking and feeling are almost indistinguishable.
>
> (Ibid: 15–18)

Criminal pathology could also be traced to a maladapted suckling period: 'Habitual criminals are often people who were badly or prematurely weaned, or otherwise seriously thwarted in early infancy ... Habitual criminals are mentally ill peoples' (Ritchie 1943: 51). As McCulloch has neatly summarised: 'The African that Ritchie described was almost a parody of human shortcomings: impulsive, self-absorbed, misogynist, angry, ungrateful, sexually promiscuous, passive, ruthless, lacking in intellectual curiosity, emotionally unstable and irresponsible' (1995: 96). Ritchie's argument had a novel complexion, but its conclusions were tried and tested.

If Gordon and his colleagues defined the practice of colonial psychiatry throughout the 1930s, the 1940s belonged to his successor at Mathari Mental Hospital, J. C. Carothers. Likewise a British physician possessing no formal qualification in psychiatry or psychological medicine, Carothers took up the post at Mathari in 1938 and set about describing the mindset of the locals. His efforts throughout the 1940s were of a piece with those of Biesheuvel, Laubscher and Ritchie. But, somewhat ironically, only after returning to Britain in 1950 was Carothers commissioned to write his most definitive works: *The Mind of the African in Health and Disease* (commissioned by the World Health Organization) in 1953, *The Psychology of the Mau Mau* (commissioned by the Kenya government) in 1954, and *The Mind of Man in Africa* in 1972.

The 20-year hiatus in Carothers' writing spanned the rise of independence movements in Africa and mass black immigration to Britain. These were broad movements interconnected by Britain's imperial project but were lit by certain flashpoints, two of which I shall examine here: the Mau Mau uprising in Kenya and the tribulations and eventual death of Nigerian immigrant David Oluwale. As it had done since its inception as an amateur vocation, the discourse of colonial psychiatry and psychological medicine – the study of the African mind, brain, temperament, personality and intelligence – stood in relation to these events as a discursive and conservative force. In describing this relation I hope to show how colonial psychiatry's kaleidoscopic range of technical jargon continued to belie its narrow set of assumptions.

By the 1950s, African nationalist movements had become more organised and their calls for independence more concerted. As a vehicle for African caricature, psychiatric and psychological discourses were powerful in ensuring that these calls fell on deaf ears. By entering the African psyche and deeming its contents abnormal, these discourses could undermine colonial nationalisms; at a stroke, entire independence movements could be authoritatively defined as pathological. Statistics were marshalled to interrogate the personhood of Africans and their worthiness as citizens. In 1961 a paper read at the First Pan-African Psychiatric Conference in Abeokuta reported that the suicide rate in Western Nigeria was one per 100,000, which by comparison with Western standards was incredibly low. The implication was that Africans hadn't the depth of human subjectivity to experience the intense personal suffering symptomatic of clinical depression. For T. Asuni (who presented the paper), Carothers, and others in the ranks of colonial psychiatry, a marked absence of depression and suicide were indicators of a psychopathic population – personalities fit for colonial subjection, not independent citizenship.[10] By 1953 Carothers' work enjoyed a wider appeal, and it is perhaps no coincidence that interest in his 'findings' increased at a time when Europe's colonial powers were struggling to douse the flames of colonial nationalism. In *The African Mind in Health and Disease* he filleted the works of a number of professional acquaintances. The first colleague 'well worth quoting at length' was Westermann: 'With the Negro emotional, momentary and explosive thinking predominates ... Where the stimulus of emotion is lacking the Negro shows little spontaneity and is passive ... (and) has but few gifts for work which aims at a distant goal and requires tenacity, independence, and foresight' (quoted in Carothers 1953: 85). Next up were French neuro-psychiatrists Gallais and Planques: 'Separated from regulating influences, he (the Negro) lives essentially in the present (in this sense like a child), and his conduct submits to influences and impulses of the passing moment and thus appears explosive and chaotic' (quoted in Carothers 1953: 86). Then another Frenchman, Barbé, who described the African mentality thus: 'From the affective point of view, impulsivity violent but unsustained ... At the level of action ... lack of persistent, passive obedience to events. In general, a submission of integrative and creative power to the profit of automatisms and instincts' (quoted in Carothers 1953: 86). Biesheuvel, Ritchie, Laubscher and Vint also featured. Carothers then provided his own appraisal:

> These attributes are apparent to most observers and are worth summarizing ... The African has been described as conventional; highly dependent of physical and emotional stimulation; lacking in spontaneity, foresight, tenacity, judgement and humility; inapt for sound abstraction and for logic; given to phantasy and fabrication; and, in general, as unstable, impulsive, unreliable, irresponsible, and living in the present without reflection or ambition.
>
> (Ibid: 87)

On 21 October 1952, the Kenya government declared a state of emergency. The following six years saw 32 European settlers and 63 members of the security forces perish at the hands of the 'Mau Mau',[11] while British soldiers and the Kenyan police attempted to contain the rebellion via the killing and mass internment of Mau Mau suspects. Ostensibly the dispute centred on a land claim first made by the Kikuyu tribe in 1913. However, over the next 40 years the claim became the locus of wider resistance to colonial rule. To this end the Kenya African Union was formed in 1943, while the return of inspirational Kikuyu leader Jomo Kenyatta to Kenya in 1946 gave further impetus to the movement, as it broadened its scope and became more politically astute. Over the next six years it ground economic activity in Kenya to a virtual halt, before things eventually came to a head in 1952. Historians still argue over the number of Mau Mau suspects killed and detained during the state of emergency. Estimates of those killed range from 20,500 (Anderson 2006) to 300,000 (Elkins 2005), and of those interned from 90,000 (Anderson 2006) to 1.5 million (Elkins 2005). However, all parties agree that several hundred Kikuyu were hanged and that the use of torture was widespread in internment camps (Anderson 2006; Elkins 2005; Monbiot 2012). The affair left the British government reeling, and there is no doubt that it expedited the granting of Kenyan independence (which occurred in 1963).

In the midst of the uprising, the British both at home and in Kenya sought to enter the mindset of the Mau Mau. Colonial psychiatry provided the entry point, and foremost among its exponents was Carothers. Duly approached by his countrymen, he became a one-man commission determined to map the Mau Mau psyche. The result was *The Psychology of the Mau Mau*, an official document of the Kenya government published in 1954. The 30-page report was a summary of the African personality interleaved with more specific psychological analyses of the Mau Mau and Kikuyu.

Echoing Levy-Bruhl, Carothers viewed his project as the investigation of a dysfunctional culture: 'Studies of cultures are, in effect, studies of psychology' (1954: 2). This confirmed that the relative worth of cultural life had moved centre stage in psychological analysis of the African mind. At first he sought to describe the African mind: 'events occur by some inner "will" in these events, as is the rule in children's thinking'; 'It is an inevitable component of the type of psychology described that, where there are no simple rules, behaviour can be governed wholly by the emotions of the moment'; 'action in individuals often takes forms which are marked by the highest degree of unconstraint and violence – a common experience in psychiatric practice in Africa' (ibid: 3). Discussion then moved to the Kikuyu, the tribe enveloped by the mysterious Mau Mau. 'Can Kikuyu people ever be trusted again?' asked Carothers. 'Even if men have been screened and "cleansed", they may still contain dormant impulses to violence ... for it is difficult to imagine that contamination with this filthy thing Mau Mau could ever leave no lasting trace' (ibid: 20). In describing 'this filthy thing', Carothers forwarded (and ventured to answer) another question: 'Do brutal oaths and obscene rituals in fact occur in Mau Mau? ... They do exist, in all the depravity that is imaginable' (ibid: 15). But, however much the Kikuyu may have been in thrall to Mau Mau, Carothers used the notion of relative cultural worth to argue that they were, in fact, redeemable: 'Kikuyu people are the most like ourselves in Kenya, and are the best fitted for success within our cultural mode' (ibid: 21). They were corrigible, Carothers affirmed, because they were 'less impulsive than many other Africans' (ibid).

Throughout the 1950s and 1960s Britain witnessed mass immigration from its territories and/or former territories in Africa, the West Indies, and the Indian subcontinent (Spencer 1997).[12] The life and death of David Oluwale – a Nigerian who arrived in Hull as a 19-year-old in 1949 – forged a direct link between discourses of colonial psychiatry and the experience of Britain's black immigrants. Stowed away on a ship travelling from Lagos, Oluwale was detained on arrival in Hull and sentenced to 28 days in Armley Prison, Leeds. On release Oluwale hoped to pursue a career in engineering, but ended up working in a Leeds brick factory. His ties to the city were strengthened after he became romantically involved with a local woman.

But things took a turn for the worse after a night out with friends ended in his arrest and another 28-day sentence. Following arrest, and having been acquainted with the thick end of a police truncheon, Oluwale reportedly suffered hallucinations. This saw him transferred from prison to Leeds' Menston Asylum, where he spent the next eight years, being subjected to various courses of medication and therapy, much of it electroconvulsive. By the time of his release Oluwale had been shorn of his former personality and was thoroughly disillusioned with his prospects as an African immigrant;

destitution was almost inevitable. He lived homeless for the next four years, moving regularly between London, Sheffield and Leeds, complaining of harsh treatment by the latter's police force.

In 1965 he was taken back to Menston Asylum for a further two years' confinement. His release meant a return to the streets and doorways of Leeds city centre, where he suffered further run-ins with the boys in blue, most fatefully at the hands of Sergeant Kenneth Kitching and Inspector Geoffrey Ellerker. In 1969 Oluwale's dead body was found in the River Aire. Two years later Kitching and Ellerker were charged with his manslaughter (charges of grievous bodily harm and perjury were also filed against the pair). Oluwale's remains lay sodden for two weeks before being pulled from the pestilential Aire. This at least brought closure to a life marked by hardship, tragedy and injustice.

In revisiting Oluwale's story it may be fruitful to examine the role played by raciological discourses of psychopathology. Before being consigned to Menston Asylum in 1953, Oluwale was assessed by Michael Leahy, a psychiatrist at St James' Hospital Psychiatric Unit. Oluwale, reported Leahy, appeared 'apprehensive, frightened, and noisy without cause ... Childish and wept when talking of his fears' (quoted in Aspden 2007: 56). On arrival at Menston, Oluwale was assessed by consultant psychiatrist Dr Richard Carty: 'When he arrived at the hospital he became my patient and I examined him. I found him to be restless, noisy, and restive ... At times he was completely withdrawn and mute. At intervals of about two or three months he would relapse and become overactive, impulsive, and aggressive' (quoted in Aspden 2007: 58). A charge nurse at the facility reported that Oluwale was 'violent and unpredictable ... he came back snarling like an animal before we restrained him' (quoted in Aspden 2007: 62). As Kesper Aspden has observed: 'The Oluwale presented in the statements of the psychiatrist looks like the classic pathological African: aggressive, excitable, childish ... and so dominated by his instincts that it was dangerous to allow him emancipation' (2007: 65).

A year after Ellerker and Kitching received custodial sentences of three years and 27 months respectively for their assaults on Oluwale, Carothers published *The Mind of Man in Africa*, a version of *The African Mind in Health and Disease* embellished with ripened prose and additional data. The book's structure mimicked that of his earlier effort, with sections likewise devoted to physical anthropology, the brain and the mind. Again he cited the work of Westermann, Gallais, Planques and Barbé, though saw fit to preface their opinions with a half-hearted proviso:

Many attempts have been made to describe African mentality but, in recent years at least, usually with the reservation that these were classical conceptions, popular stereotypes, etc. These descriptions, however, are by no means false. They represent a facet of the truth and, as such, must be recorded.

(Carothers 1972: 93)

The African had become no less impulsive since his last depiction at the hands of Carothers. Indeed, new technical terms had been invented to describe this predisposition:

African adult psychology might thus be described as monoideic for, in dealing with any situation for which no pattern of behaviour is prescribed by local custom, such behaviour is apt to be impulsive and marked by concentration on immediately presenting aspects of the situation.

(Ibid: 120)

He went on to cite Vint in asserting that 'the stage of cerebral development reached by the average African was that of the average European boy of between 7 and 8 years of age' (ibid: 124).

The behaviour of the Kikuyu, Mau Mau, and David Oluwale was officially and authoritatively interpreted in modes that were strikingly similar. These modes of discourse mirrored the rhetoric of the civilising mission and its struggle with savage Africa, though images of savagery could now be etched in finer detail courtesy of the psychological sciences. Carothers' certified pronouncement of the Mau Mau as depraved and barbarous, along with the manner in which Oluwale was buffeted by police officers, judges and evaluators between shop doorways, prisons and psychiatric wards, demonstrated how the 'African minds' of those seeking independence and black newcomers to Britain were made psychopathic. They had been stamped with the twin faces of savagery: the child and the criminal – immature, lazy, dependent on others, emotional, unstable, unpredictable, violent, and of course, impulsive. One of Britain's black sportsmen came in for similar treatment.

Today in Market Square, Warwick, a statue – duly poised for fisticuffs – commemorates the life and death of a man once given the accolade of being 'the greatest pound-for-pound fighter produced by these British Isles' (Birtley 1975). This was Randolph ('Randy') Adolphus Turpin, a young boxer whose star was on the rise around the time that Carothers and his professional opinion were being repatriated. Randy, or 'the Leamington Licker', was born in Leamington Spa in 1928 to a Guianese father and an English mother. Following his older brother into boxing, Randy turned professional in 1946 and thereafter enjoyed mixed success; from the ecstasy of beating Sugar Ray Robinson in 1951 to the ignominy of swapping gloves for wrestling trunks as he lived out his last days scampering from the taxman. In 1966 he was found dead in a room above his struggling backstreet café. Two gunshot wounds – to the head and chest respectively – had undoubtedly proved fatal. But the question remained whether Turpin himself had inflicted the wounds or whether another, most likely one of Randy's many creditors or debtors, had paid him a fateful visit.

Commentary on Randy's turbulent existence contained timeworn themes. His life has been relayed as a never-ending struggle to harness his 'famous "killer instinct"' (Birtley 1975: 62) to productive ends; in short, to brutally demolish opponents in the ring but otherwise avoid petty skirmishes and the situations which might bring them about. Felling opponents was never a problem, particularly at the start of his career:

> full of hate and suddenly raring to go on ... suddenly the killer instinct in Turpin was unleashed and he let go a tremendous right hand which landed flush on the falling Dutchman's [Luc Van Dam] jaw – and he hit the canvas like a sack of coal.
>
> (Ibid: 34–6)

In this kind of mood, and when confined to the boxing ring, his 'instinct' served him well. However, according to reports, Randy was just as likely to fire up his 'machine of destruction' (ibid: 60) in the kitchen or living room. For the women in his life, this didn't make for domestic bliss.

His 'strange, inexplicable moods' (Birtley 1975: 77) were brought to the attention of the authorities by his first wife, Mary Stack, who alleged that Randy punched her violently in the stomach following a confrontation over her falling pregnant. But it was in 1953 that his domestic violence came under international scrutiny. Following a humiliating defeat to Carl 'Bobo' Olsen in New York, Randy was arrested. Serious charges had been brought against him by a Miss Adele Daniels, a clerk in the State Department of Labor with whom Randy had enjoyed a fitful relationship since meeting her on a visit to New York two years before. According to Miss Daniels, the nature of her relationship with Turpin had taken a sudden and drastic turn: 'I begged them to have him examined by a doctor because I thought he was a sick man ... a dangerously maniacal person' (quoted in Birtley 1975: 92). Her representative called for Turpin to be detained in order that a full psychological examination be carried out: 'He is definitely mentally ill – psychopathologically ... a jungle beast in a human form, and a dangerous killer ... This man is bestially primitive' (Sala quoted in Birtley 1975: 102–3). The case was eventually settled out of court, but Randy continued to protest his innocence until his death.

One-time business partner Leslie Salts described Turpin as 'intelligent in some respects but childish in others'. His biographer, Jack Birtley, thought Randy was the 'victim of a humble upbringing which left him totally ill-equipped to face fame and fortune' (Birtley 1975: 152). But the final say was had by coroner Mr S. Tibbets, who concluded his findings by suggesting that

'Randolph Turpin appeared to have been an impulsive and generous man who had given away a large part of his earnings in the ring, and in some ways this had led to the present tragedy' (quoted in Phillips 2007: 153).

By the time of Randy's untimely death, the 'expert' opinion of Carothers no longer attracted much attention. Many African nations had become formally independent – between 1956 and 1968 no fewer than 35 freed themselves from formal European control – and this is not a development to be skirted around or passed over without due critical consideration. It is important to reflect on the implications of this momentous period for the theoretical underpinnings of the study and, more specifically, the conception of power it borrows from Foucault.

As Foucault argued, 'Where there is power, there is resistance, and yet, or rather consequently, this resistance is never in a position of exteriority in relation to power' (Foucault 1978: 95). Resistance, therefore, is intrinsically reactive – a reaction to power rather than action which is positive on its own terms. This account of power[13] has been criticised for foreclosing the possibility of traditional forms of resistance and, of course, this criticism could be levelled with regard to the movements which fought for independence from Europe's colonial powers. However, in some ways Foucault's description of power as productive can help us make sense of the relationship between discourses of 'race' and raciology and the fight for independence from colonial rule.

For Kwame Nkrumah, who led the Gold Coast to independence from Britain in 1957, the 'African Personality' would be instrumental in the reawakening of African self-consciousness and somehow manifest the bonds which united African people – their history, culture, shared experiences and aspirations. The key conceptual ingredients of Nkrumah's 'African Personality' were inspired by a variety of other Pan-Africanist scholars. The man who laid the most clearly articulated intellectual foundations for Pan-Africanist ideology was the polymath and civil rights activist W. E. B. Du Bois. Building on work conducted by black nationalist Alexander Crummell and Liberian statesman Edward Wilmot Blyden, Du Bois' efforts to produce a coherent Pan-Africanist ideology – contemporaneous with almost the entire period of European colonial occupation of Africa – developed alongside what he called the 'autobiography of a race concept' (Du Bois 1983 [1940]).

In 1897 Du Bois delivered a paper titled 'The Conservation of the Races' to the American Negro Academy in Washington DC. He noted that, 'in our calmer moments we must acknowledge that human beings are divided into races' (Du Bois 1897: 75). This didn't mean that he subscribed unerringly to the view of those colleagues who defended the integrity of biological 'races'. The notion of 'race' he accredited was (ostensibly) socio-historical: 'races ... while they perhaps transcend scientific definition, nevertheless, are clearly defined to the eye of the historian and sociologist' (ibid: 75–6).

He went on to list eight 'distinctly differentiated races', the task for each being the discovery and articulation of its message – as a race. Ghanaian philosopher and novelist Anthony Appiah (1992) has argued that Du Bois' socio-historical version of 'race' relies on many of the same presuppositions as the scientific, biological conception he was at pains to distance it from. Appiah contends that to talk of 'a family of human beings, always of a common history' and 'sharing common impulses and strivings' would mean that these common impulses have no place among the criterion for membership of a group – to be part of any socio-historical definition of 'race' they would have to be identified *a posteriori*. 'If that is so', Appiah continues, 'we are left with the scientific conception (of race)' (ibid: 52).

Nkrumah shared Du Bois' concern to emphasise that his concept of the 'African Personality' was free from any biological undercurrent:

> the African Personality is merely a term expressing cultural and social bonds which unite Africans and people of African descent. It is a concept of the African nation, and is not associated with a particular state, language, religion, political system, or colour of the skin.
>
> (Nkrumah 1973: 205)

Defending the notion against charges that it bore the imprint of a biological conception of 'race' – and writing from an avowedly 'Afrocentric' perspective – Daryl Zizwe Poe has stressed that the African Personality was 'not essentially a race-based one but a race conscious one' (2003: 10).

However, the choice to focus on a unitary 'African Personality' was curious given the term's use by proponents of colonial psychiatry to describe a generalised African mindset – as we have seen, likewise predicated on assertions about group culture – which lacked all balance and initiative, lived in the present, and was abandoned to momentary passions (McCulloch 1995; Mahone and Vaughan 2007). So, though Foucault's domains of reference are limited to the Western world (Spivak 1988), his conception of power is useful in understanding the relationship between the history of raciology and elements of colonial nationalism. As Robert Young (1995: 15) has argued, 'Racism and racialism must be one of the best – or the worst – examples of the silent and stealthy operation of this Foucauldian form of power/knowledge.'

However, it was not only imperial Britain which faced challenges to its supremacy; discoveries in both the 'hard' and 'soft' sciences were beginning to question the legitimacy of modernity and the great edifice of 'certain' knowledge which stood at its foundation.[14] It is to the implications of these queries for the 'impulsive' black male that discussion now turns.

Modernity and its discontents: the criminal, family values and 'good instincts'

After the basic oppositions between 'higher' and 'lower' life had been translated into Darwinian terms and were being put to work in justifying the Scramble, the intellectual underpinnings of the modern period were being called into doubt. The version of psychology pioneered by Freud – though only cherry-picked by most proponents of colonial psychiatry – contained possibilities for a more radical view of the world. As noted earlier, Nietzsche's monism smashed the opposition between reason and passion. Freud took on this monism in overseeing psychology's move away from biology and underlining the importance of culture as an object of study. His successors emphasised that the psychology of the individual was a product of the cultural representations with which it interfaced; biological difference did not come into it. Some practitioners of colonial psychiatry were true to this universalism; although Carothers labelled swathes of the African population as pathological or criminal, their lot was not biologically fixed. If their psychological characteristics were dysfunctional, it was because of their cultural modes of representation. In many ways this shift from biological to cultural analyses was consummated by the UNESCO statement of 1950.

In the aftermath of World War II, the victorious allies – within the forum of the United Nations – were eager to trample on the embers of Hitler's racial fantasy. They rallied members of the scientific community into producing a statement on 'race'; an epistemological decree designed to banish 'race' to the conceptual scrapheap (Haraway 1990). The statement sought to demonstrate that 'race', when viewed as an object of scientific knowledge, was not 'true':

> Scientists have reached general agreement in recognizing that mankind is one: that all men belong to the same species, Homo sapiens ... From the biological standpoint, the species Homo sapiens is made up of a number of populations, each one of which differs from the others in the frequency of one or more genes. The biological fact of race and the myth of 'race' should be distinguished. For all practical social purposes 'race' is not so much a biological phenomenon as a social myth ... National, religious, geographic, linguistic, and cultural groups do not necessarily coincide with racial groups; and the cultural traits of such groups have no demonstrated genetic connection with racial traits.
>
> (UNESCO 1950)

However, rather than achieving its ambitious objective, in many ways the statement inaugurated culture as a new register of raciology. Colonial psychiatrists had already shown that 'race' could be articulated on the terrain of culture – although this was less sturdy ground for the assertion of racial difference.

Hot on the heels of the UNESCO statement on 'race' came Crick and Watson's discovery of the structure of DNA in 1953. This presented some urgent questions and made others inevitable. Immediately the relationship between humanity and nature was thrown into question, along with methods of calibrating human similarity and difference. Focus shifted from phenotype to genotype, from the scopic to the molecular, and from the immediacy of visible cues written on the surfaces of the body to an invisible, omniscient code secreted in the genes (Rose 2006). In more remote terms, Crick and Watson's discovery enabled the mapping of the entire human genome and made a crisis of raciology unavoidable. Indeed, the transformations their discovery set in train are still being realised today.

By the 1960s various quarters had begun to voice concern about the conduct of arrivals from the 'New Commonwealth'. Criminologists set about enumerating their crimes and making sense of their behaviour as part of a trans-Atlantic conversation about the violent black criminal. Here researchers were concerned with relationships within the family unit characteristic of certain cultures, with levels of impulse-repression used to distinguish between one culture and another.

Many researchers now explored the assertion that black minority groups were over-represented among violent offenders. In 1963 F. H. McClintock pointed to a proportionally higher rate of violent crime among London's West Indian and Irish minorities. In 1970 Lambert replicated this finding in Birmingham. Three years earlier A. E. Bottoms had concluded that though delinquency rates were generally low for immigrant groups from the New Commonwealth, violent crime was a notable exception. In their attempts to explain the behaviour of violent, psychopathic (black) criminals, criminologists turned to the issue of impulsivity.

In 1969 the *British Journal of Criminology* published 'Some Thoughts on the Unstable Offender', a paper written by Herschel A. Prins. Prins cited Cyril Burt's definition of the unstable juvenile offender:

> Affection and anger, assertiveness, fear, curiosity and disgust, submissiveness and sex – all the human emotions, and all the animal instincts, are inherited by them to a degree unusually intense ... First one impulse, then another, then a third ... explodes forthwith into action ... like the pops of a Chinese cracker.
>
> (Burt quoted in Prins 1969: 54).

The cause of this instability, Burt contended, was to be found at home: 'There is little doubt that youngsters who commit acts of a violent and impulsive kind frequently come from home backgrounds which readily foster this kind of behaviour' (ibid: 55).

A year later educational psychologist Neville J. Jones had a paper titled 'Difficult Boys in Approved Schools' published in the *British Journal of Criminology*. In underlining the nature of psychopathic behaviour and relationships, Jones discussed:

> [those] boys who do not profit by, or use experience, and do not respond to punishment. They lack drive or motivation and this leads to general inadequacy of conduct so that apparent abilities are not used. Liable to act on impulse and without forethought ... boys [they] form hetero-sexual relationships for crude gratification at an instinctual level.
>
> (1970: 139)

Again, the cause was dysfunctional family life: 'The majority of mothers were described as being incapable of giving affection to their sons ... Many of the fathers in this group were described as "weak and shy" or were not actively involved in the lives of their children' (ibid: 144).

By the mid-1970s the term 'mugging' had been imported from the United States, and thereafter all manner of 'urban' crime was listed under this rubric. The term, already loaded with racial connotations, allowed social commentators and enforcers of law and order to make effortless compar-isons between black communities in the United States and those in the UK. In this way they could stand black youths apart from the Irish and other members of 'the lower orders', strengthening the bonds of signification between terms such as 'urban', 'black' and 'mugging'.

In 1973 a White Paper on police–immigrant relations complained of 'the small minority of young coloured people apparently anxious to imitate the behaviour amongst the black community in the United States' (cited in Hall *et al.* 1978: 329). Responding to a report on street crime in South London, Derek Humphrey, writing in *The Times* (5 January 1975), lamen-ted that 'of 203 muggings' in Lewisham in 1974, '172 were committed by black youths'. He then mused on the problems behind the figures, com-, plaining of 'broken families'. An unnamed prison psychologist blamed 'immature, irresponsible types' who act 'in a spontaneous way', while for a social worker (also unnamed) the issue was 'psychological impulse' (cited in Hall *et al.* 1978: 126). This zeroing in on young black men in urban areas was an opportunity to question their desire to seek gainful employment. In 1976 *The Telegraph* reported that in urban areas such as Lewisham, Brixton, Bradford and Liverpool, black unemployment was 'at least twice the national average' (cited in Hall *et al.* 1978: 336).

That same year an article titled 'Criminal Impulsivity and Violence', written by A. B. Heilbrun, I. J. Knopf and P. Bruner, appeared in the *British Journal of Criminology*. The authors were interested in mechanisms of self-control and their absence in delinquents and psychopaths: 'It has long been assumed that crimes committed by delinquents or psychopaths could be understood in part as a product of faulty development of self-control mechanisms. Poor impulse control would be considered a pervasive characteristic' (Heilbrun *et al.* 1976: 368). Using ten indices including premeditation, delay of gratification, the role of emotional arousal, and of course, impulsivity, the authors sought to investigate the degree to which black and white criminals had their behaviour under their own control during the commission of a crime. After crunching the numbers, the authors let the results speak for themselves: black offenders committing violent crimes exhibited less self-control (2.77) than white offenders (3.00) who had perpetrated similar acts. They concluded that 'violent crimes are less under the control of the offender than are non-violent crimes ... While the results seemed to hold for both black and white prisoners, the relationships seemed especially salient for blacks' (ibid: 376).

Heilbrun provided a more detailed psychological portrayal of the violent black criminal the following year. The article, co-authored by Kirk S. Heilbrun and entitled 'The Black Minority Criminal and Violent Crime: The Role of Self-Control', emphasised that the issue of violent black criminality straddled the Atlantic:

> United States crime reports consistently show that the rate of violent crime for blacks involving aggression towards a victim (e.g. homicide, assault, rape, robbery) far exceeds the rate of violent crime for whites ... However, the phenomenon of a high violent crime rate among minority group members is not restricted to the United States.
>
> (Heilbrun and Heilbrun 1977: 370)

The authors went on to cite the studies of McClintock, Lambert and Bottoms before hypothesising that:

> The attitudes and values reported to be more characteristic of blacks ... suggest that they might have special problems in establishing and maintaining self-control systems within which deferring motivated action, delaying gratification, experiencing guilt, and acting independently from peer pressures would play prominent roles.
>
> (Ibid: 370-1)

Using the same ten-item index as the previous study – though this time billed as 'Impulsivity of the crime' – the authors wanted to 'get at that aspect of self-control involving the ability to delay a motivated or habitual instigation to act given the presence of a deterrent to such action (impulse control)' (Heilbrun and Heilbrun 1977: 371). Seeking a more comprehensive set of measurements they also employed a 'psychopathic deviate scale', as it 'has been found to be an especially sensitive index of impulsive anti-social behaviour when used in combination with ... the basic hypomania scale' (ibid: 372). The latter had been pioneered by Dahlstrom, Welsh and Dahlstrom in 1972, and included a moral/ethical dimension:

> the hypomania seemingly energising or activating the pattern related to scale 4. That is, these people tend to be overactive and impulsive, irresponsible and untrustworthy, shallow and superficial in their relationships. They are characterised by easy morals, readily circumvented consciences, and fluctuating ethical values.
>
> (Dahlstrom *et al.* 1972: 273)[15]

Black prisoners met the authors' experimental hypotheses in all three measures of impulsivity: psychometric, behavioural and the impulsivity of the crime itself. 'The results of this investigation, garnered from three different sources of data, point towards a single conclusion. Black criminals who have committed violent crimes are characterised by poorer impulse control than white violent criminals' (Heilbrun and Heilbrun 1977: 376).

In 1978 the impulsive criminal was recodified once more, this time by Barry McGurk, senior psychologist at HM Remand Centre in Durham. Drawing on the work of Megargee, who had created the categories of over-controlled and under-controlled individuals in 1966, McGurk set out to investigate the personality types of the centre's inmates. In the case of over-controlled inmates, a high level of instigation was necessary to overcome rigid inhibitions, while their under-controlled counterparts required little instigation to behave aggressively because of minimal aggressive inhibitions. Following a bout of analysis, a group of prisoners was rebranded as 'Type NH4', its distinctive features being 'impulsiveness, anti-social attitudes and a moderate degree of hostility which is directed at other people. This type has characteristics which conform to Megargee's notion of under-control and has been called a "psychopathic" type by Blackburn' (McGurk 1978: 158). Experimental psychologist Monika Henderson (1982) subsequently endorsed the applicability of the under-controlled/over-controlled typology for a population of mixed offenders.

The family remained the locus of explanation, central to which was the relationship between family culture and the psychological development of the child. As the doyen of delinquency, D. J. West, put it:

> chaotic upbringing by inconsistent, changing, uncaring, rejecting or erratic parental figures, with whom the infant cannot form close ties, is said to lead to the development of an impulse-ridden character with a weak conscience and noticeable absence of guilt about breaking social rules that have never been properly absorbed.
>
> (1988: 84)

In other words, such an upbringing meant the child would never grow up.

It is clear that from the 1960s to the 1980s, the issue of black criminality, having some of psychology's canonical texts and figures as its epistemological authority, was hived off into expert discourses of criminology. This influence meant that discussions retained a psychological feel and a concern with family culture. It was not only that criminology continually conjured the violent black criminal into being. Its institutional language and peer-reviewed exchanges signified a figure that, more so than representatives of any other group, epitomised the child-like, violent male and his psychopathic criminality. If impulsivity was an institutionalised index of the immature, psychopathic, hypomaniacal, unstable, delinquent, Type NH4, under-controlled, unpredictably violent criminal, then black males would surpass members of other 'races'. At bottom, impulsivity had become a byword for black criminal psychopathology.

As criminologists were using the interaction between family culture and individual psychology to diagnose the impulsively violent black criminal, in sport, discourses of regional and family culture were emerging that reinforced raciological assumptions by pointing towards individual exceptions. The subtle ways in which these supposed exceptions underlined stereotypical notions of the 'black' family and 'black' culture illustrate the insidious nature of appeals to raciology.

For the first black footballer to represent England – making his debut for England Youth in 1963 – the cultural particularities of a local area trumped assumptions about 'race'. John William Charles was born in Canning Town on 20 September 1944. An early school report praised Charles's impeccable attendance record as well as his 'neat, careful and intelligent work ... he is in the top section in the class' and 'is very popular with boys and masters in this school and in West Ham ... We are sure that he will make a sound, reliable employee, and can recommend him with pleasure and confidence' (quoted in Belton 2004: 26). His teachers were right; Charles made his debut for West Ham in 1963, eventually leaving the club in 1971 after making nearly 150 appearances in League and Cup. As a player he was a 'cultured, no-nonsense ... dependable full-back who got on with the game without complaint and his style of play could perhaps be described as uncompromising'. As a man he was 'strong, loyal, protective, and joyful' (Belton 2004: 8–12). Explanations as to how he managed to confound the stereotype of the impulsive black male were twofold. As Charles's biographer Brian Belton has written, 'It is impossible to write about John without some consideration of the area he was born into' (ibid: 12).

During World War II the East End was ravaged by repeated bombing. Amid the rubble and the frugality of Britain's post-war economy, many of East London's inhabitants were forced into prefabricated housing. Beneath their mass-produced, flat-roofed exteriors, these buildings had the further demerit of being lined with asbestos. Though things were beginning to ease, purse strings couldn't be loosened just yet.

But according to Charles a sense of solidarity prevented anyone from feeling poor:

> no-one worried about money yer know, we were glad just to have a bit of grub and go out and play football. Everybody was in the same boat. The rationing was still going of course. We used to take the old ration book over to our corner shop for half of lard or whatever.
>
> (Quoted in Belton 2004: 20)

Neither were racial differences an issue at school: 'I was the only black kid in my school. There was no problems with that. None at all' (ibid).

His upbringing was also important. Though Charles's mother had married on two previous occasions before meeting John's father, Moister Leopold, their subsequent family environment has been described as exemplary: 'I was me dad's first son, so I was looked after and made a bit of a fuss of ... he was very strict ... My mum was great, she was brilliant' (Charles quoted in Belton 2004: 16–17). Childhood friend Charlie Green was equally effusive: 'They are a lovely family. He was lucky, John'; 'She was lovely, his mum, she was a cracker. Something else' (ibid: 29).

In 1978 Vivian Alexander Anderson became the first black footballer to represent England in a full international. Charles and Anderson had a fair deal in common. Both were pioneers, and both had their successes explained through a discourse of exceptionalism which centred on regional and family culture. Anderson's biographer Andrew Longmore has emphasised the 'stability' of 'Big Viv's' upbringing: 'Andy (Viv's father) had managed to get a job as a porter in the general hospital ... their lives had taken on an air of stability which has stayed with them ... Stability is important to the Anderson family' (1988: 10). This was a view echoed by Anderson himself: 'My mother, being a teacher back in Jamaica, was very aware that I ought to get some qualifications behind me, of course, she was right' (ibid: 12). Like Charles, Viv's colour was rarely an issue at his local school. 'There were very few black children in the school then', commented Viv's former PE master, 'everyone liked Viv because he laughed and smiled so much. It's as simple as that' (ibid: 12).

According to Longmore, this sturdy upbringing had a profound influence on Anderson; as a man he was not 'typically West Indian ... He knew his place at home and now he knew his place at work' (Longmore 1988: 18).

> Anderson fits the stereotype of the black footballer neither on the field nor off. His relationship with his parents is firm and respectful. He has always accepted authority, be it parental or managerial, and far from having a Rastafarian notion of "let it be", he had inherited a strong sense of the Protestant work ethic.
>
> (Ibid: 104)

On the pitch Viv was 'fast and instinctive but he plays full-back, a position of responsibility and intelligence, and he happens to play with a devilish Anglo-Saxon consistency' (ibid: 103). If Anderson's restless industry, consistency, responsibility, intelligence and respect for authority were products of a 'childhood remarkable only for its ordinariness', one wonders what conclusions should be drawn about a 'typically West Indian' upbringing, or that of the 'stereotypical black footballer'.

Though Longmore's assessment of Anderson in 1988 underlined the tendency for black players to be labelled 'impulsive' or 'instinctive', it also indicated that, within sport, these traits were being reappraised. This reappraisal is best understood through the phenomenon of 'stacking', which, much like discussions in criminology, involved a trans-Atlantic conversation begun in America. By the early 1970s researchers in the US suspected discrimination on the part of team coaches with regard to the likelihood of members of certain 'races' filling certain positions on the field. Loy and McElvogue (1970) sought to describe this likelihood of racial over- and under-representation, and to this end turned to the work of Blalock (1962) and Grusky (1963), which concerned organisational structure. This literature was concerned with calibrating individual output, and viewed a team as a larger or smaller economy of individual performances. The aim of the coach or manager was to devise a division of labour within which each team member could maximise his/her output. In synthesising this work and applying it to the phenomenon at hand, Loy and McElvogue borrowed the concept of centrality as a way to determine levels of racial discrimination in US professional sport. Measures of centrality were determined by how close a member was to the centre of the team's interaction, how frequently that member interacted with a greater or lesser range of other teammates, and the degree to which he or she had to co-ordinate tasks and activities with other members (Grusky 1963). Central and non-central positions were defined accordingly.

Armed with a means of defining centrality, researchers began to measure the phenomenon in US professional sport. They found that, within the organisational structures of teams, blacks were over-represented in non-central positions and under-represented in central positions; for whites the patterns were reversed. Coaches were then asked to define the ideal qualities for central and non-central positions. They listed intelligence, emotional control, and the ability to make decisions under pressure as desirable qualities for central positions. Among those desirable for non-central positions were strength, speed, quickness, high emotion, and 'good instincts' (Brower 1972; Edwards 1973; Eitzen and Tessendorf 1978; Williams and Youssef 1979).

Joseph Maguire became the first researcher to apply the centrality (or 'stacking') thesis to British sport in 1988, with his study on English professional football. His analysis supported 'the contention that there is a connection between "race" and occupancy of central positions. It is evident that among black players registered, 28% occupy central positions and 72% play in noncentral positions' (Maguire 1988: 264). In another British study which asked coaches to define the role of black players, the American coaches' appeal to 'high emotion and good instincts' appeared verbatim (Lashley 1989).

In the phenomenon of 'stacking', a calculus of individual and team output was used to deposit the black male in the spaces of the field, pitch, court, etc. in which his 'instinctive' nature could be harnessed for the maximum gain of his team. This begs the question of how a trait imputed to black males so doggedly throughout the course of British history in the immediate service of exploitation and control, had suddenly become 'good'. The 'impulsive' or 'instinctive' streak in black players had seemingly become a matter of individual expression, flair or artistry which went unrepressed by certain cultural formations. This was reflected in remarks emanating from the world of sport and in commentary on sporting phenomena.

In *Black Sportsmen*, Ernest Cashmore argued that black athletic supremacy is determined by cultural rather than biological factors. In doing so he considered the issue of impulse-repression:

> a combination of factors, including ... a distorted appreciation of the parent's function *vis-a-vis* education crystallize to release the black youth from the influence of his parents and jettison him into a world in which his peers, with whom he shares the common experience of being black in a white society, are the dominant force. Such forces carry him away from the mainstream of Caribbean life into the tributaries of a distinct black youth culture. In many cases, the work ethic is denigrated and impulse repression replaced by an incitement to self-expression. Sport is one vehicle for such expression.
>
> (1988: 87)

Three years after the book's publication – and as detailed at the outset of the study – Crystal Palace chairman Ron Noades appeared on *Great Britain United* (Critical Eye 1991), a documentary addressed to the issue of 'race' in football. 'I don't think too many of them can read the game', Noades said of Palace's black players. 'When you're getting into the midwinter you need a few of the maybe hard white men to carry the artistic black players through.'

It would appear that whereas the only option for Randy Turpin was to instrumentalise his 'killer instinct' in codified acts of violence, through sport the black male's untamed impulses could now be transfigured into unpredictable but effective forms of spontaneous self-expression; they could now be economised for the team's maximum gain. The outline of Nietzsche's 'overman' and Freud's artist, transforming powerful impulses into dazzling acts of individual performance, can almost be made out.

As it became possible to behave instinctively or impulsively without being accordingly devalued, black sportsmen began to identify themselves as such:

> I'm not the best tactical player – tactics bore the life out of me because I've no appreciation of them. I'm an instinctive player who does things off the cuff, and those sorts of players have never made great coaches or managers.
>
> (Former Arsenal and England striker Ian Wright (1997: 223)

In making this statement Wright was not perched on any philosophical peak. The remark grounds the workings of historical ontology in the context of everyday choice and self-awareness. It illustrates how Wright's 'ways of being, chosen freely or not, are from possible ways of being' (Hacking 2002a: 23), and how this sense of himself disclosed possibilities for action.

John Barnes followed suit in 1999. 'If a really hard tackle came in, I took evasive action', said Barnes. 'I knew when bad challenges were imminent. It's animal instinct. In the jungle, animals sense when a lion prowls nearby' (1999: 146). Surveying the same career, Dave Hill described Barnes's time at Liverpool under Kenny Dalglish:

> Dalglish's belief was that Barnes was a player whose potential could be liberated and whose talent could be improved. While he could not be called upon to dominate proceedings, given the right service he could dominate them. He needed the ball at his feet. Liverpool were the team to put it there for him. Ability, timing, and instinct would do the rest.
>
> (2001: 205)

In 2007 Ian Wright's adopted son Shawn Wright-Phillips was described by journalist Ian Ladyman as a 'wonderfully instinctive and impulsive winger, a player whose dexterity, pace and unpredictability made him such a devilish opponent' (Ladyman 2007). However, this evident reappraisal of impulse and instinct is just that: the reworking of a raciological idea rather than its retreat. For those like Wright and Barnes who have identified with it, the idea's format may seem benign, even complimentary. But any idea whose content holds racial boundaries in place and whose 'truth', however rearranged, testifies to clefts in humanity, is sure to have a sinister underside.

In Britain, so-called 'black' culture – and the absence of impulse repression therein – was used to explain the 'good instincts' of black athletes. However, this reasoning also saw young black males targeted because of their alleged propensity to commit acts of violence. Evidence of this logic can be found in Britain's newspapers and, more specifically, the comment and opinion columns which often appear in the aftermath of a high-profile incident (or spate of incidents) involving knife and/or gun crime as well as instances of 'rioting'. In many cases these contain raciological undertones. Aside from the gun- and knife-toting offenders themselves, the problem identified by many experts and commentators is fractured family units ill-equipped for the business of child rearing. This has the effect, so the argument runs, of driving youngsters into the clutches of a nihilistic youth culture whose ringleaders, typically excluded from an ailing state education system (predominantly in urban areas), loiter, cause a nuisance and ask the same of their deputies. Furthermore, having never learned to repress their impulses via the interventions of parents and/or teachers, they are forever liable to attack others with childlike abandon.

'It has been recognised for some time – including in such quarters as The Voice, the leading black newspaper – that the majority of suspects in muggings in inner London boroughs are young black youths and men', wrote John Steele, Crime Correspondent for *The Telegraph* in January 2002. 'A hard core, left to drift by years of family breakdown and school exclusions, is particularly prolific.' A Home Office Research Study, *Black and Asian Offenders on Probation*, published two years later, described a rehabilitation programme for black and Asian offenders. Its leaders emphasised one purpose of the programme more often than any other; this was 'to teach participants to be less impulsive and to think of the consequences of their actions' (2004: 35).

In May 2005 Detective Inspectors Steve Tyler and Gerry McGowan of Operation Trident (a Metropolitan Police initiative set up to investigate gun crime in London's 'black' community) addressed a Haringey Community and Police Consultative Group. They put forward their account of the problem:

> At the start of Trident the problem was largely Jamaicans coming into the UK and causing gun crime, but today the problem is home-grown. Regrettably there is a disproportionate amount of gun crime in the black community. There is a breakdown of family values, particularly lack of male role models and significant socio-economic deprivation in gun crime hot spots. The young people in these areas are also educational under-achievers which in turn leads to lack of job opportunities and low aspirations ... Gun crime is chaotic, disorganised and impulsive.
>
> (Haringey Community and Police Consultative Group 2005)

That year Emma Hern, Will Glazebrook and Mike Beckett, emergency consultants at a London hospital, published a brief editorial on 'Reducing knife crime' in the *British Medical Journal*. 'Many assaults are impulsive', they wrote (Hern *et al.* 2005: 1221).

A report by the Home Office Statistical Bulletin, *Violent Crime Overview, Homicide and Gun Crime 2004/05*, was published in 2006. The ensuing barrage of statistics showed that 'non-whites' had committed a disproportionate number of violent offences in the last year. Furthermore, violent offenders aged 16 to 25 were three times as likely to be 'highly impulsive' as opposed to 'not impulsive' (Coleman, Hird and Povey 2006: 36). Later that year forensic psychologist Dr Derek Indoe gave his appraisal: 'Deterrence only works if you've got someone who's prepared to weigh things up rationally. A lot of stabbings are on impulse' (quoted in *The Independent* Editorial 2006). Next to interject was Cressida Dick, Deputy Assistant Commissioner of the Metropolitan Police, who told a seminar held in early 2007 that violence was becoming 'very chaotic, impulsive'. At the same seminar a number of community leaders warned that Britain was creating a generation of 'urban child soldiers' (quoted in Glover and Travis 2007).

In 2007 an Essex County Council initiative listed 'Risk and protective factors for young black men' in response to a disproportionate number of the latter being excluded from local schools. Among these factors were 'Having aspirant parents who show their support by venturing into the world of education with their children', the 'Ability to manage feelings and emotions so that they are appropriate to the situation', as well as 'Being self motivated and able to control impulsive behaviour' (EstConnexions 2007: 7).

Both the criminal and the child figured in the appraisal of Peter Squires, Professor of Criminology and Public Policy at Brighton University: 'The police have already targeted some of the main gang players very effectively. But one of the consequences is that those criminals have had to get rid of their guns quickly, handing them on to kids, who pass under the police radar. For them it's an induction into the culture, and part of the impulsive nature of youngsters is that they try to prove themselves' (quoted in Arnot 2007). Writing in *The Times*, Minette Marrin's proclamation that 'Britain is creating youths who have nothing to lose by crime' centred on the 'normal' thresholds of a child's upbringing:

> Libraries of research have been done into this. For babies and young children, a failure to bond with their mothers, or constant separation anxiety, lack of attention and stimulation or actual abuse do permanent damage to the brain, just as bad parenting and lack of good male role models do other kinds of damage. Two common outcomes are a lack of empathy and impaired impulse control, both of which are associated with violent crime. Such children may be very much less capable of personal responsibility, or of rational choice, than children from more normal homes.
>
> (Marrin 2008)

A 2008 report by the National Audit Office, *Violent Crime: Risk Models, Effective Interventions, and Risk Management*, substantiated Marrin's claims. A child's early years were crucial, but school-based interventions also had a role to play:

> Early interventions (before age five or even 'true' early, meaning before age three) are the most effective at preventing violent and criminal behaviour. However, there are evidence-based and evaluated interventions during the school years that have also been shown to be effective. Some of these have been specifically aimed at violence prevention or reduction. For example, the Second Step curriculum was implemented with a randomised control trial in which primary school students were taught anger management, empathy and impulse control.
>
> (2008: 25)

Later that year a report was released following a Home Affairs Select Committee Inquiry into 'Young Black People and the Criminal Justice System'. The report outlined a 'new regime' for the National Offender Management Service whose main theme was: 'adolescent-specific development needs, such as social skills, impulsivity, relationship management, education, communication skills and vocational training' (HM Government 2008: 58).

The following year saw King's College's Centre for Crime and Justice Studies conduct a 'comprehensive review, analysis and critique of gun and knife crime strategies'. Titled *Young People, Knives and Guns*, its authors recited the findings of Lipsey and Derzon (1998) and Derzon (2001) which listed impulsivity as one of the individual characteristics which, in turn, was a major predictor of serious and violent offending for young people (Silvestri *et al.* 2009). They subsequently detailed school-based initiatives aimed at addressing or preventing violence. These included training in social skills, 'anger management and impulse control' (ibid: 63).

In 2010 the House of Commons Committee of Public Accounts discussed 'The Youth Justice System in England and Wales: Reducing Offending by Young People', the proceedings of which were published the following January. The Committee lamented the fact that the Youth Justice Board had 'conducted insufficient research to provide strong guidance on commonly available and used programmes, such as anger or impulsivity management' (2011: 12). The summer of 2011 would provide the Committee with plenty to consider.

On 4 August 2011, Mark Duggan was shot dead by armed police in Tottenham, North London. Two days later local residents staged a peaceful protest in response to the killing. However, that evening violence broke out in the area. Over the subsequent four nights disorder spread to other parts of London and districts of Bristol, Manchester, Birmingham and Liverpool.

The disturbances provoked a period of questioning and reflection in which the rehearsal of particular themes was inevitable: impulsivity and dysfunctional families. A story in the *Daily Mail*, accompanied by a photograph of looters in Hackney, glossed the findings of researchers at Cardiff University in proclaiming that 'Rioters may have "lower levels" of brain chemical that keeps impulsive behaviour under control' (Daily Mail Reporter 2011). The researchers themselves, Petroc Sumner, Frederic Boy and Chris Chambers, complained in *The Guardian* that these findings had been distorted. The fact that *The Guardian* carried the researchers' renouncement was curious given that the same day as the original *Daily Mail* story it had published an article on 'the psychology of looting' (again accompanied by an image of looters in Hackney) which contained the verdict of forensic psychologist Kay Nooney:

> In constituency, it's most similar to a prison riot: what will happen is that, usually in the segregation unit, nobody will ever know exactly, but a rumour will emanate that someone has been hurt in some way. There will be some form of moral outrage that takes its expression in self-interested revenge. There is no higher purpose, you just have a high volume of people with a history of impulsive behaviour, having a giant adventure.
>
> (Quoted in Williams 2011)

Prime Minister David Cameron also mulled over the possible causes of the disorder. He bemoaned the 'slow-motion moral collapse' of Britain, though eliminated race, poverty and spending cuts as precipitating factors. His response was a pledge to put 'rocket-boosters' on efforts to rehabilitate 120,000 of the UK's most 'troubled families'; more specifically, each of these families would be subjected to some kind of 'family-intervention' programme prior to the next general election (Travis and Stratton 2011).

For those brought to justice in connection with the 'riots', the penalties were harsh. A mother of two, Ursula Nevin, was given a six-month sentence for accepting a pair of looted shorts from a friend, while two young men, Perry Sutcliffe-Keenan and Jordan Blackshaw, were told they would each serve four years for using a social networking site to incite a riot (which never materialised) (Bowcott 2011). In March 2012, 18-year-old Beau Isagbo was convicted of the assault of Malaysian student Ashraf Rossli. The attack had taken place in Barking, East London, amid the previous summer's disturbances. Being sentenced to a total of seven years in prison, Isagbo was told the following by Judge Witold Pawlack: 'With one punch you fractured his jaw in two places, leaving him dazed and bleeding. Two days later he had surgery, and two metal plates inserted which will remain with him for the rest of his life as a permanent reminder of your brutal and impulsive behaviour' (quoted in Moynihan 2012).

We can see how the criminological discourses of 20 or 30 years ago have survived 'the tyranny of political correctness' (Johnson 2006): in the public arena they operate via allusions and distinctions which are ever more subtle and rarefied. And though culture continues to trump biology as the explanatory medium for behaviour, some are eager to fill in the gaps and make criminology's appeals to raciology more explicit. For example, the following appears on the personal website of Martin Sewell, a Research Associate at the University of Cambridge, as part of an entry on 'Race':

> Anthropologists claim that race does not exist, they are wrong ... Blacks are more impulsive than other races, and the unwillingness of blacks to delay immediate gratification for a long-term advantage shows up from an early age ... blacks are 3.4 times more likely than whites to be arrested for a notifiable offence in England and Wales (Home Office 2006). The most likely reason for the high incidence of black crime is blacks' lower intelligence and greater impulsivity.
>
> (2008: http://race.martinsewell.com)

As a figure, the black male is continually etched through the enumeration of crime rates and summoned into being through bywords such as impulse, impulsivity and instinct. Unless his unrepressed, childlike psychological urges meet with modes of legitimate expression – transfigured through music, art, sport, or instrumentalised through the military – a life of violent criminality beckons. The twin faces of savagery loom large and the choice is a stark one: sublimation or incarceration.

Concluding remarks: knowledge and power ethics

It is now important to revisit the three axes of historical ontology and, more specifically, to consider how they have figured in the history of the 'impulsive' black male. The nature of Foucault's three axes means that one is not easily cleaved from the others; each helps to sustain and extend its fellow axes in the production and effects of 'truth'.[16] Nevertheless, I am eager to structure a brief overview of the chronology according to these three dimensions, and in this way underline how they have articulated throughout history to give depth to the raciological ideas of instinct and impulse.

First: knowledge. We have seen the abstract thinking of Plato, the 'modern' philosophy of Descartes, the hard scientific principles of Newton, the evolutionary theory of Darwin, the monism of Nietzsche, and the psychological analyses of Freud and Jung, each to a greater or lesser extent, lay down frameworks of knowledge approaching the depth of *savoir*. These frameworks contained the systems of regularity according to which peddlers of surface knowledge constructed their neat theories and hypotheses.

Thus members of the plantocracy, colonial psychiatrists, psychologists, criminologists, journalists and social commentators have indulged their prejudices and short-term professional concerns in constituting the impulsive black male as an object of knowledge. This has landed him within numerous epistemological categories: material, passive, inert, immature, savage, psychopathic, primary functioning, monoideic, hypomaniacal, unstable, delinquent, Type NH4, under-controlled, violent criminal. But he could not have become an epistemological artefact without first having his name repeated within certain institutional settings.

Second: power. By singling out a raciological idea one can see how the diffuse effects of discourses have their origins in multiple institutional sites. While these can be buildings and other material structures or instruments, they can just as feasibly be the sentences and utterances of reports or articles. In short, wherever the name or idea in question appears as an object of knowledge, and with institutional authority. In this vein we have encountered (among others) the reveries of explorers and travel writers, the gripes of plantation owners and investors, the mental asylums, hospitals and psychiatric wards of Britain and its colonial territories, the peer-reviewed research papers of criminologists, and the deceivingly arid proclamations of government reports. Codified in epistemological terms and licensed by institutions and practices, impulse and instinct have been wielded as yardsticks of civilisation. This has seen members of the 'lower orders' usurped, enslaved, displaced, sectioned, surveilled and imprisoned. As an object of knowledge, the impulsive black male epitomised these lower orders. The founding rites of capitalism saw him dispossessed of his own body; he now occupies the margins of capitalist society – hooded, immature and liable to end up in its houses of correction. In ontological terms, the idea's conditions of possibility are sustained by a host of institutions whose pronouncements imply that the black male's best prospect of law-abiding, tax-paying, economic independence lies in transfiguring (read economising) his impulses through sport or the arts.

This brings us to our final axis: ethics. In the case of the 'impulsive' black male, knowledge and power have worked together to constrict the space wherein moral and ethical questions are formulated and judgements made. The authority of certain epistemological categories makes some questions and judgements seem urgent and inescapable, while others are quite unfathomable within the discourses available to us. Amid a historical legacy of compulsive counting and classifying, the accusatory finger now points at the abnormal, dysfunctional family background from which the psychopathic, unstable, impulsive black male emerges.

Reproduced within various institutional sites, more or less codified notions of impulse and/or instinct have helped to define these figures and classifications, and continue to do so today. For a long time they ensured that behaviour animated by impulsive or instinctive urges languished at the base of ethical and moral hierarchies. It was Britain's obsessive desire to be *the* pioneer of capitalist expansionism which led to Francis Bacon's denigration of those ruled by 'the instincts of the spirit', and his chilling injunction to 'cut them off the face of the earth' (1868 [1622]: 33). His clarion call answered, impulse and instinct continued to justify in ethical terms the treatment of those who were enslaved, who rebelled, who were sectioned, and who called for independence from British colonial rule. In the aftermath of independence they defined the black males arriving from Britain's former territories and tallied up their crimes; a second generation was similarly defined by the criminology of the 1970s and 1980s. In a contemporary setting, those who fail to suppress or economise their impulsive/instinctive urges – who lack any work *ethic* – are marked off as morally depraved. However, today's surface knowledge with its dual emphasis on the family and individual psychology means that parents are also subject to criticism on ethical and moral grounds, as impulsivity is called upon to define the 'normal' child, the 'normal' family, and the 'normal' upbringing, along with their criminal-producing antitheses.

In the history of the 'impulsive' black sportsman lies a blinding paradox: the epistemological categories which in earlier incarnations had acted as moral guarantors for imperial power – which had such professional, political and economic utility in response to the urgent institutional demands of British colonialism – now point us in the direction of anything but that power to make sense of Britain's socio-economic complexion, and the threats which supposedly issue from its margins. Today's versions of these categories are used as part of a continued effort to show that the social and moral world we inhabit stands outside the shadow cast by a fallen empire. This is possible because certain institutions and practices, those from which our taxonomies draw their historic power, have been forgotten.

But perhaps there is cause for guarded optimism. Today's experts and specialists have accommodated the raciological idea of impulsivity to the conditions of their institutional and epistemological settings. The idea has incorporated psychoanalytic principles, namely the interface between the family culture in which a child is raised and the development of that child's individual psychology, while retaining the implication that black males – motivated by impulses that went unrepressed during crucial periods in their upbringing – are more likely to carry out violent attacks than any other group. However, we should question whether the musings of elite sports coaches and professional pundits, the conclusions reached by government committees and the pronouncements of the tabloid press lag behind everyday explanations of behaviour and performance.

The role of articulations of knowledge, power and ethics in the emergence of the 'impulsive' black male has been charted. We must now discover whether these orders of knowledge, power and ethics hold outside of the 'expert' institutional settings so crucial in constituting the 'impulsive' black male. Away from the rigorous standards of epistemological exactitude and refinement which saw the idea transformed into an object of knowledge, do different conceptions of human difference come to the fore? Could these conceptions be shaped by epistemological regimes, relations of power and sets of ethical standards which conform to different institutional requirements, with 'expert' pronouncements framed and qualified differently?

To explore this possibility we now head to the inner-city. Here I undertake ethnographic research, again within a sporting setting, to see if the totalising claims of raciology have any purchase on the consciousness of a set of young Londoners. Put in ontological terms, I question whether these individuals' possibilities for being are conditioned by the claims of raciology. Do notions such as impulse and instinct operate as placeholders in the constitution of self and others as objects of raciological knowledge? If not, what conceptions of human difference figure in this constitution, what possibilities for action are disclosed, and how might we go about explaining them (along with the absence of raciological ideas)?

Finally I should reiterate that the chronology presented here is necessarily abridged and incomplete. I hope it may prompt the writing of alternative accounts which engage with the historical record rather than invoke the idea they should seek to explain. Indeed, a large step will be taken in the battle against raciological ideas when people's default reaction is to explain, rather than simply invoke anew.

Conceptions of human variation at Oldfield United FC

Part 2

Conceptions of human variation at Oldfield United FC

Chapter 4

Setting the scene

In this chapter I prepare the way for a detailed analysis of the conceptions of human difference on show at Oldfield United Football Club (OUFC). I begin by describing the environs of the club and, more specifically, the socio-political complexion of Oldfield. The focus then turns to the people who make the club tick: its board members and players. It is important to offer a description of the people and relationships that hold the club together, as these provide the key to understanding the methods of human classification employed by club personnel. As later chapters describe, for the players of OUFC it was the intimacy of these relationships along with a detailed inventory of the local landscape that framed and modulated the issue of human variability. The conceptions of difference to which players subscribed imply a complex interweaving of space, knowledge, ethics and power that I will attempt to describe and disentangle in the chapters that follow.

Mirroring the structure of Part 1, at the end of Part 2 I revisit the study's three ontological axes in drawing conclusions with regard to the notions of human variation encountered at OUFC. But before delving into these notions, it is necessary to examine the nodal points which made them legible, beginning with the physical and social landscape of Oldfield itself.

Oldfield: the landscape, the people and the football club

The district of Oldfield is located in the London borough of Bridgegate.[1] Its main thoroughfare is Oldfield Road, which links Bridgegate Central in the south to Hurstmoor in the north. Because of continual streams of immigration Bridgegate is one of the most ethnically diverse boroughs in the country, and this is reflected in the demographic profile of Oldfield's 15,000 residents.

The eighteenth and nineteenth centuries brought émigrés fleeing the French Revolution, liberal Spaniards on the run from absolute monarchy, and navvies from all over the United Kingdom who arrived in Bridgegate looking for work on the London to Midlands railway line being driven through Bridgegate Central and Jameson Road. In the 1950s came settlers from Ireland, Greece, Cyprus, Portugal and the West Indies. These were joined in the 1970s by migrants from the Sylhet region of Bangladesh, who would open many 'Indian' restaurants in the borough. Following the collapse of the Eastern Bloc, Polish men and women arrived in equal number; the latter to serve in bars and cafés, the former to work in engineering and construction where they became worthy successors to the Irish. The 1990s Balkan conflicts saw the immigration of thousands from that region, while people fleeing war in Afghanistan, Sudan, Congo, Algeria and Somalia have settled in the borough over the last decade. Data relating to the ethnicity of Oldfield ward residents (compared to borough-wide statistics) are listed in the table below:

If the district is home to a wide range of ethnic groups, no such diversity is evident in its socio-economic complexion. Levels of economic security are polarised; and this is reflected in the condition of the local housing market. Within the district of Oldfield a one-bedroom flat fetches an average of £250,000, while families wishing to purchase a four-bedroom house have to stump up around £950,000. Indeed, the code for the postal district is shared, somewhat ironically, as a territorial badge of honour by local street gangs and those affluent enough to afford an abode on the private market. There is thus an overwhelming demand for local council housing – Bridgegate Council's waiting list numbered 16,000 applicants at the last count – and, though plenty of local authority-owned flats and houses are situated in the borough, supply is hopelessly strained.

Table 1 Ethnicity in Oldfield Ward: breakdown of ethnic groups as a percentage of total population (versus borough-wide statistics)

		Oldfield	*Bridgegate*
White	British	59.0%	52.7%
	Irish	5.6%	4.6%
	Other White	12.0%	15.8%
Mixed	White and Black Caribbean	1.3%	0.8%
	White and Black African	0.8%	0.6%
	White and Asian	0.9%	1.0%
	Other Mixed	1.0%	1.3%
Asian or Asian British	Indian	1.3%	2.3%
	Pakistani	0.3%	0.6%
	Bangladeshi	5.0%	6.3%
	Other Asian	0.8%	1.1%
Black or Black British	Caribbean	2.3%	1.8%
	African	6.6%	6.0%
	Other Black	0.5%	0.5%
Chinese or Other	Chinese	1.0%	1.8%
	Other Ethnic Group	1.5%	2.7%

Source: 2001 Census Ward Profile

The ecology of this London district bears the hallmarks of the neo-liberal policies implemented successively by Conservative, New Labour, and Tory-Lib Dem coalition governments (Hall 2011; Harvey 2005). The High Street tells a confused story of consumption. Pound stores and cheap cafés neighbour exclusive furniture shops and health-food outlets, their price lists reflecting a yawning gap in the amounts of disposable income available to their respective clienteles. This gap is indicative of the poverty and prosperity which rub shoulders on the High Street and reside cheek-by-jowl in the area's dense network of private and council housing.

In an inversion of the district's socio-economic hierarchy, the inhabitants of Chorville and Blake Tower – council-owned redoubts whose hulking concrete exteriors dominate the local landscape – gaze down upon ribbons of expensive private housing. Blake Tower stands at the centre of the most notorious estate in Oldfield, Rydal Grove, formerly a vibrant centre of social housing which hosted a weekly street market, but now a drab collection of low- and high-rise apartment blocks, its labyrinth of alleys and walkways strewn with refuse and policed by street gangs and drug dealers. Indeed, the recent social deterioration of Rydal Grove has seen it dubbed a 'no-go area', with murder rates the second highest in London and 23 per cent of young residents having been mugged.

Gianni Zola and Geoff Phillips founded OUFC in 1994, concerned that youngsters in the local area (their sons included) had too few opportunities to play competitive football. Initially attracting only a ragtag collection of parents, the fledgling club played its first competitive fixture in the Bridge-gate & Highfield Midweek League – three of the 11 players who started the match that evening were still involved with the first team squad in 2010. The club then began to expand, subsuming other local teams which had disbanded. It had three representative age-group teams (under-12, under-13 and under-14) by 1998; a year later it had eight, competing across the Bridgegate & Highfield Midweek League and the Teddingham & District Youth League. By 2003, with the original nucleus of its players growing older, the club now needed a senior side and to this end joined the Allied Districts League (ADL). The team consolidated its position by finishing tenth in the ADL Second Division, but excelled in 2004/05, gaining promotion to ADL Division One. It soon found its feet in the division, finishing the 2007/08 season as Champions and thereby gaining promotion to the ADL Premier Division. OUFC's maiden season in the Premier Division brought disappointment and controversy, with the club finishing bottom after receiving a ten-point deduction for fielding ineligible players. It also suffered because of the semi-professional status conferred by membership of the ADL's top division. Already running at a considerable loss, the club were unable to remunerate players for their services. Sixteen of the 38 players registered in the summer of 2008 left during the course of the 2008/09 season, being offered paid contracts or 'boot money' by other clubs in the division.

For Gianni and Geoff, Rydal Grove (aka 'the Grove') was the club's spiritual home. A handful of players in the youth team that eventually grew into OUFC hailed from the estate. Many current first and reserve team players lived there, although took great pains to stress that their lodgings were situated at the 'good end'. When Geoff carried out the pre-match pick-up in the vicinity of the Grove, outside a church on Vicars Street, he would invariably curse the absence of the two or three players who failed to present themselves at the appointed time. Reaching for his mobile phone to bellow the customary, 'Allo, where are ya?!' the lads would eventually appear, scurrying along the estate's warrens or emerging from one of the convenience stores which line its western perimeter.

Oldfield United FC: the board

Though he had since moved to Shinewater, a mile or so to the north-east of Oldfield, in 1962 Geoff was born in the dreaded Chorville, the area's tallest and most dingy tower block. 'My sister's still there. She moved out but eventually went back, got a decent place … (I) don't go down there very often these days.' Before settling in Shinewater he rode the council-housing carousel, and openly admitted that he and his wife Shirlie's decision to have their first child was influenced by the council's point system which measured a tenant's eligibility for larger accommodation. Horrified at the prospect of a young family occupying a room which contained one bed, a cooker and a bath (concealed by a curtain) – a curious take on 'studio living' – a visiting council representative duly reassigned Geoff and his pregnant wife to a two-bedroom flat in Shinewater.

> I could see her looking at her form and knew she was gonna ask, sure enough: 'it says here you have a bath in this room but I can't see one', she said. So I pulled the curtain back, shoulda seen her face!

Their son Alex was now 16 years old and preparing to enter sixth-form college.

In 1997 Geoff qualified as a bus driver and worked for Transport for London (previously London Regional Transport) until 2003, when a controversial public–private partnership meant he had to reapply for his job on lower pay, and was eventually made redundant. Having met Geoff in the early 1990s, Gianni pulled some strings at his own place of work, *Bridgegate Meat*, a meat wholesaler situated on the eastern margins of Bridgegate Central, to secure Geoff a job. He now worked 12am till 9am, six nights per week. 'Been there for a few years now. Some nights it's murder, others there's nothing to do. Bit of a killer after midweek games though, like, know what I mean?' Indeed, after many midweek away fixtures Geoff headed straight to work.

Geoff had a calm demeanour but wasted no time in making his mind up about people: 'I can tell pretty quick if they're gonna stick around, what they're in it for, know what I mean?' If he identified reliability and trust-worthiness in a newcomer to the club he had a knack for short-circuiting the formative stages of friendship. Part of this knack was an ability to make people feel at ease. When telling a story or trying to get across a point, to compensate for his lack of verve in delivery Geoff would bow his head very slightly, fixing his discussant with a confiding stare that didn't leave hold until his trademark, 'know what I mean?' appealed for the appropriate response, whether it be laughter, sympathy or shared indigna-tion. He anticipated this shortcoming in others and, sensing immediately whether a statement was being made for comedy's sake, would let out a hearty chuckle just before the delivery of the punchline, as if his fondness for the teller had already vouchsafed the quality of the joke.

Standing around 5 foot 8 inches with short, thick grey hair, his paunchy torso was normally decked in a polo shirt which, according to players, had the 'wrong' animal sewn onto its left breast: a dolphin or shark instead of a mounted horse or crocodile. His bottom half came clad in black slacks: heavy, thick trousers which gave Geoff's already purposeful gait a soldierly bearing. Geoff soon became my match-day companion and in the early days (before I was given a lift to matches *ex officio*) I often arrived at stadiums after kick-off and wondered as to his whereabouts in the stands. His location was soon given away by the long, primordial yells which, if they did not follow an individual error by one of OUFC's players, were – by quickly unleashing a wave of panic and indecision – almost certain to precede one. Each yell began as a deep grunt in the pit of Geoff's stomach but quickly rose to a volume and pitch commensurate with the severity of the mistake which had been made. If the blunder was particularly serious, resulting in the concession of a goal or penalty kick, for instance, Geoff's mouth gaped and the back of his throat gave a warbling intonation to what, by then, had risen to a blaring roar.

Geoff's role of Club Secretary (which he had fulfilled since the club's inception) was downgraded to Match Secretary in 2009 after the club was found guilty of fielding ineligible players.

It was either that or cancel the fixtures, we had no other goalkeepers … was ridiculous in the end. We had a new player – you know "Netti", Netanel – but we was all calling him Neil from the sidelines, the name of the fella who'd gone away but hadn't cancelled his registration.

His duties now included confirming the dates and times of fixtures with officials and opposing clubs as well as ensuring that a clean, correctly colour-schemed kit was available on match days. He was present at every home, away and reserve team fixture, and had to work in the café when needed. Gianni and his partner (and club Chairwoman) Deborah owned the franchise for this café, relying on large athletics meets and school sports days for any profit.

His relationship with Gianni had the characteristics of any long and durable friendship; one could usually forecast the antics of the other, though such behaviour was no less infuriating for having been anticipated. One evening after a match in Shoreston, Gianni jumped over the advertising hoardings in order to remonstrate with officials who, in his opinion, had 'given us nothing all game'. After a half-hearted attempt to hold him back, Geoff uttered, one second shouting, the next mumbling: 'No, fu ... ! I knew he was gonna do that ... Gianni! It's not you that has to deal with the fucking fines! Fuck's sake.' After Gianni had said his bit and retreated from the pitch, the pair had a row outside the boardroom of the opposing team, Shoreford Town:

Gianni: He was shit that ref, I've gotta tell ya.
Geoff: You're not s'posed to be on the pitch Gianni, you're not manager no more. Now we better hope the ref don't recognise you from last year and puts it in the report.
Gianni: What *can* we do then Geoff!?
Deborah: I'm not getting involved.

Gianni stormed off to his car with Deborah following a couple of seconds later, concurrently shaking her head and raising her eyebrows. This left Geoff and I to carry out the necessary particulars in the boardroom with the opposition and match officials. Gianni's foray didn't make it into the referee's match report – it was difficult to tell whether Geoff was relieved or disappointed. On the drive home Geoff predicted that he and Gianni would 'get on alright' when they encountered each other at work early the next morning. Indeed, the altercation didn't shadow their friendship for long, and in many ways this summed up the ties which bound the pair together: old and inextricably tangled.

The club staged its home fixtures at Churchfield Stadium, an arena designed primarily for athletics and shared with local athletics club Churchfield Chasers. Churchfield is located in Wish Hill, well outside the borough of Bridgegate. Bridgegate offered no alternatives in the way of a home stadium; there are no full-size football pitches in the borough (the nearest are within the grounds of Hurst Park and come under the jurisdiction of a neighbouring borough council). OUFC paid the owners of Churchfield Stadium, Wish Hill Council, around £400 per match in rent and renewed its contract on a year-by-year basis. Having fallen out with the stadium's management team (it was run by a private company on behalf of the council), OUFC's contact at the site was 'Chemical Ali', its Iraqi groundsman. Ali was 27 and had arrived in London six years ago to enrol at college. He had since accepted a place at Churchfield University to study pharmaceutical science, taking the job as groundsman in order to pay his tuition and living expenses. Ali had grown closer to Gianni and Geoff during OUFC's three years at Churchfield. When Ali was learning to drive, Geoff gave him impromptu lessons in the stadium's sprawling car park, while Gianni had given him a key to the café so he could help himself to tea and hot snacks on mornings when it wasn't open for business. Whenever Ali returned to the Middle East to visit family the pair teased him about being off to 'Al-Qaeda training camp' or 'bomb-making school', to which he would jokingly reply: 'I've told you, I already know all I need to know.' On match days Ali's young nephew messed around with Jorge, the seven-year-old brother of OUFC midfielder Diego, harrying Deborah and acting as occasional ball boys in pursuit of free snacks.

The stadium itself was a lopsided edifice forged from enormous cinder blocks. The northern side of the stadium was home to its only stand, a two-storey structure with stairs at either end leading up to three dense blocks of blue, plastic seating. Within the bowels of the stand were located a modestly outfitted café, kitchen, boardroom, changing rooms and reception area. Newspaper cuttings and other athletics paraphernalia (medals, pendants, etc.) plastered any available wall space, and this left visitors in no doubt as to which of the stadium's tenants had made its permanent home there. The only reminders of OUFC's stake in the arena were a lock-up situated to the east of the running track – containing footballs, portable dugouts, corner flags and large bags of kit – and the faces visible through the large portal to the café. The cost of food supplies was lessened by Gianni and Geoff's employment at *Bridgegate Meat*, the café's freezer being freighted with burgers, sausages and slabs of ham and steak. In fact, meat circulated as a kind of currency within the club.

Having a home ground located more than seven miles from Oldfield proper didn't do wonders for the club's sense of place and any attendant notions of community. People taking an interest were almost exclusively the friends and relatives of players or staff; a fact which affected the club's finances. Though match days were a showcase of hurried endeavour, it was relatively exceptional to see money change hands. Despite charging an entry fee of £5 and Gianni and Deborah's complaints at the meagre profits produced by the café, the desire for earnings was outweighed by a compulsive need to identify strangers. It was an urgent task to connect everyone that attended club fixtures on more than one occasion to one of its players, coaches or officials (those who attended only once were members of that strange breed: 'the ground-hoppers'). And because 'associates' of the club seldom paid for refreshments and admission, this reduction of the unfamiliar to the familiar meant a lack of profit on match days.

As all of the club's players (despite its semi-professional status) were unpaid, and all of its staff were volunteers. When Gianni felt particularly indebted to one of his charges – for a long car journey, completing an onerous pile of paperwork, or agreeing to an improvised shift in the café – the favour was repaid in packages of meat. Typically weighing around 3 kilos and containing one whole chicken, two pork chops, two fillet steaks and a selection of burgers and sausages, these bags were discreetly presented to players and staff in club car parks across London and its suburban hinterlands. Consequently, for club personnel the invitation to 'come and have a chat outside' was akin to the sounding of Pavlov's metronome. I was presented with my first package a month into service as Club Secretary, obviously to mark the end of some informal probationary period; living the typically frugal life of a post-graduate student (in a flat with no freezer), the following week's menu laid siege to my digestive system.

Gianni had lived in London since his teenage years. His parents arrived from Italy in the 1950s. As a youngster Gianni got a job as a pizza boy, and this took him 'all over London really'. He moved to Bridgegate Central in his late teens following his parents' return to Italy, staying in the area for 20 years before moving to Winchford where he now carried on a tempestuous house cum timeshare with his ex-wife and two children. Gianni paid the rent and occupied the house (where his children lived permanently) at weekends when his ex-wife left for the suburbs. Upon her return on Monday he took up occupancy with Deborah in Wakebourne, until Friday evening came around once again. 'It ain't ideal James – we've had some messed up situations over there I tell ya. [I] pay through the nose for it but I want to see a roof over my kids' heads.' It was a funny arrangement, which left Deborah exasperated. She often asked if I had heard what 'she's done now' (referring to Gianni's ex-wife), which Gianni took as his cue to stare unseeingly into the distance. I knew the subsequent account, though directed at me, was actually intended for Gianni, as Deborah hoped her criticisms would gain momentum by ricocheting off a third party. These barbed remarks about 'her indoors' normally concerned the amount of money Gianni was required to give his ex-wife in child support payments. Because of her position at the Department for Work and Pensions (DWP) Deborah was privy to a database listing the benefits claimed by every British citizen, and she was keen to remind Gianni that an internal phone call could bring his ex-wife's dubious claims to the attention of the Benefit Fraud authorities. She never followed through on these threats, however, aware that any prosecution would be easily traceable to her and that Gianni would become further estranged from his children as a result.

Like Geoff, Gianni was 48 years-old – though he looked older. As 'Chief Executive Officer' of OUFC his photograph would appear in the local paper every few weeks, much to everyone at the club's amusement. Here, aged by the camera's flash, he cut a somewhat craggy figure, anything but the slick, polished appearance of the typical CEO. A couple of inches taller than Geoff, he had grey, thinning hair, most of it concentrated on the flanks of his scalp, and his eyes – deadened by another night shift – were saddled with purple, puffy bags. His forehead was networked by a series of deep furrows, extending and bifurcating irregularly beneath a sharp jut which gave the impression of tipping his hairline ever further from the front of his head. His arms and legs were bowed to a similar curvature and combined to produce a light, scuttling gait which (in his time as manager) carried him back and forth along the touchline, as he flirted with the boundaries of the 'technical area'. His voice was raspy, thinned by years of smoking. He struggled to raise it to an audible level in order to berate the referee's latest contentious decision. Occasionally he would vault the hoardings to feed his habit, as he and a cigarette hurriedly drained the life out of one another before he returned to the dugout. He always wore trainers, dark blue tracksuit bottoms and a charcoal coloured jumper, his defence for this dowdy look being that a nightshift or a stint in the café had always preceded or would follow the match, training session or meeting in question.

If 'you know what I mean?' was Geoff's verbal tic, Gianni's was undoubtedly 'I've gotta' tell ya', a pet expression which started or finished (and on occasion both started and finished) almost every statement he made. I noticed how he inserted the name of his interlocutor into these statements at random intervals in an attempt to give his words added sincerity. Conversations between Gianni and Geoff opened with a ritualised exchange in which call and response were spoken with affected hauteur:

Gianni: Bon soir.
Geoff: Bon soir.
Gianni: How is one?
Geoff: Maaar-ver-lus.
Gianni: Maaar-ver-lus.

Gianni had been an employee of *Bridgegate Meat* for ten years and, like Geoff, worked six nights per week (although Gianni's shifts ran between 2am and 10am).

> [The] problem is I finish in the morning and think to myself, "I've got the rest of the day now." I do a bit of running around and before I know it it's three o'clock and I've got to start at the café in an hour.

Following a shuffle in club personnel which took place in the summer of 2009, Gianni assumed the role of CEO – although, along with being First Team Manager, this had been his *de facto* position at the club since its inception. Before the reshuffle he presided over the club's finances as well as its organisation on the pitch. 'I couldn't carry on doing it James – (it) was killing me. I'd go more than 48 hours without sleep. Now at least the work's spread a bit thinner.' His duties as CEO included running the club café, securing stadia and facilities for the first team, reserves, under-18 and under-17 teams, soliciting sponsorship, and generally making sure that each team had everything it required. Succeeding Gianni as First Team Manager was Reginald Merchant, a 25-year-old undergraduate student who had known Gianni for six years during which he turned out for OUFC sporadically.

Despite Gianni's move into the background he was still very much *pater-familias*, with players more likely to approach him for help with personal issues than Reg, Geoff or Deborah. In fact, since becoming CEO Gianni had taken a keener interest in the pastoral side of running the club. 'Speaking to Gianni' was always a valid excuse for missing portions of a training session or arriving late for a squad meeting, and while Geoff and Deborah stood purposefully aloof from most players, engaging with only seasoned members of the squad, Gianni acquiesced in being surrounded by players of all ages, turning no one away. As a result he shouldered all of the club's practical and personal baggage, dealing with issues ranging from transport and money problems to unexpected pregnancies and court appearances.

> [I] get it all James. I've had people asking for money, food ... want picking up and dropping off here, there and everywhere. Get asked for references all the time, you know for jobs and that. Had to write character [witness] letters three times, go to court once to be [a] character witness. So, yeah, everything.

One Saturday afternoon before a fixture against Deepcoate FC I found Gianni and veteran midfielder Clive Linehan in deep conversation in the café. I went over to congratulate Clive on his recent marriage to childhood sweetheart, Paula, which had taken place the previous Saturday, but quickly excused myself after sensing that serious matters were being discussed. It turned out that Gianni was advising Clive on a claim for compensation following a minor car accident which took place in the days leading up to his wedding. While Clive was trying to park, another driver had collided with the back of his car. He and Paula had suffered minor injuries as a result. Gianni had subsequently advised Clive to 'ham-up' these injuries for the sake of the claim, and to this end insisted he have two sets of wedding photos taken, one with the married couple wearing neck braces, another with the braces taken off. The former could then be sent to the insurance company as evidence of the couple's emotional hardship.

Gianni wouldn't reveal the nature of his players' criminal offences. 'You'd have to ask them', he muttered with a smile. 'You know about the court appearance though!' Here he referred to an incident which took place in August 2008 during the last few minutes of an FA Cup preliminary round fixture against Heelborough Town. Substitute Gerry Linehan (Clive's older brother) became frustrated that First Team Coach, Laurent Viallon, had reneged on a promise to bring him onto the field at some point of the match to fulfil his lifelong ambition to play in the FA Cup. At the final whistle Gerry headbutted Viallon, who subsequently required treatment by paramedics and later pressed charges against Gerry. Gerry was eventually given community service and a lifetime ban from the club, while Viallon left in November 2008 following Gianni's refusal to give cash incentives ('boot money') to individual players. In addition to Gerry's brush with the law, at the beginning of the 2008/09 season OUFC's star striker, Lawrence Osment, was sent to prison for burglary, while midway through the following season midfielder Jess Reeves received a six-month prison sentence for driving offences.

The same age as both Gianni and Geoff, club Chairwoman Deborah Smyth was born and raised in Middlesborough. She had worked since 1990 as a low-ranking civil servant in regional offices of the DWP. Her youngest son signed for OUFC in 2001 after enrolling at university in London, and settled in the area following graduation. 'He doesn't play anymore. (He) has a good job in marketing and doesn't have the time what with a steady relationship and that ... wish I'd jacked it in when he did!' Initially travelling down from the north in order to visit her son and take in the odd match, in 2005 Deborah had to make the journey to London for more grave purposes. After her husband, Collin, was taken seriously ill, doctors in Middlesborough deemed that specialists in London were best equipped to carry out the urgent operation required to promote his recovery. With Collin subsequently interned in a central London hospital, the months following his operation brought serious medical complications during which Deborah was supported by her son, and more broadly, the football club. Her attendance at OUFC's matches led to a friendship with Gianni.

> I'd go up there for matches and offer to run the door or make the teas at half-time, anything to help Gianni out really. Took my mind off things and I got to know some of the players which kept me interested.

Her husband soon succumbed, dying in hospital in late 2005.

Deborah then returned to the north-east but continued to travel to London whenever OUFC's fixtures did not interfere with her commitments as a season-ticket holder at Middlesborough FC. Her involvement with Gianni (and the club) intensified over the following two seasons; her visits became more frequent and prolonged before she eventually moved to Wakebourne in the summer of 2009. With her request for relocation accepted by the DWP and her position as OUFC's Chairwoman made official, the only thing left was to relinquish her season-ticket at 'the 'Boro'.

Deborah wore an attentive look, the combination of an unthreatening frown and slightly pursed lips, and looking at her one noticed how the purple-brown freckles which mottled her lower neck matched the tint of her heavily dyed hair, like swatches of a larger canvas. As the club's vocal outrider she defended the conduct of its representatives with maternal abandon – whether on *Footy Chat* (an internet forum for followers of ADL clubs) or in the portable buildings which passed for boardrooms at opposition grounds. (The most curious of these boardrooms was found at Telwich Rovers, where the niceties of post-match 'hospitality' were observed amid the steely austerity of a disused shipping container.) 'I remember when I came in Gianni said, "Everyone hates Oldfield." He wasn't wrong. He'll just ignore it or lose his temper. I won't stand for it though.' At home fixtures she was billeted to the club café, serving tea and coffee from two huge stainless steel urns and relaying food orders to Gianni who stood behind her, manning the griddle. Away matches were a more leisurely affair, her only task being to guard a boot bag containing the players' personal effects, mostly loose keys, wallets and mobile phones (from which issued a never-ending chorus of ringtones). Clutching this polyphonic bundle of 'vallies' (valuables) in one hand and a lit cigarette in the other, she assaulted the senses of fellow spectators by shuttling between the directors' stand and areas just outside the jurisdiction of the smoking ban.

The final member of the management committee was First Team Player-Manager Reginald Merchant, a mature student reading Psychology and Criminal Behaviour at the University of Clarkborough. Reg had taken charge of the first team towards the end of the 2008/09 season, when only ground grading issues had saved OUFC from relegation. His assistant was his father, Jeremy, who had previously managed fellow ADL Premier Division club Hertfield Green, during which time Reg cut his teeth as manager of Hertfield's under-18 side. On first meeting the manager and his assistant it was difficult to tell that they were father and son. However, a measure of resemblance, if also a marked lack of harmony, showed in the instructions they bellowed from the touchline; their joint exhortations to 'squeeze!' or 'push-up!' reverberated around the stadium in conflicting tones. They lived, along with Reg's girlfriend Rachel, in Jeremy's two-bedroom flat in north Bridgegate.

Reg had earlier played professionally but, after deeming that a career as a player was unlikely, he opted to make his way in management while continuing full-time study. He struggled in his early days as OUFC manager. However, he gradually managed to combine a number of new players – recruited through his extensive network of playing contacts in the local area – with the nucleus of OUFC veterans such as Alex, Clive and Lawrence. Indeed, at first he faced an uphill battle to win the allegiance of the young men from the Grove, whose loyalty to Gianni proved difficult to override. Thus during the early months of the 2009/10 season, as OUFC languished at the bottom of the table, these lads often expressed their frustration with Reg's methods in private asides. But as the season wore on and more players were brought into the fold, Reg managed to win the respect of OUFC's more experienced players – men who were two or three years his senior – though it should be said that this respect was not exactly unflagging. They sometimes registered dissatisfaction with squad selections by threatening to sacrifice their place in the squad for another player whom they felt had been unfairly overlooked; Reg usually responded by finding a place for both players in the match-day squad, and in this way a playful accommodation of one another's assessments was slowly forged.

Reg had a big frame rooted in a Herculean pair of quadriceps and wore team apparel to meetings, matches and team outings. He arrived at the club sporting a huge mop of curly brown hair but shaved his head periodically to signify threshold moments in the season, usually following an important win or a heavy defeat. With a maturity and attention to detail that belied his age, his infectious smile succeeded in cutting through any tension that built up on the touchline or in committee meetings, particularly while OUFC was suffering a bad run of results. However, it was clear that Reg was still developing a management style that made the best of his characteristics; his inexperience counted most heavily against him in inviting criticism when it may have been better to brook no counsel but his own. But his methods were gradually honed and by the end of the 2009/10 season there were few doubts as to his abilities as a manager at semi-professional level.

I became involved with the club at the start of the 2008/09 season when I began to attend home matches regularly. After getting to know Gianni, Geoff and a handful of the players, I offered to carry out statistical analyses of the players' performances, pass completion rates, etc. I fulfilled this duty, attending every match armed with pen and clipboard, until Christmas of 2008 when Gianni and Geoff thought I could be utilised more effectively to reduce the workload of other club personnel. From then on I was tasked with 'working the door' (sitting at a table in the stadium reception area charging for admission and match programmes), locking and unlocking the changing and referees rooms, and hosting officials from the opposing team in the boardroom at half time and after matches. This latter consisted of serving tea, coffee, biscuits and sandwiches to the Chairman, Club Secretary and other board members who had travelled with the away side.

At the end of the 2008/09 season Gianni approached me with a proposition. The punishment for fielding ineligible players had prompted a reshuffle which freed up the position of Club Secretary, a role for which he, Geoff and Deborah had me in mind. I accepted the position, assuming my duties at the beginning of the 2009/10 season. These included the registration of all first and reserve team players, payment to the FA of fines for bookings, dismissals and other club misdemeanours, the completion and submission of team sheets and match reports for every first team fixture, and the overseeing of all transfers, contract cancellations and requests for international clearance.

I was around the club a lot more during this second season, attending training regularly in order to discuss fines, bans and pending international clearance requests, and could thus build on relationships I had established during the first. Initially the players were suspicious of me, curious as to why a 20-something had assumed a role normally carried out by someone in their dotage and, furthermore, why their behaviours and ideas might be worthy of considered analysis. However, with numerous training sessions and car journeys, and endless loitering in various club houses and car parks, the players got used to my presence and the gentle lines of questioning I pursued, admitting me slowly into the confidences of both changing- and boardroom. This allowed me to capture the life stories which knitted together the 'data' listed on players' registration forms.

Oldfield United FC: the players

Of the 69 players registered for the 2008/09 season, 58 per cent were in current employment, 11 per cent were in full-time education, while the remaining 31 per cent were unemployed. A number of those currently employed worked in coaching/sports development or held low-level positions in the service industry (in retail or sales). Many of the former were employed by Bridgegate Council or were used as casual labour by local youth football clubs, with most admitting that their recruitment was down to their status as a 'semi-professional footballer'. In this way, though the club hadn't the means to remunerate players for their labour, being 'semi-pro' conferred a social dividend which some converted into economic gain. However, as the neighbourhood sports centre, which acted as the hub for local sports development, was currently being privatised, a number of players had been forced into competition with one another for a reduced number of coaching and sports development jobs. Of those in gainful employment most worked either cash-in-hand jobs or were party to rolling, short-term and/or part-time contracts; since leaving the education system at 16, 18 or 21 many had known little other than working on an insecure, 'permanently temporary' basis, and as such were members of what Wacquant (2008; 2009) has called the 'precariat' – though the players opted to call themselves 'casuals'. The majority enrolled at college and university were studying sports- or leisure-related subjects, such as leisure and tourism and sports management.

Ninety-four per cent of players lived within Bridgegate or neighbouring boroughs. Sixty-nine per cent lived in council-owned accommodation, of which 78 per cent resided with parents. The other 31 per cent, those living in privately owned accommodation, did so exclusively with parents; no player who had left home had subsequently bought a flat or house of his own.

This was unsurprising given that the average age of squad members was just 21.

Players travelled to and from matches in a motley cortege of cars. The advent of satellite navigation meant some were prone to break ranks while others blazed a manual trail, using maps or their own initiative. Indeed, the lack of a team minibus rendered the few players possessing a driving licence and their own car difficult to omit from the squad. Unlike other teams in the division, club rules did not oblige players to wear formal dress – i.e. trousers, shirt and tie – to matches; most preferred the comfort of sportswear, and so arrived at matches showcasing an array of hats, headsets and other oversized accoutrements. Players' girlfriends and fiancés seldom made the trip to away matches. However, when the club had a home fixture on a Saturday afternoon one or two girls in their late teens or early twenties might appear alongside regulars in the crowd; they had invariably met a player on a night out and subsequently been invited to attend a match the following Saturday (and in some instances the following day). The player often regretted this offer. A round of virile banter followed his teammates' realisation that the female in question had no place on the club's roster of regular 'WAGs'. He was thus singled out for teasing and abuse, particularly if he had earlier bragged about the attractiveness of his lady friend only for her beauty to be dispelled by the telling combination of sobriety and unforgiving light.

With the squad containing men of 22 nationalities who between them spoke more than ten languages, players communicated using a *lingua franca* which consisted of basic English embroidered with various West Indian and Bengali terms, along with slang of more parochial provenance. This vocabulary, widely used by youth in the surrounding area, was a ledger of cultural negotiation that demonstrated how Bridgegate's version of urban English has been embellished over time. Below is a selection of terms used commonly by OUFC's players alongside my best attempt at an OED-style definition:

Bait • **adj.** Being blatant, usually in revealing one's intentions. Most commonly: 'You're bait.'

Bare • **adv.** An abundance of; an excessive amount of – e.g. 'There's bare women/food here.'

Chirpse • **v.** To chat up/flirt with someone; seemed to be a successor/ alternative to 'pull'.

Ends • **n.** One's local area or neighbourhood. Most commonly: 'My/the ends.'

Jays • **adj. and adv.** Alone; on one's own; an abbreviation of the cockney rhyming slang term 'Jack Jones'. Most commonly: 'On my/his Jays.'

Nang • **adj.** Good; latest version of 'cool'.

Peng/Piff • **adj.** Attractive; seemed to be a successor/alternative to 'fit'.

Rago/Rags • **interj. and exclam.** Whatever; 'fuck it'; usually accompanied by or following a flouting of propriety or etiquette.

If notions of human variation were articulated by players – for example, to explain the character, behavioural tendencies, etc. of certain 'types' of player or people – the ensuing explanation would usually feature one or other of these terms. Needless to say, this lexicon was a far cry from the 'specialist' neologisms which helped to constitute the 'impulsive' black male as an object of knowledge.

Most players listened attentively if a phone conversation or a chat between teammates was being carried on in a language other than their first, and as a result most had accrued a small vocabulary in each of the squad's respective mother tongues. For the most part these phrases were expressions of common courtesy and abuse; some players could translate 'Hello, how are you?' and 'Fuck off' into at least four different dialects. Diego and Jorge were particularly popular among the squad because their thick Spanish-Colombian accents allowed them to recite iconic lines from the 1983 gangster movie *Scarface* with aplomb (players weren't deterred by the fact that the film's main protagonist, Tony Montana, was actually a Cuban exile). I lost count of the number of times one of the pair was pestered into saying 'You wanna play rough?!' or 'Say hello to my little friend!' for the entertainment of the other players.

During matches the players reverted to a vocabulary familiar to anyone who has played competitive football, enjoining one another to 'walk them out', 'get tight', 'squeeze', 'drop off', 'line it', 'square it', 'switch it', 'hold the line', '[be] on toes', '[win] first and seconds', 'get an Oldfield head on this', 'ave a word', '[chuck it] in the mixer' and '[keep our] shape'. Other on-pitch parlances included 'hospital ball', 'winners' and 'back door'. The cadenced thump of R'n'B provided a soundtrack, whether blaring out of the changing room, players' cars, or the television set in the club café (tuned to 'MTV Base' between the sacrosanct *Final Score* or *Jeff Stelling's Soccer Saturday*).

With two, two-hour training sessions each week and on average three matches every fortnight, the squad spent around nine hours a week in each other's company, and when milling around before training sessions and matches gathered in groups of three or four. The odd player would prefer to remain on his own, listening to music on headphones or stealing a ten-minute nap. Other individuals sought out the company of Gianni, Deborah or Geoff. These affinities were ordered by age and length of service; the players from OUFC's early days – now in their mid-to late-twenties – clustered together in two or three core groups. A few players overcame the boundaries of seniority by quickly establishing themselves as invaluable members of the squad, and subsequently enjoyed the freedom to roam. Bonds of friendship amongst younger players were similarly formed in workplaces, schools, youth teams and local neighbourhoods.

Every month or so a row would break out on the pitch, sometimes sparked by criticism of a younger player by an older teammate, but the most intense arguments took place after a difference in opinion between two more experienced squad members. These had a recurrent quality. The same older players continually fell out because, over time, word had got round that one didn't 'rate' the other. This was a deeply felt slight which created irreconcilable tensions between players. Other squad members of all ages intervened, having their own opinion of who the better player was, whether Reg agreed or not.

As the chapter has shown, OUFC was an organisation bewildering in terms of ethnic and cultural diversity. The characteristics of the local area were reflected in the structure and composition of the club, in terms of the profile of its players and staff, as well as the manner in which it operated. Patterns were beginning to emerge along lines of seniority, individual history and units of the local landscape. Having gained a foothold in the club, the task was now to investigate these patterns and, more specifically, their role in constituting the conceptions of human variability espoused by club personnel. These issues are taken up in the following two chapters.

Chapter 5

Ways to be urban

People out of place

Now that a description of Oldfield and the club's physical and social make-up has been provided, the following chapters describe and analyse the conceptions of human difference employed by OUFC's players, and, of course, ponder the degree to which these conceptions incorporate forms of raciology.

The first section of this chapter considers the theoretical possibilities for framing the diversity on show at OUFC. I argue that only a sociological account of urban denizenship – which draws on elements of what Paul Gilroy (2004) has called 'conviviality' – can adequately explain the players' approach to this diversity. Drawing on the character of the convivial encounters described by Gilroy, I seek to distance urban denizenship from numerous previous attempts to reinvent the cosmopolitan tradition, the variants of which have adapted cosmopolitanism in so many directions that the concept risks being drained of relevance and subjective worth. Furthermore, I argue that, taken together, Kantian cosmopolitanism and the imperatives of liberalism create a tangle of the universal and particular which, in turn, acts as an incubator for denizenship.

In pursuing this line of argument I do not advocate substituting denizenship for cosmopolitanism as a dominant mode of understanding diversity in inner-city areas. Rather, my account of urban denizenship begins with individual responses to conditions that are immediate and material and wherein, therefore, subjective voices are a rightful point of departure.

The second section of the chapter describes the different ways that OUFC's players existed as resident aliens and tries to mark off the common ground in their sentiments and ways of life. This encompasses their motivations for denouncing and/or refusing to adopt British citizenship and the manner in which their everyday lives have shaped these motivations.

The final section seeks to develop the sociological notion of urban denizenship. This concept centres on a sense of feeling alien in relation to discourses of nationhood and national politics, and a subsequent refusal to meet the requirements of citizenship. Here I clear the ground for Chapter 6, where I explore the implications of denizenship for the conceptions of human difference advocated by OUFC's players.

Conviviality, liberal cosmopolitanism and urban denizenship: the (re)creation of outsiders

'Conviviality', as Paul Gilroy (2004: 167) has called it, requires a metropolis 'in which cultures, histories, and structures of feeling previously separated by enormous distances can be found in the same place, the same time: school, bus, café, cell, waiting room, or traffic jam'. Discussing the conviviality found in the postcolonial city, Gilroy has described the 'chaotic pleasures' enjoyed by its inhabitants. This conjures images of the carnivalesque and, indeed, Gilroy places faith in the 'carnival of heteroculture' to familiarise the ideal of a non-racial humanity. With OUFC's players being aged between 17 and 28, most had either grown up amid a sea of cultural and linguistic signifiers or had arrived more recently and seemed to assume that such diversity was characteristic of life in Britain's cities. Their behaviour certainly made a mockery of any fixed system of racial classification. As already discussed, the array of languages and cultures being negotiated was vast and, of course, the fact that this negotiation was carried on without ruptures along so-called 'racial' lines is reason for celebration for anyone who identifies with the cause of anti-racism. The players themselves did not find any cause for celebration here, however. They were not concerned to trace the spoor of certain cultural fragments or probe everyone about their 'real' racial origin. Though in their daily lives players were party to convivial exchanges carried out in post offices, convenience stores and other urban scenes of social interaction, their relationships with one another resulted from shared experiences which were more intimate. While these relationships cast partial light on the workings of conviviality, they seemed to lack any overtly gratifying aspect. On another register, they were free from the consumerist undertones of cosmopolitanism.

In *The Communist Manifesto* Marx and Engels famously asserted that 'the bourgeoisie has through its exploitation of the world market given a cosmopolitan character to production and consumption in every country' (2005 [1848]: 31). In more recent times Ulrich Beck has argued along similar lines:

Cosmopolitanism has itself become a commodity; the glitter of cultural difference fetches a good price. Images of an in-between world, of the black body, exotic beauty, exotic music, exotic food and so on, are globally cannibalised, re-staged and consumed as produces for mass markets.

(2004: 150–1)

Defending cosmopolitanism from the predations of consumer culture, Kwame Anthony Appiah (2007) has denied accusations that expressions of cosmopolitanism are structured by the grammar of consumption. However, despite his best attempts to salvage the concept from identification with touchstones of 'right-on' consumerism, one is never entirely convinced that 'being cosmopolitan' is about more than a lifestyle choice afforded by privilege. This criticism is not original in any way. For Craig Calhoun (2002) cosmopolitanism is the ethical orientation of the frequent flier; while it is all too easy, Saskia Sassen (2006) argues, to equate cosmopolitanism with the globalism of the transnational professional and executive class.

The scale of Appiah's ambition is admirable. He hopes people will subscribe to a universal mindset that preaches tolerance and empathy; something to be learned and cultivated the world over. But talk of 'a genuinely cosmopolitan response', 'accepting the cosmopolitan challenge', and protestations that 'the rich nations can do better' seem to address his argument to particular sections of the international community. Furthermore, the fact that his *ethics in a world of strangers* requires a cleverly expounded philosophical blueprint – which traces cosmopolitanism beyond its putatively Kantian roots to the Cynics of Ancient Greece – makes it difficult to square with people's everyday responses to specific local conditions.

Cosmopolitanism is a normative concept (Ferrara 2007); one that pronounces upon how society should or ought to operate in an ideal world. Its proponents argue that cosmopolitanism can take everyday forms. However, as Gerard Delanty contends in his book *The Cosmopolitan Imagination*, these are only the 'banal' expressions of more profound political and philosophical principles: 'cosmopolitanism is much more than what is found in individual experiences; it has major societal expressions in, for instance, establishing an international normative order based on human rights and multicultural forms of political community' (2009: 14). Despite talk of cosmopolitanism as a 'way of thinking', 'self-understanding', 'self-definition', and as being 'empirically meaningful', both Appiah and Delanty opt – avowedly and legitimately – to limit their discussions to the conceptual realm. This makes it difficult to square cosmopolitan's normative and subjective planes, particularly as more and more facets are etched onto its conceptual core.

Delanty's book alone discusses legal, political, ethical, cultural, theoretical and sociological norms; and cosmopolitanism is thereby skewered by a profusion of dimensions. There is a danger that all the positive elements issuing from multicultural engagement, and therefore celebrated by those sharing a broadly liberal mindset, are appended to a list of abstract qualities under the heading 'cosmopolitanism'. Cosmopolitanism consequently becomes a container for all that is 'good' about diversity and cultural appreciation, a fact which may explain the constant commodifying and channelling of cosmopolitan identifications into niche markets (Harvey 2009).

It is difficult to quibble with the aims of both Appiah and Delanty. However, their plans to reorient the relationship between universality and difference fail to address the responses of the state to these differences, and more specifically, how national governments have set about defining those differences recognised as legitimate and hence compatible with the requirements of dwelling within a given national territory. Indeed, cosmopolitanism's blind spot regarding the attempts of governments to categorise, manage and exclude sectors of its population from the privileges of citizenship is curious given Kant's insistence (examined in Part 1) – found within material of seminal importance for many later formulations of cosmopolitanism – that not all residents of a 'cosmopolitan' nation qualify as citizens.

In Part 1 we saw how exclusionary practices are legislated for in the structural make-up of Kantian cosmopolitanism and the canon of liberalism. The showy exterior of universalism and freedom hides an under-belly of particularity, exceptionalism and exclusion – a trade-off that increases the appeal of cosmopolitanism and liberalism because it deepens and perpetuates capitalist and state powers. As Harold Laski argued:

> Liberalism, though it has expressed itself always as a universal, has, in its institutional result, inevitably been more narrow in its benefit than the society it sought to guide. For though it has refused to recog-nize any limit in theory, whether of class or creed, or even race, to its application, the historic conditions within which it has operated effected a limitation despite itself. It is the meaning of this limitation which is the key to the understanding of the liberal idea.
>
> (1997 [1936]: 17)

This remains true today, where the values of the Kantian, inter-state version of cosmopolitanism are articulated with the imperatives of neo-liberal ideology to distribute wealth in particular ways (unsurprisingly, ways that serve the interests of political and business elites). Harvey (2005) has called this conjunction 'cosmopolitan neoliberalism'.

Here we have claims to universal justice, democracy, liberty, freedom and goodness mobilised to ensure the spread of free market protocols and private property rights across the globe. This was witnessed in the aftermath of the invasion of Iraq when Paul Bremer, head of the Coalition Provisional Authority, listed the political–economic dictates that would ensure the full liberalisation of Iraq: 'the full privatization of public enterprises, full ownership rights by foreign firms of Iraqi businesses, full repatriation of foreign profits ... the opening of Iraqi banks to foreign control, national treatment for foreign companies and ... the elimination of nearly all trade barriers' (quoted in Juhasz 2004). The usual appeal to universal, self-evidently 'good' values was used to smuggle all manner of geographical and anthropological assumptions about Iraq and the Iraqi population for the purposes of exclusion. For the newly 'free' Iraqi people, freedom and liberty would have to be exercised in ways sanctioned by the wants and needs of neoliberalism. Those who rejected the values of self-enterprise and self-responsibility would be labelled 'immature', not yet ready for the rigours of universal justice. This is a well-rehearsed argument, as we have seen. As Harvey notes, 'From this perspective it may even legitimately be claimed that (George W.) Bush is a true Kantian' (2009: 34).

Of course, the products of cosmopolitan neoliberalism can also be found at home, where the privileges of citizenship are unevenly distributed and, in some cases, refused.[1] Notions of maturity and readiness are applied to those who dwell in neoliberal states but are not amenable to the requirements of the market, in many cases the impacted minorities that inhabit poor, inner-city areas. Here geographical and anthropological assertions can be used to justify their exclusion from the (ever-narrower) trough of neoliberal capitalism. Harvey (2005) has written of how the illusions of freedom and autonomy that attach to these populations are subject to a set of individual human rights clustered around territory and capital.

Though human rights are often billed as universal, whether one possesses them or not will, at bottom, depend on whether the state in question is willing and able to enforce them. Such rights are therefore conditional upon citizenship. The territorial specifications of the state are crucial, as the question of who is and who is not a 'citizen' – the status of stateless persons, refugees, etc. – has to figure when drawing up principles of inclusion and exclusion that impact upon the spread of individual human rights.[2] The absolute space of national territory and private property, upon which the diffusion of capital has relied since the theories of Locke and, later, Kant, thus continues to provide the basic framework for these principles (Harvey 2009).

Also central to the issue of individual human rights under neoliberal regimes is the bundle of rights necessary for capital accumulation. As in the case of Iraq, top of the list of inalienable human rights are those which concern the integrity of private property and the profit rate. Affixed to these are particular 'bourgeois' virtues:

> individual responsibility and liability, freedom from state interference, equality of opportunity in the market and before the law, rewards for initiative and entrepreneurial behaviour, care for oneself and one's own, and an open marketplace that allows for wide-ranging freedoms of choice of both contract and exchange.
>
> (Harvey 2005: 181)

This system of rights is seductive, yet its appeal to universalism and absolute time and space once again means that, on the ground, it can be used to marginalise and exclude. After all, a system of rights that centres on the endless accumulation of capital and economic expansion (with little regard to the consequences) implies that this very system must be rolled out in lockstep with the expansion of the economy and the continuous accumulation of capital. Like Kant's universal citizenship which, in reality, admitted only certain kinds of citizen, the issue of individual human rights as understood under neoliberal conditions presupposes a certain kind of individual. Those failing to identify with the state and the imperatives of the market are denied these rights. They are reminiscent of Kant's exclusion of the 'rabble', those troublesome elements lacking the maturity of citizens.

As did the normative framework of liberal thought, confident in its own cosmopolitanism, cosmopolitan neoliberalism systemically creates those trapped within the interstices of its absolute space. Its myth of the free, deracinated subject located in absolute time and space has implications for how people constitute themselves as objects of knowledge, as the underlying presumptions of free market ideology come to define the 'conditions of possibility' for being. For example, the US citizens who lost their houses in the recent subprime mortgage crisis typically 'blamed themselves for their failure to live up to the personal responsibilities of homeownership' (Harvey 2010: 218).

Though Kant modified the cosmopolitan tradition inherited from the Stoics and Cynics by introducing a federal structure to the interstate system (Harvey 2009), the scope of many subsequent arguments for a cosmopolitan order makes it impractical to discuss the strategies of particular states in managing diversity and the contingencies to which residents must subsequently react. Such discussion would recognise the importance of the connections between nation, state, sovereignty and citizenship injected into the cosmopolitan mix by Kant's modification.

Weighing Ayelet Shacher's (2009) claim that citizenship is more important than ever against Peter Spiro's (2008) contention that it is in irreversible decline, Christian Joppke (2010: 11) has argued persuasively that interpretations of the significance of citizenship depend on matters of perspective, underlining the importance of 'factoring in or out host states' immigration policies'. Loïc Wacquant (2008: 38) has insisted that citizenship can no longer be viewed as a status to be granted or achieved once and equally for all. Rather he conceptualises citizenship as a contentious and uneven process that 'must continually be struggled for and secured anew' (ibid). Though a useful point of departure for a rethinking of citizenship, his approach, because directed specifically to the US (and to a lesser extent France) and how national and local government policies have effectively withdrawn the citizenship of those locked in areas of urban deprivation, fails to address the strategies of 'aliens' in other urban centres around the world. Inserting the responses of these aliens (and others) into the process of citizenship gives it a two-way dynamic and leads us to the figure of the denizen.

An English word that up to the 1840s was used to describe 'an alien to whom sovereign has by letters of patent under the prerogative granted the status of a British subject' but who was not permitted to 'hold public office or obtain a grant of land from the Crown', Tomas Hammar adopted the term 'denizen' to designate 'persons who are foreign citizens with a legal and permanent resident status' (1990: 15). This means that though they are not citizens of the country in which they live, these persons have been allowed to stay permanently (notwithstanding exceptional circumstances, e.g. the committal of violent crimes or being perceived as a threat to national security). Although Hammar is concerned to stress that his use of the term is purely technical, giving it greater conceptual texture and depth may be a worthwhile endeavour for social scientists. Indeed, in recognising that the citizens and denizens of advanced states have entered into an area of potential indistinction, Giorgio Agamben (2000) hints at such a broadening out of the concept of denizenship.

Hammar's discussion of 'denizen' as a technical term centres on a distinction between temporary foreign visitor/guest worker, denizen and citizen, with the status-bound zones inhabited by each regulated by three entrance gates: immigration regulation (gate one), regulation of domicile and residential status (gate two), and regulation of naturalisation into full citizenship (gate three). Denizens occupy the interstice between gates two and three, having been granted permanent resident status without being naturalised and hence granted full citizenship. Obviously Hammar is concerned with degrees of entrance – as regulated by his three gates – into the populace of a given nation state, and thus gives no consideration to the degrees of exit from citizenship. Indeed, his stringent assertion that 'a denizen cannot be a citizen of his country of residence' (Hammar 1990: 15) rules out any such consideration.

Here I contend that the relationships on show at OUFC were based on urban denizenship. That is, by examining the relationships of foreign players – denizens in Hammar's technical sense – with those players I shall (paradoxically) call 'native denizens', I argue that these relationships were underpinned by a sense of belonging bound up with resident non-citizenship. Further, I argue that this ontological bond, based on feeling 'foreign' or 'alien', had important implications for the way that OUFC's players made sense of human variation.

OUFC had over 60 registered players for the 2009/10 season, and as Club Secretary I held copies of each player's registration form which recorded information such as nationality, place of birth and mother's maiden name (the forms did not require a player to identify himself in terms of 'race' or ethnicity). The circumstances which united this assemblage of young men in inner-city London were bound up with movement across the world. This movement, whether by plane, train, boat or automobile, was carried out by the players themselves, or by their parents or grandparents. The conditions which prompted these movements – including the specific points of arrival and departure – could be explained by a combination of history and contingency.

Those players whose presence in Britain was explained by the circuitry of colonialism understood the motivations of their parents or grandparents in moving; others fled civil war or ethnic conflict in Africa or Eastern Europe; the remainder were economic migrants. None staked any exclusive, nativist claim to London or England by defining themselves against more recent arrivals. If anyone so inclined set out to determine which of the squad were 'most indigenous', the dubious privilege would fall to players whose Irish or West Indian grandparents arrived in Britain in the 1940s and 1950s to find that they, apparently of the same infra-human order as dogs, would struggle to find a place to stay. Any residual sense of indigeneity was free from commensurate claims to whiteness, and this meant the decoupling of Britishness from whiteness; terms which, as Gilroy (2000; 2004) points out, have in many contexts remained doggedly synonymous. This was no surprise given that 'white' British members of the squad were far outnumbered by British players who were phenotypically 'non-white' – including players born in France, Portugal, Colombia, Bangladesh, Indonesia, Nigeria, Congo, Rwanda and Liberia – and players of other nationalities who were phenotypically 'white' – from France, Portugal, Poland, Albania, Slovakia, Slovenia, Italy, Israel, Ireland, Australia and Spain. Only two players in the squad, Clive Linehan and Lee Whitton, identified themselves as being both white and English, with Clive choosing this allegiance despite his father's parents both being Irish.

In terms of religion, the squad included Christians from Britain, Spain, Trinidad and Tobago, Jamaica, Colombia and Liberia, Muslims from Britain, Albania, Togo and the Ivory Coast (and Iraq if we count Ali the groundsman), along with a number of players who were atheist or agnostic. Religious members of the squad held varying interpretations of their faith and its prescriptions. Few of the Christian players attended church each week, preferring to exhibit their religiosity by wearing crucifixes or crossing themselves as they entered the pitch. Muslim players prayed when it was practical, though a minority had no qualms about eating the ham sandwiches on offer after matches.

No metaphor of invasion framed the players' perceptions of immigration and the figure of the migrant thus lacked the physical, moral and economic threat imputed to him by the popular press, as experienced by arrivals from the 'New Commonwealth' in the 1960s (see Chapter 3). Players were mindful that their own presence in London was down to global migration and aware of continual waves of immigration into the area. They saw migration as one of the essential realities of the inner city; it was part of the urban reproductive cycle. I spoke to Abdi, a British Asian born in South London who had moved to Churchfield eight years ago, about the issue of immigration:

JRT: What d'you make of playing with so many foreign players?
Abdi: Yeah, it's good. I'm hardly gonna say throw them out [of the country] am I? Look at me for Christ's sake. I lose track of where they're all from. [I've] given up asking [to] tell the truth. As I said though, my mob came here. [So I'm] happy for them to [as well].

Ways to be alien: the native, the naturalised and the denizens proper

The native denizens

Alex (aka 'Chuckles') was club captain and had played for OUFC for 12 years. As a teenager he joined the club with his twin brother, Anton, with the pair forging an effective partnership in central defence that they would eventually carry into the men's team. Alex lived with his girlfriend on Rydal Grove, though his registration form had him living in council-owned accommodation close to Boorman Oak station. Formerly an ever-present in the side, Anton's appearances over the last two seasons had gone from being sporadic to non-existent. This followed his sentencing in May 2008 to eight months in prison for actual bodily harm. Anton's regimen in prison had involved heavy weightlifting, and the bulk of muscle he carried after being released hindered his mobility around the pitch. People could no longer believe that the brothers were twins.

Alex stood at just under six feet and had broad, square shoulders. The sharp contours of his physique looked as if shaped by testosterone. His swarthy face was weathered and marked by a small, deep scar on his forehead; the result of a headbutt which left the tooth of an opponent embedded an inch above his right eyebrow. I inquired on a number of occasions as to Alex's occupation, normally provoking a hollow or evasive response, 'don't ask' being the most common. After telling Gianni one Saturday afternoon that I was heading to a house party that evening, he told me – without prompt – that Alex could get hold of 'anything you want', while later I heard him pestering Alex for a course of Viagra he had ordered 'for a friend' in return for a package of frozen meat. Other stories, along with the wisps of pungent smoke which curled upwards from the sunroof of his car, confirmed my suspicions that Alex was heavily involved in the local underground economy.

Alex lived in his OUFC tracksuit, his hands stowed in the trouser pockets, and sported a curious limp, which wasn't an affectation, he protested, but the result of a muscle wasting disease in his right knee. This ailment offered no impediment to his running; the only time he appeared to move freely was when charging around a football pitch. Being the eldest of OUFC's squad members at 28 years old, Alex acted as its spokesperson, and his expressions of feeling in some way alien in relation to England were more clearly articulated than other players'. This feeling of detachment was illustrated one evening following a match against Hailfold Borough. After the match, players from both teams convened in the bar while club officials headed to the boardroom, in this instance a Portakabin ornamented with donated furniture and various club bric-a-brac. Having completed the routine admin tasks, Geoff and I walked to the car park where we were greeted by a group of players led by Alex (including Abdi, Micah, Derek and Chinua) who, on seeing us about to leave, had charged out of the bar to confront Geoff, their faces knotted with indignation:

Alex: What the fuck was that Geoff?
Geoff: What?
Alex: Them sandwiches!
Geoff: Oh, you had 'em as well? (Laughs) Thought they was a bit odd.
Alex: Fucking coleslaw sandwiches ... We can't be eating that shit Geoff, we're foreign man. We need meat. Make sure we give them something nasty when they come to our place.

This expression of the group's alien status led me to consider the relationship between nativity and nationality in the case of the 17 players who were born in London and listed their nationality as British on their registration forms. On paper, players such as Alex, whose Greek grandparents had settled in London in the late 1950s, were British. He was a British citizen. He, his brother and both of his parents were born in London and had attended local schools. However, being foreign was important to him; I heard him identify himself as such on many occasions. Interestingly this identification came without any avowed attachment to Greece; it was enough to be recognised as being an alien, though the entity to which he was alien was seldom mentioned. I had ample opportunities to discuss the issue with Alex while he served a three-match suspension for violent conduct in October 2009. Below is a fragment of a conversation we had about OUFC's players 'looking foreign' which took place at an away fixture against Leeford Heath:

Alex: Look at us, man. We all look foreign. I do, Gianni does, you do. Look at Nigel (an Australian who had recently signed) ... fucking size of him ... you know he's been living in the middle of nowhere munching on cows. You seen how far he can throw it?
JRT: What d'you mean, foreign?

Alex: Look at our team-sheet! There ain't no English players on there. Look at theirs. That's what I mean, Jay.

JRT: But you're Oldfield born and bred though, right?

Alex: Of course, man. You know how much shit I have to take because we're bottom of the league?! Wish the paper'd stop fucking writing 'bout us. But that don't mean I'm English, no way. I'm local and foreign, everyone round my way's foreign. You think I'm cheering for England next year (in the 2010 World Cup Finals)?! I'll watch and get lagging, but I ain't cheering for them.

JRT: So you don't see any difference between yourself and Mariusz, for example?

Alex: Well, yeah. We come from different places. He's from Poland, int' he? He won't try and pass himself off as English. Good luck to him. Same here.

JRT: Who does look English, then?

Alex: Look at him there (points to an opposition player warming up for the match). (He) looks like a fucking farmer's son.

This emphasised how important the opposition between urban and suburban/rural space was to Alex and, furthermore, underlined the assertion that the 'English' supposedly dwelled in regions outside of the city.

So although Alex was nominally British, he took pains to distance himself from discourses of Englishness and carry on a lived sense of being alien in relation to England, yet native to Oldfield. Like every other member of the squad, he had never voted. The prospect of him doing so in future was undermined by the fact that he (like the vast majority of other squad members who were enfranchised) lived on an estate deemed by local government to be of little electoral value. This meant political pamphlets were only delivered if enough volume remained after rounds of distribution to roads containing private housing (the same principle applied for the free local paper). On marginal estates like the Grove, the only political ephemera to make it through people's front doors invariably belonged to parties at the further reaches of the political spectrum.

While Alex continually sought to renounce his stated nationality, other players had no desire to become naturalised and gain full citizenship. One such player was Stephen Johnson, a 24-year-old who lived in Lonsworth Park. Gianni had signed Stephen three years ago on the guarantee that he would score 15 goals a season. Since then, however, the tall, lithe mid-fielder – considered in both his appearance and style of play – had been used as a utility player, shunted between the first and reserve teams, and preferred to get more match time with the latter rather than sit on the substitutes' bench for the former. When called up to the first team, Stephen would meet Geoff and I on Shinewater High Street, and as a result we spent a fair amount of time together travelling to one away ground or another.

I quickly noticed that Stephen and Geoff had a relationship analogous to that of frustrated father and wayward son; each continually requested things the other thought entirely unfeasible, whether this was Geoff bellowing demands from the stands or Stephen pleading with Geoff to stop the car so he could empty his bladder. This latter scenario happened with comic regularity, and resulted from Stephen's obsession with being fully hydrated before first team fixtures. He thus arrived in Shinewater clutching a two-litre bottle of water and took regular, generous swigs during the journey – the first request for a comfort break normally came around half an hour after our departure. Despite pleas that he was 'busting', Geoff angrily explained the impossibility of stopping on whichever A-roads his sat-nav had prescribed, but eventually gave in, deviating from the route so Stephen could relieve himself in an alleyway or the front garden of an unsuspecting suburbanite.

As I was present during their numerous tiffs, both liked to protest to me about the other being unreasonable, and I used this time to chat to Stephen about his loyalties to nation and state:

JRT:　So I saw on your registration that you've got Nigerian nationality.
Stephen:　Yeah.
JRT:　How long have you been in London then?
Stephen:　All my life man. Was born round my way.
JRT:　You never thought about naturalising?
Stephen:　What d'you mean?
JRT:　Getting British citizenship?
Stephen:　Not really, don't see the point. My parents never have and they ain't had no problems, you know? I can still travel alright when I get on holiday or whatever.
JRT:　You feel no attachment to Britain, then?
Stephen:　No, not really. I'm from Lonsworth Park, play for Oldfield United, support Man United (laughs).
JRT:　Nigeria?
Stephen:　There neither. My parents do a little I think, I have no need for that you get me?
JRT:　Do you feel at home here though?
Stephen:　Shit, not here! (We were having the conversation in Oxenhead, a small town located over 30 miles outside London.) But I do in my ends, yeah.

He went on to reveal that his parents had travelled to London from Nigeria in the late 1970s, both to pursue careers – his father in British Rail, his mother as a nurse in the NHS – but had never become naturalised citizens. Indeed, the prospect of naturalisation had never been discussed in the Johnson household.

Players like Alex expressed a repudiation of Englishness. However, this was not a momentary purge. It was an ongoing affirmation of being alien in relation to the nation-state to which they nominally belonged. Alex's expressions of alienation from Englishness corresponded to actions which might be interpreted as degrees of exit from citizenship. He was, to all intents and purposes, a native denizen. Stephen also fell within this group, but his membership came via a refusal to take citizenship in the country of his birth rather than from a renouncement of this nationhood. Though he had a 'nationality of origin', he had in effect given up the right of protection offered by his own nation-state – Nigeria.

These native denizens break the link between nativity and nationality and challenge the 'fiction that ... *birth [nascita]* comes into being immediately as *nation*, so that there may not be any difference between the two moments' (Agamben 2000: 21). Unlike refugees, native denizens need not pass outside sovereign territory to relinquish their nationhood and thus become non-citizens. Indeed, their assertion of being native to Oldfield, Lonsworth Park, etc. yet foreign to England calls the hallowed trinity of nation-state-territory – the very foundation of the nation-state as a legitimate political unit – into question.

This attachment to a specific locale or neighbourhood is a clear obstacle to cosmopolitanism's injunction to abjure local allegiances and particularities in the name of a rootless humanity (Held 2010). Perhaps the demand – which places urbanites in the vanguard of the cosmopolitan movement – pays too little attention to the spatiality of the city. It certainly doesn't allow us to view the city as an intersection of space, knowledge and power, nor allow for the fact that space, time and being are the formative dimensions of human existence (Soja 1989; 1996; 2000). The playing out of these intersections not only sets the stage for everyday urban encounters, it directly influences their character. Individuals such as Alex, as we will see, had a complex and conflicted attachment to the areas in which their attitudes to life had been forged. More specifically, these urban areas – as conjunctions of spatiality, temporality and social being – had acted as the privileged media through which sameness and difference were wrestled with.

Just as the immediate, short-term, professional and political tactics of the specialists and technocrats encountered in Part 1 were conditioned by the institutional settings within which their statements were made and disseminated, the spaces of the city inhabited by players had offered up the challenge to which denizenship was a response. Asking that they relinquish this mentality and make the high-minded commitment to becoming a 'citizen of the world' was a tall order.

The naturalised denizens

Eighteen-year-old Diego Cortes was born and had lived most of his life in Colombia, moving to London four years ago with his mother, brother and girlfriend in order to join his uncle who had made the journey three years before. After being allocated to various council-owned dwellings throughout London, the family had settled in a rented council flat a stone's throw from Meadson village, and thus shared a postcode with a number of celebrities, diplomats and other wealthy luminaries. Diego was studying for A-levels at a nearby sixth-form college and worked a couple of evenings a week (along with Saturday mornings) coaching football to youngsters. He was always immaculately turned out; though he never wore expensive clothes, he paid meticulous attention to his facial hair – a thin strip of which served to clarify his jaw-line – while the hair on top of his head was coiffured with similar care and precision. He normally came to matches with his brother and girlfriend who were charged with looking after his dog, a puppy pitbull terrier, for the duration of the fixture. In many instances his girlfriend was forced to rely on her dusky good looks to get the puppy admitted to away grounds. As a player Diego was a refined, right-winger who hit the ball crisply but was forever being criticised for his work-rate. The impression of effortlessness communicated by his technique could, when the chips were down, quickly be interpreted as a sign of laziness. This did not correlate with any 'racial' or raciological stereotyping, however. In being identified as lazy, Diego was normally classed together with other young players who still harboured hopes of a professional career. Older players sometimes complained of having to 'carry the bags' of these talented youngsters, or, alternatively, of having to 'do their running for them'.

On arriving in London as a 14-year-old, Diego was enrolled at a state school in Bridgegate, where he completed the final two years of his secondary education:

JRT: What was it like at school?

Diego: Difficult man, at first anyway. I didn't speak hardly no English. Spanish classes were easy (though)! Their football team was shit so I didn't bother with that. Found (out) about Hertfield (Borough) and started playing for their youth side.

JRT: Your registration says you're British, did you have to naturalise then?

Diego: Yeah, my Uncle had done it ... (he) talked to my mum. I didn't know what was happening really.

JRT: Would you have done it, given the choice?

Diego: Don't know ... Mum was pushing you know, saying it's better for us. (I) don't feel like it's that much easier ... you know? How many of these guys have it? Bare people don't I bet.

JRT: About half I think.

Diego: Yeah, ok, right. How many of them are liars (laughs)? None of them is really English anyway.

JRT: You wouldn't call yourself English then, no?

Diego: Nah, I do on forms. What's the point in having it if I ain't never going to use it? But apart from that, no. (If) people ask me when I'm out or wherever, I say Colombian.

JRT: You feel like you have two nationalities then?

Diego: ... Not bothered about them really, don't feel like I need to be. Everyone's from someplace else ... No big deal.

Along with the wages Diego received for his coaching job (£8 an hour paid cash-in-hand), his family relied on his mother's earnings as a cleaner and his girlfriend's as a waitress. As far as Diego was aware, the family claimed no money in benefits.

Another player to have naturalised was the club's substitute goalkeeper and goalkeeping coach, Max Nkundo. Max was born in Rwanda in 1985 to parents belonging to the Tutsis, an ethnic group that – along with the Hutus – can trace its formation to the census-taking of Belgian colonial administrators who in the nineteenth century sought to classify everyone in Rwanda-Burundi according to a single taxonomy (Khan 2000). In 1994 he and his mother fled the Rwandan Genocide[3] and sought refuge in London. Here they were given council accommodation in Bridgegate, where Max subsequently attended primary and secondary school. He now worked as a salesman in a high street electronics store and had recently married a local woman, Gina, who came to watch home fixtures occasionally if Max had been selected. Following their marriage the couple decided to remain near to their families and to this end took up a rented council flat in Bridgegate Central.

Evidently Max struggled to balance the demands of married life with those of playing semi-professional football. He complained of having to act as a 'fucking taxi service' for his wife, who had repeatedly failed her driving test. This ferrying around caused him to be late to many a fixture or team meeting, though he protested that his wife getting to work on time was all-important. Tall yet stocky, and possessing an infectious work ethic, Max was combative both on and off the pitch. His calm demeanour gave way to paroxysms of anger if he felt wronged in any way. This wasn't helped by his role as perennial substitute, as when positioned in the dugout he would often get involved in arguments with opposing managers and substitutes. His determination stoked by verbal exchanges between dugouts, when he was called upon to enter the fray he would invariably seek to vent his aggression, but had a knack of doing so within the laws of the game; he only received one booking during my time as Club Secretary despite his tactile approach to goalkeeping. That said, Max was not averse to getting involved in scuffles with opposing players, and took the invitation to 'see you afterwards?' literally. On one occasion Alex had to prevent Max from sprinting to confront an opposing striker at the final whistle. 'I told the guy', said Alex, 'he'll [Max] fucking kill you, man. Max don't give a fuck, I wouldn't touch him bruv. No fucking way.'

Max had become a naturalised citizen in 1996, in response to his mother's desire for a 'new beginning':

Max: She thought it was a good idea, to start completely afresh – a new beginning she called (it). (I) think people did it more back then. Was more common ... there were other kids I knew (doing it). Why d'you wanna know?

JRT: I'm interested in how many of you guys have become British citizens.

Max: Oh, ok. How many have then?

JRT: Not many I don't think; you, Diego, maybe one or two others.

Max: Yeah, but as I said, no one's seeking out that kind of thing now. For us I think it was 'bout getting rid of something, trying to forget the past rather than ... you know, really becoming something else.

JRT: So you don't really feel English or British then?

Max: ... What does that even mean? No, I don't really. It meant something to me ten years ago maybe. Not now though, (not) even on forms! That one you mentioned (registration form) was the first I've done for time! Apart from that, (it) ain't something that comes up round my way.

The denizens proper

Mariusz Adamczyk was one of the club's star strikers. He signed during the summer of 2009 but could not play for the first team until international clearance had been received from the Polish Football Association. The 23-year-old marked his first appearance in September that season with a goal against Rayham in the FA Cup and thereafter went from strength to strength, scoring numerous more and quickly establishing himself as a talismanic figure in the side. He was tall, deceptively strong and possessed remarkably quick feet. However, these were a mixed blessing. His attempts to dance and shimmy his way around opponents resulted in frequent injury, as defenders took aim at the ball only for it to be whisked away. His absence through injury left a gaping hole which only underlined his importance to the club. Effortlessly amiable, he was on good terms with club personnel at all levels, but was particularly close to first-team goalkeeper Neti Amsellem, a French–Israeli who made a living working for National Rail and was known for the orders he bellowed out in quasi-operatic tones.

Mariusz had arrived in London only a couple of months before signing for OUFC, again following a family member to the city, this time his older brother. Like Stephen, he and his brother had settled in Lonsworth Park, where they lived with Mariusz's Slovakian girlfriend. He explained his decision to move to London to Geoff, Neti and me during a journey to Northbourne:

Mariusz: My brother come a few months (before). They say at home it's not good time to come, so I wait for my brother to say how it is. He has no problems getting in or with work, so I come.

Neti: Where do you work?

Mariusz: I work at a restaurant for Italian family. I am a waiter there. (I get) fifty pounds per day (cash).

JRT: Monday to Friday?

Mariusz: Yes, mostly. Sometimes I have to go (in) on Saturday, late. That is hard after football.

JRT: How many hours a week normally, then?

Mariusz: Fifty. More if I do some shift on Saturday. But then I get more (money).

This worked out at £5-an-hour, eighty pence below the legal minimum (taking no account of tax deductions), but Mariusz had neither the appearance nor the demeanour of somebody toeing the poverty line. While he shied away from excess, he reported that he and his brother – who also worked as a waiter – afforded the rent of their two-bedroom, sublet council-flat with relative comfort. He had recently opened a bank account for the sole purpose of signing a mobile phone contract; he could consequently get his hands on the latest *Apple iPhone* he had seen flaunted by teammates.

Unaware that he was from Poland, most other squad members called him 'Mario' – which became 'Super Mario' after a few weeks of displaying his abilities. Mariusz embraced the new nickname and on one journey joked about attending a Halloween fancy dress party in the blue overalls and red cap sported by his pixelated namesake. I asked him about his plans for the future:

JRT: Do you think you'll stay over here?

Mariusz: Yes, for sure. For some time at least. My girlfriend is here, my brother also. I have friends at football, and work. I like my area. But I may go back (to Poland) someday, I don't know.

JRT: So you'll be calling this place home at some point?

Mariusz: Here? No! I read what happens to us in Pixford! But in London, Lonsworth Park or near? Yes, I like it. Maybe.

Here he referred to an incident that occurred in October 2009 in Pixford, immediately after an ADL Premier Division fixture between Pixford United and Brentwich Sports. A Pixford player had confronted Brentwich midfielder Aleksy Gryzbowski while players were shaking hands after the final whistle, calling him a 'fucking Polish bastard'. Things quickly escalated, with the two players having to be separated by their teammates. As the referee and his officials were apparently out of earshot, the exchange could not be reported to the Football Association. However, a member of the Brentwich Sports board had heard the remarks and took it upon himself to disseminate his version of events to all members of the league via email. The board members of Pixford United took great umbrage at his chosen course of action and immediately sent a detailed reply, again with the entire ADL mailing list 'copied in'. This set in train a litany of correspondence between the clubs, with each episode being added to a thread created on *Footy Chat*. The Club Secretary of Pixford United offered no defence for the player's 'disgusting comment', incredulous that a man 'born and raised in Dolebury – the most diverse town in the East of England in terms of race and culture' could have made such a remark. In apologising for his behaviour she noted that 'the comment came from someone who cannot express his frustrations in anything but ignorant, mindless fashion'.

Sphresim Sfarca, a classy midfielder born in the disputed Balkan territory of Kosovo in 1991, was another of OUFC's denizens. In 1999 his mother decided to flee the Kosovo War,[4] travelling with Sphresim to London where they were given council accommodation in Oldfield. She quickly enrolled Sphresim at a local primary school and he had since attended secondary school and sixth form college in the area, though recently left college because of football and work commitments.

Like many of OUFC's other players, Sphresim worked as a youth football coach, being paid £10 per hour, cash-in-hand to run training sessions and matches at Hurst Park. He would often arrive late to matches or meeting places on Saturday afternoon because of his coaching job in the morning. 'It's ok,' he said of the work. 'I have to do around two evenings a week and then usually just Saturday, but sometimes Saturday and Sunday mornings.' Whenever he travelled with Geoff and me to away matches, Sphresim's boss would phone to tell him when and where he was coaching over the following week. I asked him about this casual arrangement:

Sphresim: I love it, man. Love working with the kids. Plus, I need the money. Have to help with rent.
JRT: You don't mind working on a week-to-week basis then?
Sphresim: Nah, course not. I never have no credit [on my phone] though!

Sphresim was a liked member of the squad, though was often criticised as being a lightweight, luxury player. Geoff particularly enjoyed home matches when Sphresim had been named in the squad as, being tasked with announcing the team line-ups over the stadium's tannoy system, over the course of the season he had mastered the correct pronunciation of Sphresim's name, despite continually forgetting that he was Kosovan, not Greek. Players called him either 'Sphres' or 'Spesh' and, aside from a minority, did not inquire as to his 'country of origin'. It was difficult to see why any would feel inclined to make such inquiries. Sphresim spoke perfect English and was more fluent than most of his teammates in the local argot described earlier. This was because he had attended the same schools as some of them, had played youth team football with them, dressed like most of them, and shared an occupation and the same religious convictions (those of Islam) as many of them.

I broached the issue of citizenship and politics with Sphres:

JRT: Are you tempted to get citizenship so you can vote next year?
Sphresim: I'm tempted, because I hear they're all chatting about throwing us out! But nah, not into that shit, man.
JRT: Would you take up citizenship for any other reason?
Sphresim: Nah, not really. Don't feel like I need to. [I] just get on with it. I don't feel no less worthy than any of these other guys, man. So why [bother]? So [I] just move on, keep going and don't think about it.
JRT: You're not going back to Kosovo anytime soon though?
Sphresim: Fuck no. That weren't ever really home, you know. I came here so young that this feels more like me, you know? I have friends that come from there also, but we don't never talk about it, we don't know. [We're] more about what's happening here: football, work, girls whatever ...

Denizenship: towards a sociological understanding

Like Mariusz and Sphresim, many other squad members fitted Hammar's technical description of the denizen. But a certain frame of mind shared by the vast majority of the squad – whether individuals were classed as native denizens, naturalised denizens or denizens proper – seemed to unite them. The signal feature of this mindset was a sense of belonging based on the feeling of being alien; alien to mainstream discourses of nationhood, to politics, to the basic functioning of the nation-state and, at bottom, to the qualifications and requirements of being a British citizen.

Depending on their condition as denizens – whether they were native/naturalised denizens or denizens proper – this mentality involved either a renouncement or a refusal of citizenship, marked by a paucity of taxable income, reluctance to gain/exercise the right to vote, and other degrees of exit from/strategies of refusal of citizenship and its requirements. Unlike Bell Hooks' arguments for choosing marginality, 'to be part of the whole but outside the main body' (1984: xi), the denizen's frame of mind bore a twin-faced alterity: individuals from elsewhere occupying 'other' spaces (areas of urban relegation). In some senses the players' stance approximated to Walter Mignolo's notion of 'border thinking' (2000a) or 'border epistemology' (2000b). That is, 'the recognition and transformation of the hegemonic imaginary from the perspectives of people in subaltern positions' (ibid: 736–7). However, while Mignolo sees his epistemology as an alternative to separatism, the denizens of OUFC – though undoubtedly occupying a subaltern position – chose to exploit the opportunities that separatism afforded, using spatial borders in complex ways: in some instances as a means of asserting difference (via the boundaries of the Grove or the M25), in others to promote solidarity via an imaginary contiguity (via the 'shared' boundaries of the Grove and Avant Crescent [another notorious local estate] despite the distance which separated them).

That this was witnessed in one of the world's most 'cosmopolitan' cities (Storkey *et al.* 1997; Harding 2007) may surprise some people. However, if we consider the exceptions to the status (and rights) of citizenship laid out by one of cosmopolitanism's early apostles, Immanuel Kant, the (self) exclusion of the denizen becomes a little easier to understand. As we saw earlier, Kant held that cosmopolitan government would only work if based on a federation of independent nation-states, units which he conceived in vague anthropological terms:

> By the word people (populus) we mean the number of inhabitants living together in a certain district, so far as these inhabitants constitute a unit. Those inhabitants, or even a part of them, which recognize themselves as being united into a civil society through common descent, are called a nation (gens); the part which segregates itself from these laws (the unruly group among these people) is called rabble (vulgus), and their illegal union is called a mob (agree per turbas), a behavior which excludes them from the privileges of citizenship.
>
> (Kant 1974 [1772]: 86)

Here the requirement of common descent is inconsistent with the permanent residence of aliens, while the exclusion of troublesome 'rabble' because of its insufficient 'maturity' could easily be read as an allusion to a recalcitrant underclass.

The appeal of Kant's cosmopolitanism owes much to its commitment to a vague theory of universal goodness. Though as Harvey (2009) has argued, this theory can also permit exclusions on the ground that are deeply prejudicial; as a poor resident alien, Alex would not have fared much better in one of Kant's abstract cosmopolitan nations than he did in contemporary London. However, though some inhabitants of the former would be denied the privileges of citizenship because they failed to meet the necessary requirements, individuals like Alex had no desire to fulfil these responsibilities and thereby gain access to any related benefits.

Most of the squad seemed to evade the state's dragnet of citizen-making and subjection, a web whose series of obligations and conditions are, as outlined by Nikolas Rose in *Powers of Freedom* (1999), laid between the poles of the 'community' and the 'excluded' – I draw extensively on Rose's account in what follows. For Rose, the community has emerged in the context of debates about the governability of liberal, democratic, market-based societies as a natural, extra-political unit within which citizens are bound by human ties and affinities. These bonds keep a check on the impulses of personal interest and advantage incentivised by the free market. However, occupying a place supposedly 'outside' the realm of politics does not buy immunity from political power, power which continually seeks to make an object and target of one or other 'community'. These units have been woven into the state's attempts to maintain surveillance and adherence via national citizenship and institutionalised identity politics. In this way, both acts of good citizenship and resistance to state measures, in defence of civil freedoms, for example, were to be seen in the context of and/or organised around the locus of the community. Thus expressed, the properties and activities of a given community become the focus for political programmes dreamt up by local and central government. The political rationality of the day has chosen to treat those situated outside the 'community', individuals who fail to exhibit the behaviours of an enterprising, self-sufficient citizen, as the 'excluded'.

Exclusion from a community is viewed as an inescapable consequence of market individualism. Those hobbled by unemployment and/or poverty lack the resources needed to assume a meaningful role as a full citizen in the community, and therefore dwell in the marginalised zones of society: the council estate, 'the street', etc. This exclusion must be counteracted by inclusive measures aimed at drawing the excluded into a 'stakeholder economy' and hence back into one or other community. The unemployed are recast as 'jobseekers' and consequently forced to provide continued evidence of their attempts to re-enter the labour market (and hence the zone of citizenship); the neoliberal state thus treats certain members of its population as clients or subjects before they can be rightfully be considered as citizens. Some never cross this threshold. As Rose has stated:

> It appears as if outside the communities of inclusion exists an array of micro-sectors, micro-cultures of failed citizens, anti-citizens, consisting of those who are unable or unwilling to enterprise their lives or manage their own risk, incapable of exercising responsible self-government, attached either to no moral community or to a community of anti-morality.
>
> (1999: 259)

A speech delivered by British Prime Minister David Cameron to the Munich Security Conference in February 2011 is illustrative of this political logic. 'What I am about to say is drawn from the British experience, but I believe there are general lessons for us all', Cameron began:

> In the UK, some young men find it hard to identify with Britain, because we have allowed the weakening of our collective identity ... we

have encouraged different cultures to live separate lives, apart from each
other and apart from the mainstream. We've failed to provide a vision
of society to which they feel they want to belong. We've even tolerated
these segregated communities behaving in ways that run completely
counter to our values.

(Prime Minister's Office 2011)

Cameron's solution was the introduction of a two-month National
Citizen Service to be undertaken by 16-year-olds from 'different back-
grounds' to school them in the tenets of Britain's 'common culture'
(Cabinet Office 2010; Conservatives.com 2010; Quigley 2010; Weakly 2011;
Woodcock *et al*. 2010). This came amid a more or less vague reiteration of
liberal tenets:

> Frankly, we need a lot less of the passive tolerance of recent years and
> a much more active, muscular liberalism ... I believe a genuinely
> liberal country does much more; it believes in certain values and
> actively promotes them. Freedom of speech, freedom of worship,
> democracy, the rule of law, equal rights regardless of race, sex or sexu-
> ality. It says to its citizens, this is what defines us as a society: to belong
> here is to believe in these things.

The notion of muscular liberalism – originally coined in the 1850s by
members of a Tory party split over Corn Law reform (White 2011) – was
subsequently echoed by Deputy Prime Minister Nick Clegg (Oglaza 2011).

If the realities found at OUFC are anything to go by, flexing the muscles
of liberalism more intensely may only accelerate the atrophy of Britain's
body politic. As already noted, a large proportion of OUFC's players went
about their lives outside of the web of governmentality which aimed to make
subjects, clients or citizens of them. The word 'community' was never used
at OUFC, let alone employed strategically as a container or rallying point
for the players' sense of being alien. Neither did they constitute failed
citizens, unable to manage their lives according to a calculus of enterprise
and risk. By identifying themselves as local by virtue of being 'alien', and
carrying on an enterprising life according their own, non-resident logic,
these individuals pre-empted the state's attempts to characterise them as
outsiders – members of the 'excluded' – in order to incorporate them into
the body politic according to certain conditions. Here we are reminded
of Said's compelling argument in Orientalism: 'What it (Orientalist
discourse) is trying to do ... is at one and the same time to characterize
the Orient as alien and to incorporate it schematically on a theatrical
stage whose audience, manager, and actors are for Europe, and only for
Europe' (1978: 71). This testifies to the 'critical ambidexterity of the resident
alien' (Soja 1996: 31) in resisting the quasi-evolutionary version of change

which sees migrant arrivals 'catching up' with host majorities in terms of equality and community recognition (Keith 2005: 18).

Thus Hammar's definition of the denizen is helpful in terms of identifying the growing number of aliens who reside permanently within the territory of a given nation-state. However, the attitudes, motivations and everyday social realities of OUFC's wilful aliens spilled beyond the categorical boundaries he lays down. We should nonetheless be cautious in extending these boundaries for the purposes of sociological inquiry. As Rainer Bauböck has rightfully argued:

> Many scholars have analysed denizenship as a quasi-citizenship status that diminishes the value of national citizenship in the country of immigration. What they have tended to ignore is that denizens are at the same time foreign nationals of a country of origin.
>
> (2010: 848)

While taking such criticism into consideration, we might move the analysis of denizenship beyond mere legal status to examine the cast of mind which informs the attitudes and modes of belonging of the resident non-citizen. The condition of the denizen can no longer be identified solely with numbers; it has become a state of mind for many city dwellers in 'advanced' nation-states. The category therefore needs, literally, fleshing out. That is, it needs to be given human texture and depth through sociological analysis. Such analysis would record the personal stories of urban aliens which have contributed to the denizen becoming a central figure in charting the future of 'advanced' urban areas. More specifically, though historians of Western civilization describe citizenship originating as membership in the city as an institution, in the Greek polis or the Roman civitas (Isin 1992), the city may now be subject to an emptying of citizens. We should take seriously the prospect of urban space as increasingly comprised of denizen enclaves – urban denizenia – each embedded in networks of global settlement but united in their residents' renouncement or refusal of national citizenship.[5] As such, and if the current realities of urban life do not do so already, this prospect would see the definition of the denizen as either citizen- or deportee-in-the-making strained and eventually exhausted. We are then left with the sociological phenomenon of denizenship, a mindset and corresponding set of everyday strategies for dwelling peaceably within a specific urban setting as a non-citizen.[6]

Descriptions of denizenship must always begin with the voice of the subject and the methods employed in navigating a given urban area as a resident alien. Because of their everyday nature, the subjective accounts of urban denizens are untidy and contradictory and it is therefore difficult to list many generic elements which exist beyond the specific, local co-ordinates whence these voices emanate, let alone express these elements as norms.

Certain trends observed throughout the course of my time with OUFC, such as involvement in the underground economy or evading the monitoring techniques of the state, could hardly be considered norms. They were strategies. It follows that instances of denizenship are difficult to translate into political capital and will not likely resonate beyond local horizons. However, these should not be seen as insurmountable problems, or even as weaknesses. Rather, denizenship might be viewed as an honest account of life for a growing number of urban dwellers.

I hope the ethnographic observations recorded here, brief and incomplete as they are, contribute to an understanding of what it is to be an urban denizen in a given inner-city area. I emphasise the rooted nature of these observations, resisting the temptation to abstract from the particularities of time and place. These were the conditions to which the players' distinctive brand of denizenship was a response, while in a related move these specificities also shaped the conceptions of human variation to which players subscribed. Henceforth it is the manner in which OUFC's denizens made sense of human difference and, more specifically, of the behaviours, strengths and shortcomings of their fellow aliens, that is my principal concern; although, of course, these conceptions will also help in constructing a more detailed picture of the players' general mindset.

My early inquiries, rather than leading me to the heart of denizenship, seemed to (re)inscribe its limits. That is, certain events underlined that the acceptance of urban denizenship – of contentment amid a sense of being in some way alien – was uneven; it was geographically and generationally specific and subject to many anomalies. Though they constituted a minority, those who felt excluded from this sense of comfort with ethnic and cultural diversity were more strident about their beliefs than were its exponents. The more they felt their worldview and its simple conceptions of human difference to be challenged or threatened, the louder and more explicit were their (re)assertions of these differences.

The first of these events came in Shoreston, after the loss to (the all-white) Shoreston Town, and again centred on the issue of post-match cuisine. The protocol following games meant that players retired to the bar after showering while officials from the two clubs – as well as the referee and his assistants – went to the boardroom of the home team. Refreshments were then served in the respective rooms courtesy of the home side. These normally comprised a tray of sandwiches filled with either ham or cheese, cut with geometric accuracy into equilateral triangles and occasionally garnished with a dozen sausage rolls, cocktail sausages, onion rings or potato wedges. Approaching me with a heaped tray that had been covered with cling film and marked 'players', a Shoreston Town official asked if I would deliver the tray to our squad, which had gathered in the adjoining bar. 'Not sure how much of it your lot will eat though', he mumbled as I turned away. 'How d'you mean?' I asked, turning to face him once again.

'Well', he replied, 'the teams from down London normally want pizza and bhajis, not sure what they'll make of the pasties and sandwiches we do up here'. As was invariably the case – the only offending variable being coleslaw – after two or three minutes the players returned an empty tray to the bar.

On another evening OUFC were hosting ADL Division One club Ivestone in the ADL League Cup. As they were members of a lower division, everyone expected the opposition to be swept aside fairly easily and Reg therefore took the opportunity to field a number of reserve team players alongside a few first team regulars. After 20 minutes Ivestone had scored twice without reply. Attending the match that night was Ian, a 40-something construction worker who acted as Secretary for OUFC's under-17 and under-18 sides. 'Who's the captain?' he asked loudly while sat amongst a group of us watching from the stand. 'Derek', replied one of a group of Ian's under-17 players who had also come to watch, Glancing left and right, Ian queried: 'Which one's he? Can't see the armband.' 'Number eight', replied another member of his squad. 'That's gonna be his (Reg's) problem this year', he uttered quietly after a few seconds delay, 'too many brothers in the team'. At first I thought Ian's comment had provoked no reaction, carried off by the autumnal wind before registering any effect. However, I then saw Elliott's dad, Elliott senior, nodding in silent agreement. I decided to broach the issue with Ian after one of the club's management meetings:

JRT: What d'you reckon was the problem the other night?
Ian: What, against Ivestone?
JRT: (Nods)
Ian: No leadership, manager looks like he doesn't give a shit. Also, you got players in the side who can't concentrate. That number two [Richmond]. Useless. Always ball-watching and has no idea what's going on around him. No idea why he keeps picking him. Also, that Derek's a good player but he's no captain is he? Don't look at me like that. [There's] no use denying it James. Something has to change.

As well as performing his secretarial duties for OUFC's junior sides, Ian acted as Assistant Manager for both teams. There was a preponderance of 'black' players in both teams and each enjoyed considerable success in their respective leagues, with many players consequently being drafted into the first team. This made Ian's opinions somewhat baffling. It was clear that only a tiny minority of the crowd were prepared to coddle his gripes. However, the fact that those nodding in quiet affirmation were a generation older than the youngsters who looked on with indifference underscored the uneven nature of the denizenship evident at OUFC, and how this distribution could be partially explained by generational attitudes to raciology.

His salvo didn't provoke the reaction he was looking for, and though it was fired while sat among a group of ten or 12 fellow spectators, I became aware that there were three parties to his statement: those who nodded in agreement, those for whom the argument lacked cogency, and those for whom it lacked intelligibility. For these latter, OUFC's urban denizens, Ian's argument did not stick. He reacted with the frustration of someone trying to explain to a group of nihilists why they were 'wrong' and he was 'right'. The only argument to ensue would have been between me on one side, and Ian and on the other.

OUFC's young denizens didn't reside in Ian's ontological universe; theirs was of a different order. Unlike Ian, their view of the world did not rely on 'racial' markers to make it navigable and hence comfortable to inhabit. Unlike me, they felt no need to celebrate the phenotypical confusion evident in their surroundings, nor were they obliged to defend it from others who failed to accept such an untidy reality.[7] Their comfort in these surroundings was no lifestyle choice or a calculated expression of ethnic harmony. It simply worked for them; it was part of their ontological view of the world. The next task was to map this ontology and find out how it framed the issue of human variability. My attempts at doing so are the subject of the following chapter.

Chapter 6

Denizenship, ontology and human difference

As we have seen in previous chapters, ontology is the branch of metaphysics which concerns the study of being in general; being in general, that is, as opposed to philosophical reflection on ultimate entities such as the soul or God. Here we are dealing with reflection on 'what there is' in the world – all classes of objects – and the conditions under which they come into being. Most attempts at ontological study have focused on the most general kinds and classes that exist in the world, and as Ian Hacking has pointed out, 'usually the emphasis has been on demarcation' (2002a: 2). Indeed, in Part 1, a programme of ontological study attempted to show how a certain 'kind' of person – the 'impulsive' black male – came into being as an object of knowledge, shedding light on the institutional settings within which his name was repeated, and the ethical values which sprang up around him. The notion of ontology can also be employed to make sense of the uneven denizenship on show at OUFC.

Most subjective accounts pay little mind to academic divisions, particularly where issues of knowledge, difference and related lines of demarcation are concerned. I have therefore chosen to present the study's ethnographic findings according to themes that emerged out of the research itself. This is not to abandon the ontological axes that oriented the foregoing analysis; in concluding the chapter I will address the axes of knowledge, power and ethics.

The first section of the chapter explores the ways in which OUFC's players attempted to classify people and their related methods of rationalising the behaviour of self and others. The second section examines the effects of the local underground economy upon players' conceptions of human variation, and describes how competing notions of 'home' framed their moral judgements when it came to human difference. As already noted, in the final section I revisit the study's three ontological axes in drawing tentative conclusions about the versions of human difference expressed by OUFC's personnel.

'Freshies' and flatulence: ontological security and the classification of difference

Various philosophers, sociologists and psychologists have tried to capture what it is to be ontologically secure. The sociologist Anthony Giddens defines ontological security as 'a sense of continuity and order in events, including those not directly within the perceptual environment of the individual' (1991: 243). He elaborates:

> To be ontologically secure is to possess, on the level of unconscious and practical consciousness, 'answers' to fundamental existential questions which all human life in some way addresses ... freedom is not a given characteristic of the human individual, but derives from the acquisition of an ontological understanding of external reality and personal identity.
>
> (Ibid: 47)

Such answers provide the silent backdrop which allows individuals to focus on specific tasks. The fundamental questions to which they are addressed concern the basic existential parameters of self and social identity, the formation of self and others according to the fundamental classes and orders that exist in the world. For OUFC's urban denizens, these parameters were not shored up by 'race', ethnicity, nationality or religion, but this isn't to say that the club was some sort of humanistic commune. The players drew upon these categories but were aware that each could be played with, offering opportunities for experimentation and subversion. Each player knew he couldn't be nailed down by these categories, that ultimately his identity could never be reduced to a triangulation of 'race', nationality and religion.

Though the majority of players identified themselves as British, the Football Association did not ask for any proof of their nationality, and I was witness to conversations between players who, after brief deliberation, thought it better to state British as opposed to their 'real' nationality on their registration forms. For example, I noted the following exchange between Emmett and Derek while overseeing their registration:

Derek: What you putting?
Emmett: For what?
Derek: Nationality?
Emmett: Well I ain't putting fucking Turkish am I? British innit?
Derek: You from Turkey though, right?
Emmett: I always put British though, less hassle.
Derek: Fuck it, I'm putting Jamaican.
Emmett: But you're British, Del.
Derek: Yeah but I wanna play for them.
Emmett: Whatever ...

A similar conversation took place between Patrick and Daniel, with Patrick opting to list 'British' despite having dual Irish-Polish nationality. When Patrick queried as to the location he should list as his place of birth, Daniel advised: 'just put Royal District like me' (referring to the Royal District Hospital in Meadson). Of course, the players' creativity in filling out these forms affects the validity of the information these forms contain. However, this creativity along with the management's blasé attitude towards capturing such information was interesting in itself. I was the only member of club personnel interested in where players were 'really from', a fact reinforced whenever I tried to quiz players about their identity and that of other players. A conversation with midfielder (and resident of the Grove) Daniel typified these early attempts.

JRT: Who's he then?
Daniel: Who?
JRT: The black guy, tall fella?
Daniel: That's Stephen, plays on wing, been here for a couple of years.
JRT: Where's he from?
Daniel: Round Shinewater somewhere I think.
JRT: What about his parents?
Daniel: I don't fucking know, Shinewater probably.

A shrinking of reality is needed to protect feelings of ontological security (Merleau-Ponty 1973). As such, certain referents and rules of thumb are used to stabilise reality and reduce the dimensions of the challenges it often presents. On this score, it wasn't that OUFC's players treated the dimensions of diversity surrounding them as somehow unfit for shrinking. However, only a tiny minority of people at the club, like Ian, used raciology as an interpretive key. His version of ontological security meant the diversity of club personnel was made manageable by overlaying a raciological frame. However, if his perception of the world relied on raciology to make it ontologically stable, when OUFC's urban denizens had learned to live they had done so with the raciological stabilisers off. It frustrated Ian that I rejected his arguments; it infuriated him that the young denizens did not understand them.

Methods of classification: frontiers, stairwells and the suburban 'Other'

The raciological bonds which elsewhere connect the categories of ethnicity, nationality and religion, and in doing so renew 'race' with elemental force, were largely absent among OUFC's players. Nevertheless, quirky schemas of difference were espoused by squad members. The most interesting of these belonged to Anis-Islem Anouar ('Slemie'), a 21-year-old striker of Algerian descent who had moved to Bridgegate via Paris as a child. He signed for OUFC in November 2009 after being released by a professional club.

Slemie had a sharp nose for flatulence, quickly detecting a foul emission and guessing at the culprit. As I saw before an away fixture at Halwyn Green in March 2010, these guesses could also be used as a means to comment on the lifestyle of other players. Slemie was suspended for the match but travelled with the team to lend his support. As Alex was heading out of the changing room to begin his warm-up routine, he passed Slemie in the corridor. 'What the fuck Al? That's a black man's fart. What you been eating? Fucking beans, fufu and that shit?! You need to clean that shit up. I'll give you some couscous next week.' Alex laughed and jogged away to join the rest of the squad. I asked Slemie about his olfactory detective work while waiting to exchange team sheets with my opposite number:

> I've spent bare time in changing rooms, here, in France, even when I go Algeria, so I know about that. The Muslim boys normally have alright smelling ones, have a clean enough diet, the Caribbean boys like Del [Derek] theirs [will] be bad, you seen the shit they bring to eat? And the boys from the Grove, fuck knows what they're eating – when I play up-front with Giro I can smell him coming!

This classification of flatulence, which fractured totalising categories such as 'black' and 'white' via confusing allusions to lifestyle and culture (as correlative to ethno-national, religious and even neighbourhood referents), was difficult to make sense of. This perhaps explains why Slemie's guesses at the originator of a given waft were almost always incorrect (though on most occasions it was near impossible to determine who the guilty party was).

But this didn't frustrate Slemie as much as the fact that players and officials of certain other clubs sometimes identified him by referring to the 'black fella/player'. 'Are they fucking stupid?' he would protest, struggling to understand why his phenotypical markers could be read in this way. Indeed, the issue of identifying and classifying such bodily signifiers was dealt with in interesting ways by OUFC's players. The grammar through which they expressed human difference was constructed according to their everyday ecology and, as a consequence, phenotypical signifiers were becoming illegible. Like Slemie, their socio-cultural surroundings had thrown up interesting ways of classifying the differences on show, and it was becoming clear that these folk schemas of difference were as haphazard as those dreamt up in the laboratory or the anthropology department. However, the players seemed comfortable in their failure to essentialise other squad members and thereby modulate the flux of experience. Whereas scientific attempts to redefine 'race' now appeal to multi-polar models of human difference (Gilroy 2009), the attempts of these young men to understand the behaviour of others relied on layered referents to origin that resisted any principled academic understanding.

The central paradox was that to be local was *ipso facto* to originate elsewhere; to come from Oldfield, Bridgegate, Lonsworth or Shinewater was to trace one's ancestry to a foreign territory, as the British 'Other' lived in the suburbs or the countryside. This meant that players' ideas about human variation were ordered by an interesting set of nodal points; generalised attributes were not oriented around 'racial' poles, let alone ascribed value according to distance from a cluster of so-called 'white' traits. Less a tidy pentagram than a misty and muddled constellation – where the touchstones of identity burned brighter or dimmer according to social context – the players' methods of registering of difference were mediated by a combination of queries as to where someone lived, how long they had lived in the area, etc. This was a system of referents where much was left to guesswork and contradictions and inaccuracies were legion.

Oppositions between various locales emerged throughout my time with the club. Geoff complained of a drop-off in levels of 'tolerance' when OUFC travelled to away grounds situated outside the bounds of the M25.[1] Others at the club – as well as officials from rival clubs in inner London – reaffirmed the frontier effect of this ring-road. As a spatial boundary, the M25 was important. As we will see, OUFC's players posited urban zones of exclusion relative to those of suburbia and, more specifically, the places beyond the M25 where 'farmers' sons' went about their lives according to the dictates of 'Britishness'. Attached to the coordinates of the inner city and outer suburbia was a set of assertions relating to the issue of human variation. This was ironic, as a road designed to improve access to and from London has come to be represented as a boundary separating the urban from the suburban.

When playing away from home, officials of hosting clubs often signalled their intolerance by complaining that the names which appeared on OUFC's team-sheet sounded insufficiently Anglo-Saxon; whereas Geoff enjoyed the challenge posed by the pronunciation of a name like 'Sphresim', those in charge of the microphone at other clubs didn't share his relish. 'Your lot are bad', alleged an official of Halridge Town, 'but that mob at Brentwich, I fucking give up'. Here he implied that, because of patterns of local settlement, Brentwich Sports – begun by a group of Bangladeshis in 1986 with the aim of providing young Bangladeshis with the opportunity to play organised football – now had a squad heavily comprised of players from Eastern Europe.

Heated encounters between players and supporters often underlined this opposition between metropolitan interior and outer city suburbia. At away grounds, OUFC's players often reacted to taunts about the number of 'immigrants' who played for the club by alleging that the parochial nature of the host town was reflected in the breadth of its gene pool.

Closer to home, the folds along which players shrunk social reality were conditioned by their everyday experience of the city, using the districts and estates from which players hailed as well as the schools they had attended and the teams they had played for in the past in order to 'place' people. In time, a finely differentiated series of micro-locales emerged which centred variously on streets, council estates, as well as each estate's individual buildings.

A new player would often be known to one or a number of existing squad members. Alex took up a typical line of inquiry with Terry, a player who joined in September 2009:

Alex: You live up Chorville don't you?
Terry: (Nods)
Alex: Ohhhh shiiiit … careful of this one then lads.
Geoff (eavesdropping on the conversation through the portal to the kitchen): Where'd you live Chuckles? Up the Grove isn't it?
Alex: Yeah, used to Geoff, USED TO. Live up Boorman Oak now … Look at Geoff sticking up for Chorville! [You're] representing, Geoff! (Everyone erupts into laughter)

This patchwork of estates didn't lay flush with the boundaries of respective London boroughs, local council wards, etc. or any ethno-national allegiances (Wacquant 2008; Ackroyd 2000). Because of the metonymic power of terms such as 'the Grove' and 'Avant', these words designated an epicentre whose outposts could be located some distance away.

The above exchange between Geoff and Alex was curious given that the latter – despite listing his parents' address on club registration forms – lived with his girlfriend on Rydal Grove, as I discovered when Geoff dropped him home late one evening after an away match. As we were approaching the point where he had asked to alight, Alex, having recently discovered that his girlfriend had fallen pregnant, expressed dismay at the prospect of raising a child on the estate. 'I'm praying for a girl, man. You can't raise a boy round here. It's a shithole, absolute fucking shithole. You'll get stabbed or shot for looking at someone.' However, while on this evidence and that of his registration form Alex seemed ashamed of living on the estate, at other times he enjoyed the status which accrued to hailing from the Grove. When status inhered in aspects of social identity associated with masculinity – more specifically being able to 'take care of himself' and having the 'hook-up' – Alex's identification with the Grove intensified. In this context, being an experienced resident of the estate was empowering. It afforded the ability to negotiate the area safely and expediently, even if the power of state agencies was instrumental in reproducing the dangerous spaces to be negotiated. If less 'macho' traits were praised by teammates or other club personnel, his affiliation faded.

This identification, alternately declared and denied, was reflected in Alex's conception of the local landscape, which focused on individual blocks, alleyways and the spaces outside certain shops in and around the estate:

Alex: Down there (points to the southern portion of the estate) are the crackheads, crackhouses, the blocks on the outside are ok, ones near the middle are shit mostly. You don't want to be heading up some of them stairs [stairwells] that side (motions to the east of the estate) where the Somali boys hang around.

JRT: You steer clear of the Somali lads then?

Alex: Yeah, some of them man. [It's] only some the fresh kids [that] you need to watch though; they're crazy ... Kosovan, Somalian, wherever they're from. Trying to make a name and that, some of them even if they've been here for time, let everyone know that they won't take no shit. The boys that been here longer are mostly cool. We play football, we all sell and swap stuff with them and that. Known them for time, from school and around the Grove.

Alex conceived of his situation relative to several different phenomena. First, players like Alex imagined their plight relative to other migrants (and their descendants), and this entailed a string of perceived commonalities. Alex noted that the ambition of the Grove's 'fresh' Somalis and Kosovans was to 'make a name' for themselves, but explained this desire by invoking their status as recent immigrants. He positioned them at a relative distance from himself, as dwelling in a different zone of the Grove. However, he argued that being 'fresh' was an attitude which many migrants adopted, regardless of their ethnic background, and that in due course the 'freshness' of new arrivals and the attendant attitude of 'taking no shit' may abate. His argument was underpinned by the perception that all residents of the inner city were, at bottom, alien, and that consequently they (or their forebears) may once have been 'fresh'. No notion of absolute, progressive time, or any Lockean sense of maturity, would guarantee the conversion of the 'fresh' teenager's attitude into that of a more senior resident, however. As we will see, this depended on how the youngster responded to the challenges of life on the estate. Being 'fresh' was an attitude that could be adopted by anyone, at any time. It was by no means the preserve of recent migrants.

Looking at the large collection of buildings that comprised the Grove – both high- and low-rise flats as well as small houses – led me to question the official statistics relating to criminal activity on the estate (as recorded by the Metropolitan Police and compiled by government departments such as the Office of National Statistics). Indeed, locals protested that the crimes supposedly committed on one street – Rydal Grove – actually took place on a number of other streets constitutive of and situated on the margins of the estate. However, these were conflated because 'the Grove' had come to stand for the network of streets branching-off Rydal Grove proper. That said, despite the way residents of the Grove such as Alex differentiated between the estate's 'good' and 'bad' zones, in Alex's eyes these locations were united in being spaces of alterity and exclusion:

Alex: Everyone over there's poor, man. They've [the council] stuck us there, refugees always coming in, the Somali and Kosovan boys, then there's the crackheads. Them people won't travel or ever move [out of the area], they [the council] know that. Shit, most people [have] never been out of the borough!

JRT: How do you deal with that, then?

Alex: Just keep my head down, do what I have to ... You see these mugs like Geoff paying 50 pound or whatever for a *TomTom* [satellite navigation device]? Got mine for a fiver off a crackhead.

The players travelled little, following the trend of those living in pockets of urban deprivation. On the journey home from Hailfold, Lawrence reflected on the impossibility of travelling abroad:

I can't barely afford to go out on a Saturday night mate, fucking forget about [a] holiday. Forget it! Besides, you think I can get out of here while I'm on parole? No chance. I'm stuck in the manor, man.

Alex elaborated: 'No way, man. There's no way me and my missus got the money for that. She's on about getting out to the country but I can't handle it, I'd get so fucking restless and bored out there.'

Alex described the Grove as a dumping ground which allowed those with the power to do so (the local council) to deposit and (with the help of other state agencies) contain undesirables, whatever their 'origin'; he felt that the boundaries demarcating these areas served to confine alien elements – durable margins of the inner city left to the 'foreign' and 'poor' – and was keenly aware of his status as an occupier (i.e. as a council tenant) rather than an owner.

The estate didn't enjoy much in the way of capital investment. The shops on the perimeter of the estate were mostly bookies and off-licences, while the narrow, leafy streets of Boorman Oak and the bustle of the financial sector, though located nearby, seemed an eternity away. As Alex argued, inhabitants of the Grove were unlikely to possess the tools needed to climb the social ladder and as a result its borders (along with those of similar estates) were marked by considerable friction.

Indeed, for the players that lived there – some of whom exploited the fact – the Grove had been surrendered to lawlessness, a space marked more by exclusionary power than disciplinary networks of surveillance; it was one of those urban spaces which, as John Berger has put it, 'hide consequences from us' (1974: 40). 'You never see the police round our way', complained Alex.

> There ain't hardly no cameras but there's bare crime! They don't ever chase it up anyway, if someone gets robbed or whatever. [They're] not bothered. But see when it's one of us getting in bother somewhere else watch 'em get there in no time at all.

The law seemed to be enforced at the edges of the estate and, more specifically, at its interface with the affluent neighbourhoods that hemmed it in.

In linking the plight of its residents under the touchstones of alterity and exclusion, Alex spoke of a shared ethic of survival. This common ground emerged from residents' position relative to the job market, capital investment, waves of immigration, and to the places where mainstream discourses of 'Britishness' thrived. This did not foreclose the possibility of relative differences being asserted; they clearly were – between 'fresh' residents and calmer residents, as represented by the respective positions they occupied on a given estate. But these relative positions still allowed for commonality.

Alex's comments revealed more about the sense of belonging he experienced. As Nadia Lovell has remarked, 'Belonging to a particular locality evokes the notion of loyalty to a place, a loyalty that may be expressed ... through narratives of origin as belonging' (1998: 1). In line with the twin-faced alterity of the denizen outlined in Chapter 5, Alex's expressions of belonging to his locality invoked origins which might be characterised as doubly elsewhere. His foreign heritage and the allocation of his parents to a marginalised, inner-city estate were the touchstones of this belonging. It wasn't linked to any celebration of the area's landscape or certain 'local' objects. Instead it was based on a sense of experience, a phenomenology of belonging centred on the ideals of the Grove and similar zones of urban relegation (Tilley 1994).

The individual and the group

We saw in Part 1 how the labelling of the black male (and black sportsman more narrowly) as 'impulsive' or 'instinctive' entailed ways of being which disclosed certain possibilities for action. In this way the individuals so labelled had their sense of agency restricted and, with this, the terms of their individuality circumscribed. Recall the decision of Ian Wright to forgo a career in management because he was 'an instinctive player ... and those sorts of players have never made great coaches or managers' (Wright 1997: 223). His (elective) membership of a particular group had reduced the scope of his individual agency. At OUFC I witnessed a more complex conception of the relationship between the individual and the group.

Alex's dissimulation with regard to the Grove was paralleled by other squad members when it came to evaluating their own capabilities as players and, more broadly, as human beings. When players accounted for valued attributes such as masculinity, toughness and being well-connected, whether in terms of access to the underground economy or networks of local hard-men – usually signified by boasts about 'my boys' – these did not issue mechanically from being resident in a certain area or estate. Rather, these traits were the reward for an individual's successful negotiation of local conditions. This empowered the individual rather than valorised the area in which he lived. So being a wily or 'cute' player could result from being streetwise, a trait nurtured by successfully managing the risks posed by a given urban area. However, these same risks may have been managed differently by other young men in the squad, leading to the cultivation of different, but similarly valued, character traits – varied responses to a kindred set of stimuli. This came to light during my discussions with players from the Grove, principally Alex, Clive and (later) Lawrence:

JRT: What type of player would you describe yourself as being?
Clive: I'm cultured mate, like Beckham. Simple … but accurate, you know?
Alex: You're cute Cli, bare sneaky out there. Like as a kid when it was all kicking-off you'd be out of it somehow, [you] weren't coming away hurt or getting involved 'cos you always saw it coming!
Clive: Yeah, unlike you. You're still starting [initiating confrontation] on players twice your size – like you and your brother when we was younger. Whenever I heard anything kicking-off at school or around the estate I knew it'd be one of you.
Alex: Usually both! (Laughter)

In this way traits and attributes considered valuable on the pitch were cast in individual terms, being related to a player's nous, bravery, etc. Conversely, if a player was identified as possessing characteristics considered a hindrance on the pitch, he usually explained them away by invoking his membership of one group or another. This way responsibility for the perceived weakness was deferred to a given collective – because if all members were to blame, no one was to blame:

JRT: Reg is forever complaining that you two are always late.
Alex: He can fucking wait. We're from the Grove mate, what have we got to rush for?
Clive: Yeah, exactly. What does he expect? We never have to hurry for nothing, we have all day. Don't know why he's bitching anyway, we've never missed a kick-off before.

Alex: Yes Cli. It's them boys who work that come late for games ... [us] casuals always make it. We just walk out! But I ain't got nothing at the moment anyway so ...

Here the pair blamed their alleged tardiness on the exclusionary nature of the estate. This afforded them time to, well, take their time. This fact was also important in relation to money and the market. As already noted, OUFC's players were mostly unemployed or employed as casual labour, and enjoyed little geographical mobility in relation to capital (Harvey 1973). Because of their absence from the labour market, their lives were not ensnared within the chronological net used to mark off and impose productive labour time in the workplace (Harvey 1990). Time was not money in the sense of undertaking a specified amount of paid labour in a given day or week.

The tendency to cast strengths in individual terms and weaknesses in terms of a given group was widespread within the squad and so greatly influenced the conceptions of human variation articulated by its members. I asked Alex which players were most important to the squad:

Alex: Easy: Mariusz, Derek and Josh Lindsay.
JRT: What do they bring to the side?
Alex: Josh is lightning quick, great finisher. When he's fit that is.
JRT: Him and his brother are both quick aren't they? Think it has anything to do with their background?
Alex: What d'you mean? Like, their parents and that?
JRT: Yeah. What d'you reckon?
Alex: I know they're local. Live up Aspern Hill near Meadson. Not sure if they're milky bar [a term which seemed to denote an ethnic mixture partly constituted by white heritage] part Spanish, Portuguese or what. Anyway, they're fast. Probably to do with running up all them stairs! Like some of them Irish boys, Duff, Bobby and that, don't look that quick when they're jogging but you put 'em in a foot race or have someone chase 'em, fucking lightning ... [They] grew up round Avant Crescent and playing at Aldwick Street ... [they are] used to running from the feds [police] and them awful tackles you get down there!

It was interesting that Alex made reference to the Irishness of Bobby (Clarke) and Carl (Duff) – though, in fact, only Carl could trace his ancestry to Ireland – yet appealed to the area in which they grew up when trying to explain their deceptive speed. In Josh Lindsay's case, it turned out that the parents of his mother were German, which he told me after asking around at home. What both of Alex's explanations had in common were references to local conditions and individual agency rather than the fixed endowment of biological or hereditary factors. In the absence of certainty with regard to the issue of ancestry – the only certainty being that the ancestral trail would lead abroad – Alex lent explanatory weight to what he was sure of: the places where he had encountered other players while growing up.

The groups alluded to when trying to explain perceived weaknesses had to be units compact enough to fit the local landscape, itself comprised of numerous micro-locales. This helped to defer responsibility and promote a feeling of solidarity among members of the group being invoked. As already noted, perceived strengths were explained by an individual's skill in navigating this landscape. Any appeal to raciological explanations would rob players of agency by predetermining their capabilities and, on the other hand, undermine the membership of those groups which afforded solidarity amid perceived weakness. Indeed, the clumsy logic of 'race' would dissolve such groups whose criterion for membership was based on more contingent factors. Alex, Clive or any player labelled 'white' in terms of racio-logic reacted with horror at any supposed solidarity with the 'farmers' sons' who dwelled outside the confines of the M25, just as Lawrence Osment bridled at the suggestion that his agility or finishing abilities were the rightful biological endowments of a 'black' man. To be given any credence these explanations first had to make sense, and they succeeded in doing so because they threatened neither the players' nuanced view of the local area nor their ability to negotiate the risks and opportunities it threw up. Raciological explanations were largely unreadable in this context, partly because, as already noted, the legibility of racial markers was under threat.

Alex's comments indicated that, for OUFC's players, phenotypical markers had become red herrings; they were unreliable as clues to a player's ethno-national background. Their view of the world thus contradicted the proponents of 'implicit racial bias' who allege that an optic ordered by racial – phenotypical – differences continues to dominate people's coding of urban terrain (Bobo 2001; Sampson 2009; Sampson and Raudenbush 2004). The 'racial' categorisations inherent in this optic, so the argument runs, issue from an 'implicit bias' (Banaji 2002; Bobo 2001; Fiske 1998) whose attendant set of cultural stereotypes is difficult to confront (and hence redress) given the subconscious level at which it resides; one can hold fast to such stereotypes without possessing any conscious racial prejudice (Devine 1989). Taken together, these implicit biases, cultural stereotypes and racial categorisations promote a 'laissez-faire' racism (Bobo 2001) and a relationship between diversity and decline in public trust in urban areas.

The players' attitude to ethnic signifiers was evident in their relaxed, almost resigned reaction upon discovering that their guesses about another squad member's ethnicity were incorrect. A warm-up drill performed before matches demonstrated these almost comical attempts to pin down someone's ethno-national identity based on the information available. In this drill players lined up facing Reg or one of his assistants – who stood around 15 yards opposite – and waited for the name of a nation to be called. Upon the call every player sprinted towards Reg barring those with allegiance to the stated nation. (I use the word allegiance as players like Alex stayed put on hearing Greece being called out rather than England, despite being a British citizen and listing 'British' as his nationality on club registration forms. The same was true of other 'British' players who identified with foreign nations, such as Derek with Jamaica and Diego with Colombia.) On reaching Reg the players turned and jogged back to join their teammate(s) who remained at the starting point because of their national loyalties. The name of another nation was then called and the drill continued in this fashion.

One day as I stood watching the drill I noticed that Reg was struggling to involve Slemie, who had signed for the club only a few days before. As no name had been called that identified Slemie's ethno-national allegiance he had yet to be spared any of the group sprints, and I could see players exchanging snatches of dialogue with Reg while performing their collective volte-face, obviously suggesting the name of a nation that would afford Slemie some respite. By this point Slemie looked shattered, but later admitted that he was enjoying the manager's bungling attempts to determine his origins.

So it went on: 'Lebanon!' Everyone sprinted towards Reg, turned, and ambled back to the starting point. 'France!' Again Slemie began sprinting, leaving a grateful Arthur behind to catch his breath. 'Argentina!' This time the whole squad took off, leaving no one behind. Reg eventually gave in, and, knowing Slemie supported Tottenham Hotspur, shouted 'Spurs!', whereupon Slemie and one or two other players remained on the starting line. The players, along with Reg, immediately looked quizzically at Slemie, who barked 'I'm from Algeria for fuck's sake!' After the match, while he and the players loitered in the café, I asked Reg what had happened:

JRT: What happened with the sprinting drill earlier on? Looked like a bit of a commotion!

Reg: I know, I saw you watching and nearly called you over to ask about Slemie's registration form.

JRT: Oh right, to ask about his nationality? (Reg nods) French I think but I'd have to check.

Reg: That's what I thought at first, because he looks like [French footballer] [David] Trezeguet, Micah said [that] as well because he's light-skinned. See I read that Trezeguet is really from Argentina so tried that as well – didn't work. What did I try before that? You said it Alex?

Alex: What, with Slemie? (Reg nods) Lebanon. His first name's Anis, he told me earlier on today. I've got a friend called Anis, [he] looks real similar, even has the same lines shaved in his hair! He's from Lebanon.

The squad's joint efforts at identifying Slemie's ethno-national identity provided an illustration of how they tended to read phenotypical markers.

These markers were nested within a web of other identifications, various morsels of information deemed relevant to the individual in question. As the story above shows, clues issued from the experiences of whoever was making the guess. In Slemie's case these included his likeness to a prominent French footballer of Argentine descent, his name, and his haircut. In this way the enigmatic air which attended a newcomer like Slemie was quickly debunked; his background and characteristics being related to players' own self-identifications, or elements lent significance by their day-to-day lives, along lines of almost petty equivalence. Their suggestions had local inflections and a texture forged by everyday encounters; such a nuanced, confused set of signifiers and the differences they muddled towards were a far cry from the grander and more destructive scale of 'race' and raciology encountered in Part 1.

Lawrence 'Giro' Osment, the underground economy and qualitative uniqueness

On 2 March 2010 the most prolific striker in OUFC's short history was released from a low-security prison in Dorset. Speculation on internet (non-league) football forums was rife as to whether the 27-year-old, born on Rydal Grove, would re-sign for his boyhood club or opt to join one of the professional clubs which now coveted his signature. The conjectural murmurs were fuelled by reports from those who had visited Osment during his 18-month sojourn for burglary on a house within a one-mile radius of the Grove. Among the visitors were representatives of various amateur and professional clubs located in and around the Greater London area. On being released he began training with Topsham Manor, an amateur club situated on the outskirts of London (whose secretary, Tony, had been to see Osment so frequently during his incarceration that other friends and family struggled to secure a vacant slot during visiting time), but after only a week decided to return to OUFC where his 'recapture' was greeted with joy. It was not misplaced; the club's fortunes enjoyed an immediate turn-around.

Lawrence's grandparents had moved to London from Grenada in the 1950s. His parents had been allocated a flat on Rydal Grove in the late 1970s where Lawrence and his brother, Jamie, were later born. Besides tending to the follicles of his trademark moustache, Lawrence wasn't as considered in his appearance as the majority of other players, turning up to matches in grubby jeans or tracksuit bottoms and a large hooded jumper. Gianni immediately took measures to ensure that Lawrence was looked after, making contact with his best friend (and former OUFC midfielder), Shaka, and entrusting him with the job of keeping Lawrence out of trouble on Friday nights – principally this meant staying away from the bookies. He also saw that Lawrence received a club tracksuit free of charge (other players had to pay around £40 for theirs), donating Deborah's club polo shirt in the process.

After hearing about the 'Prodigal Son's' prowess as a footballer with increasing regularity in the weeks leading up to his release, I questioned whether these reports could refer to the man who heaved his carriage through the doors at Churchfield Stadium early in March 2010. However, it wasn't long before I jumped on the bandwagon. As a player Lawrence had an exceptional touch, and therefore insisted that everyone 'fizz it in' to him whenever possible. He was the only OUFC player that other clubs legislated for in their tactics, whether through double-marking or making substitutions to find personnel more suited to stifling his efforts. Like Anton Christou, Lawrence had put on a considerable amount of 'prison weight' while inside, and at first sight Geoff doubted if Lawrence's body was still up to it. 'Fuck's sake, look at his gut … I'm telling you though, James, this boy is class', he said with glee. Indeed, Lawrence's excess weight didn't hamper him to any great degree, as he spun, twisted and accelerated with unlaboured finesse, making a fool of defenders in the process.

Word of Osment's release had spread throughout the league, and on numerous occasions I heard fans and representatives of other clubs mutter, 'He's just got out of prison you know … ' as soon as Lawrence's name was mentioned, 'bet he'll have problems with the refs'. In fact, when addressing referees Lawrence struck notes of entreaty that seldom led to cautions for dissent.

Going underground: the ethics of exit

Osment had been at the club since he was 13 (following his release by a local professional club), playing football and growing up alongside other OUFC veterans such as Alex and Anton Christou and Clive Linehan. His younger brother Jamie (whom Gianni deemed an inferior player) had also played for OUFC as a youngster before signing for a professional club of considerable standing. Lawrence had scored 30 goals in OUFC's promotion year (season 2007/8), during which he was on probation for another burglary offence. This brought a 9.30pm curfew, which meant at evening fixtures he was unable to see out the entire match; the half-time whistle saw him hasten back to Oldfield at the wheel of Gianni's car. The conditions of his latest probationary period didn't include a curfew but did demand that he 'sign on' to receive unemployment benefit if unable to secure gainful employment. This made sure that he remained on the radar of the probation service (and more broadly speaking, the state). He thus picked up the nickname 'Giro',[2] coined by Alex (who prided himself on creating sobriquets which stuck) but quickly adopted by everyone else at the club, even if they were unaware – like many of the younger players – of the meaning of the term. Alex meant it as a playful jibe; he knew Lawrence resented the risk of compulsorily signing on. All of the other players who were unemployed had not (or refused to admit that they had) signed on, chief among whom was Alex, who explained his decision thus:

Alex: I don't want them fuckers asking what I'm doing all the time ... you get fuck all anyway. Ask Giro! He spends all his money in one day! [I] just wanna stay out of it you get me? Just do my own thing?

JRT: What's that then?

Alex: Don't ask them questions, Jay. You know ... I got my schemes.

Later Alex revealed that he had been doing mentoring work with local children who had been excluded from school, but that he preferred to do so on a voluntary basis to avoid 'the system'. 'They sort me out every now and again [cash-in-hand]', he admitted. 'But I ain't interested in it being official. If I stay in all day I get fucking bored, keeps things interesting having to man-mark one of them kids. Some of them are crazy, man.' A full-time job was a dim prospect: 'I ain't got no GCSEs, no A-levels. What the fuck am I goin' to do? I do alright.'

The fact that Lawrence was unable to resist the monitoring techniques of the probation service didn't prevent him from quickly re-entering the local underground economy. Indeed, on meeting me he asked whether I was interested in his latest service:

Lawrence: What's your name bruv?

JRT: James.

Lawrence: You a player, yeah?

JRT: No, Club Secretary.

Lawrence: You got [a] pay-as-you-go [electricity] meter?

JRT: No, why?

Lawrence: I've got a key innit, will get you fifty pounds' worth every time [it is used]. Selling it (£50 of credit) for a score (£20). Let me know if any of your people want it yeah?

This turned out to be a popular scheme. On the way back from away games Lawrence received repeated requests – many from fellow players, and one from Geoff – for cheap electricity and when dropped off at the Grove (before getting a cab to his girlfriend's flat in Boorman Oak) would dash from house to house collecting money or goods from friends and acquaintances in return for delivering cheap electricity.

Such trading between players and their associates was common. Having an effective strategy of survival in material terms meant forming and sustaining a complex set of human relationships over time, which, in turn, structured exchange relations. This set of relationships and the fluid conception of value it promoted entailed a corresponding bundle of assertions that influenced the players' approach to human variation. As in the café, money seldom changed hands; whether it be electricity credit, clothes, meat or marijuana, exchange relations coincided with social relations with the result that personal and subjective relationships between players and club associates were unmasked by the exchange of money. That is to say, a reliance on social relations rather than impersonal notions of exact value and market exchange – on trusting relationships with people rather than fleeting and objective allegiances – had a profound effect on the way players conceived of human difference.

For the economy to hold together, bonds of trust had to be maintained by all parties, and these seemed to centre on an ethic of survival linked to the areas of deprivation wherein such informal networks operated. The totality of personality thus remained within relationships of exchange, as dependency on a function was bound up with the bearer of that function and an awareness of the contingencies that bore upon him/her. This was illustrated towards the end of my fieldwork when, after learning that he would soon be a father, Alex vowed to 'go straight'. As I discovered, this did not mean extricating himself entirely from branches of the local economy which could be deemed illegal. Rather, Alex sought to distance himself from those niches which fed directly into wider networks of gang- and drug-related crime. Immediately he struggled to live with such reduced means, but after a month or so was managing with the help of friends from the club and the estate. He relied on Lawrence to provide credit for electricity in return for driving the pair to training, while he would do shifts in the café at Churchfield in exchange for meat and extra 'petrol money' from Gianni. Gianni also suspended the repayment of any money that Alex owed the club in fines for cautions (yellow cards) and dismissals (red cards).

Here personalism overcame impersonality, as deep-seated personal relations led to agreements and deals shot through with mutuality and charisma. To thrive within in the local underground economy of trade and casual labour required knowledge of the places that constituted the 'hubs' of this economy, as well as the relative position of the actors it contained. Most fundamentally, however, to succeed in entering and navigating the economy one had to cultivate a detailed knowledge of individual personalities. This entailed the integration of one's needs with the memories of past experiences pertaining to a given set of individuals, which, in turn, depended on a detailed and enduring engagement with the people concerned. It was through such an engagement that, over time, others were constituted as objects of knowledge.[3]

The sacrifices and benefits of exchange were experienced with a subtle and grateful 'being-for-one-another' not possible within reciprocal monetary exchanges (Simmel 1969).[4] And because players accepted that certain parts of reality – such as their personal relationships – could not be expressed according to logical or calculable operations, nor be reduced to accord with the axiomatic precision of money, the individuality and qualitative uniqueness of other players were incompatible with racial logic. That is, in players' evaluations of life and human difference, the individual wasn't levelled down to the generalised attributes of one 'race' or another. As already noted, the notions of difference they drew upon afforded more scope for individuality and, therefore, inaccuracy and confusion.

Attempting to pursue the issue of individuality further, I spoke to Reg and Gianni about the demands of running a club comprised of unpaid employees. Roping both men into the conversation was fruitful, as they quickly began swapping managerial anecdotes:

Reg: I have to be aware of as much as possible, otherwise it's chaos ... whether players work regular or casual, about their relationships, family life – you know, whether they have kids, how many ... Remember, they haven't signed a contract so don't have to turn up. It's up to them, and if they're quality I have to pick them or we're getting relegated. There's two different worlds in this league. You've seen it.

JRT: How do you make life easier for yourself in terms of building trust then?

Reg: I'll be honest, as far as possible I sign people I know ... or the mates of other players.

Gianni: It's always been like that at this level. Look, here, players all come in groups of three, four, five. Then there's the hardcore from the Grove, those from the old days.

Reg: Yeah, that way I know all about them. But I take it one hour at a time, let alone a week or a day at a time. How many times have we had to start matches with one or two players missing? But I can't be angry when they're struggling to get lifts or running for trains ... and this is a semi-pro league!

JRT: So you can't lump players together in terms of how reliable they'll be?

Reg: Not really. If anything the guys that work casual are the best because they're flexible. I mean look how many in the squad have coaching jobs or, you know, try to live week to week. But even then, I know that if a job comes up and they need the money, they might not be available. They have to live. We can't help with money.

Gianni: Yep. I'm happy to dish out meat and the odd packet of fags but we can't afford to pay players ... not sustainable James.

JRT: So there's no real profiling in terms of ethnic background as there seems to be at other clubs in the division?

Gianni: Not a chance. It won't work here. You should have seen what happened with the under-18s last year ... Andy and Ian had a proper falling out.

Having narrowly avoided 'a falling out' with Ian myself, I invited Gianni to elaborate:

JRT: What went on there then? I knew the under-18s more or less folded earlier this season but wasn't sure why.

Gianni: It was fucking hilarious I've gotta tell ya. Last season, that team played the best football I've seen in that league. Knocked the ball around, was really fluid ... Andy [the team manager] really had them playing. But then they lost a couple of matches and Ian [Andy's assistant] thought it was because some players were too laid back ... he meant the black players. Now you've got to remember that Andy's a Rasta, proper dreads and all that. But he's just laughed it off. At the beginning of this season, though, things were getting a little strained. Andy had to do something to change things, so he signed up his son, Jess – he was only 17 but was a quality little player.

JRT: Yeah, I remember. He played once for the first team this year.

Gianni: Yeah, that's him. Anyway, Ian has turned up to the game late because of work and so sat in the crowd. They're losing 1–0 with around 20 minutes to go so Ian is motioning to Andy to get some subs on. He sends Jess on, he sets up a goal for Felix [a 'white' player] and they get a draw. After the match, Ian goes up to Andy and says, 'I told you about having too many brothers in the team, look which two players combined for the goal.' So Andy's turned round and said, 'Jess ain't white, Ian, he's my son.' Ian had never met Jess before you see. They lost the replay and the side pretty much disintegrated after that.

JRT: That sums it up pretty well, then? No real shortcuts?

Gianni: As Reg said, you have to know each player and his circumstances.

Reg: Besides, if you're asking what I think you're asking, how am I supposed to know where every player is from? I don't think half of them know anyway. Trying to guess only ends up in problems, look at Ian ... As I said, the best way to get an advantage is to know each one. Taking note of which players they're close with, where they're living, what the work and family situation is. I've known most of these [players] for years anyway so it comes natural. Even then it's hard, what with players staying at their girlfriend's or mate's all the time, like Lawrence. I'm always getting confused. Things change, you know?

The conversation was telling. First, it reinforced the marginal position of Ian relative to others at the club in terms of understanding human variation. As observed in Chapter 5, the way Ian framed the issue was almost unintelligible to his own players, just as he struggled to understand why they didn't endorse the lore he used to frame this issue. Second, his error with regard to the ethnicity of Jess strengthened the impression that phenotypical markers were misleading in indicating membership of one or other 'racial' or ethnic group. He continued to draw simple links between these markers, the 'racial' groups which they supposedly signified, and the stereotypical traits of these groups. His method of framing experience therefore chimed with arguments attached to 'implicit racial bias'. However, as already noted, Ian was in a minority. Other figures at the club did not understand his view of the social world; for them, individual qualities were paramount in understanding a player's behaviour.

This foregrounding of individuality and a related sensitivity to the changing circumstances of one another meant it was difficult to see how any political orientation could crystallise or take hold in the players' lives. Indeed, the nature of the local underground economy shielded its participants from any direct political participation. By entering this economy, players opted to carve out niches for survival within rather than publicly challenge the polarising logic of neoliberal government (Soja 1989). Trading in the underground economy was therefore another facet of the denizen's rejection of a collective ideology and a culture rooted in the extension of *polis* (politics, policy, polity, police) and *civitas* (civil, civic, civilian, citizen).

It was the workings of this economy that led to Lawrence's conviction for burglary in 2008, after he resorted to illegal measures to repay a gambling debt to a local heavy. The spoils of the robbery meant Lawrence escaped the wrath of the neighbourhood gangster – but not the clutches of local law enforcement. This was Lawrence's third prosecution for burglary. On the second occasion he had been trying to acquire a 'plasma' television for Gianni, who later protested that a 36-inch device would have sufficed rather than the hulking 42-inch unit which Lawrence tried unsuccessfully to carry away from the scene of the robbery. By the time the set had been uninstalled from its wall brackets and was being manoeuvred out of a nearby window, the police had arrived at the property. Lawrence managed to flee, but not without kicking a pursuing police officer in the head. The police caught up with him only days later, whereupon the charge of assaulting a police officer was duly appended to that of burglary.

Gambling was Osment's vice, so on being released he vowed to steer clear of betting on horses and stake money solely on what he knew – football.

The Cheltenham Festival[5] came round less than two weeks after Osment had re-signed with OUFC, and the club held its collective breath to see whether he would stick to his resolution. He was aware of this concern and on the second day of the festival sought to ramp up the suspense before OUFC's away fixture versus Pixford United. Geoff and I were due to meet Lawrence, Alex and Josh at 5pm at the Patient Oak pub, adjacent to Boorman Oak station – a short walk from the Grove and Lawrence's favourite branch of *William Hill* – before setting off on the 80-mile round trip.

At 5.20pm Lawrence had yet to arrive. Alex repeatedly tried to phone him, but he didn't answer. Geoff was now approaching boiling point and on the verge of driving to the Grove to search the aforementioned bookie. 'Fuck it. Let's just go', said Alex. 'We've got enough. I'll text Reg and let him know.' 'No!' Geoff exclaimed. 'Remember what happened last week when he never played [OUFC had lost 3–2 to bottom of the table Halwyn Green]. We fucking need him ... Get in, we're going down there [to find him].' He started the engine and began a three-point-turn in preparation for the short journey to the Grove. A beaming Lawrence then emerged from the pub clutching a half-pint of lager. 'There he is, fucking joker!' Alex shouted. 'Where?!' replied Geoff. 'Oh for fuck's sake. Lawrence! Fucking get in!' Lawrence jumped in the front passenger seat and exchanged platitudes with us. 'What's that?' asked Geoff, managing to kindle a smile. 'Only a cheeky half, Geoff', Lawrence answered blithely. 'I'll be alright.' OUFC won the match 2–1, and despite remonstrating with himself about changing the meeting place from the Patient Oak (it had switched from Shinewater after Lawrence's release), Geoff had amassed nearly a dozen half-pint glasses by the end of the season.

The incumbencies of home

By the end of the season Lawrence had signed a pre-contract agreement with a professional club situated elsewhere in London, but vowed to help OUFC fight relegation for the remainder of the 2009/10 season. News of the signing quickly spread around the division and thereafter Lawrence was singled out by opposing clubs. This became obvious during a match against Winchford Tigers in April 2010, an encounter that underlined the clash of cultures evident when inner-city clubs came up against teams located towards and beyond the M25 ring-road. After the match kicked-off I noticed the manager of Winchford instructing his central defenders to commit fouls against Lawrence behind the referee's back in the hope he would retaliate. It wasn't long before these tactics had the desired effect. Lawrence began to push and pull the defenders, and at half-time things came to a head.

OUFC's substitutes and management, located in the home dugout, pro-tested to the referee that Lawrence was being targeted for rough treatment, and the Winchford manager couldn't resist adding his tuppence worth: 'Your lot are a bit fucking chirpy for a team stuck at the bottom', he said towards Lawrence, who reacted by striding towards him while unleashing a volley of abuse. The pair was separated by players of both sides, which rather than meliorating the situation only set off another series of minor skirmishes. Abuse was now being hurled in all directions, but one comment resonated beyond the standard vitriol heard at matches up and down the country every Saturday afternoon. Having come to his manager's defence, the captain of Winchford (who was also a central defender) became involved in an altercation with Lawrence, repeatedly imploring him to 'Fuck off and get a home life!' This infuriated Lawrence, who demanded that his disputant elaborate. 'What's that supposed to mean you little boy?! You don't know nothing about me', he replied.

The referee asked the managers of both teams to come to his room at half-time in order to be reprimanded and give their account of what had happened. Interestingly, only the manager of Winchford Tigers was cited in the referee's report and therefore faced an FA charge of misconduct for his part in the quarrel. The Winchford captain's refrain, despite being directed unequivocally at Lawrence, had obviously annoyed OUFC's other players, particularly 'Giro's' close friends. Alex had been ruled out of the match because of an injury picked up during a fixture the previous Saturday, and though in attendance (and well within striking distance) he had stayed out of the scuffle until the Winchford captain's remarks to Lawrence. At this point he charged into the fray to confront the captain, a cocktail of adrenaline and testosterone providing momentary relief from his ankle complaint. 'What the fuck do you mean by that you prick?!' Geoff immediately waded in to retrieve Alex, aware that the penalty for failing to control home fans was particularly harsh. The second half of the match was a non-event, and at the final whistle players exchanged the usual curt acknowledgements.

Lawrence was unavailable for the match the following Saturday (away at Langworth FC) because of a hamstring injury, but decided to make the trip in order to lend the team his support. Before away matches kicked off Geoff and I would have a beer together – our reward for successfully performing the routine preliminaries – and on this occasion Lawrence joined us holding a clutch of betting slips. As he sat rifling through them I asked about the scuffle the previous Saturday:

JRT: What was he saying to you, that defender?
Lawrence: Something about a home life ...
JRT: What did he mean by that? Strange one ...
Geoff: That's the problem with this league, everyone knows about everyone else ... Like a fucking mothers' meeting. On that *Footy Chat* there's pages of chat about him [Lawrence] and

him getting out. Who's he going to play for and all that, know what I mean? So ...

JRT: So word's got round you reckon?

Lawrence: Yeah I seen that Geoff, some people have nothing else man ... And that fool's telling me to sort out my home life. He don't know nothing about me ... I got a kid now. I'm not going back there Geoff ... [it was] the worst time of my life in the pen.

As the dialogue indicates, Lawrence was slightly unsure of me, perhaps because I had suddenly appeared at the club after his recent stint in prison. He registered this uncertainty by addressing his answers to Geoff, whether or not I had posed the questions. 'That kid had no idea what I have to do, how I get by ... I'm getting by every month, gonna get fit so I can earn money playing next year, man.' His complaints about a lack of understanding exhibited by people hailing from the suburban outposts of the Allied Districts League even extended to those who offered him assistance:

Lawrence: You see Tony, Geoff, from Top-Shop [Topsham] Manor?

Geoff: Yeah, for better or worse!

Lawrence: He came to see me all the time in the pen. He wants to fucking save me ... support me and that. That's fine, but he don't listen to me, man. Not hearing what I'm trying to say. I know it's because he feels sorry for me ... But you know what? I feel sorry for *him*. I knew when I came out I'd have my boys, my missus, my little boy. What's he got? Nothing, bruv. I feel sorry for him, that's what I'm saying. That's why I still return his messages now; he ain't got nothing else. But I signed for Gianni when I got out, because he knows me. He's known me and my brother from day. He listens to me and knows how to help me out, I know Oldfield (United) ain't got no money but he'll give me things here and there. And he knows I'd get more playing somewhere else, but I want to help him out and I feel like we appreciate each other.

In this way OUFC's players felt deeply misunderstood by the representatives of suburban clubs. The key here was the deep mutuality which marked the players' relationships with one another. These relationships were held together by intimacy, dialogue and negotiation, hardly values compatible with the notions of pity or charity which, according to Lawrence and his fellow squad members, characterised the attitude of suburban outsiders.

One of Winchford's substitutes on the day of the fracas was Edward Price, a right-back and native of Winchford who had started the season with OUFC before rejoining the club he had played for at youth team level. I spoke with him briefly in the café after the match:

JRT: What was the spat all about at half-time?

Edward: Not a lot, our manager's a lairy bastard.

JRT: What was all that about a 'home life'? That comment seemed to start things off among the players.

Edward: Everyone knows Lawrence's history. I don't think he's (Winchford's captain) meant anything by it. We know what it's like growing up down here.

JRT: How d'you mean?

Edward: (It's) mad down here for a youngster. It's easy for him to get in those situations. We understand that. A lot simpler up our way, I could see that when I was playing down with Oldfield.

JRT: So that's what he's getting at you think?

Edward: Yeah, I would say so. He just means – fucking – living within the law, holding down a job and relationship. D'you know what I mean? Look, when I was here, I had my parents and grandparents coming to watch every week. There wasn't ever any other family here … never. Just the same old few familiar faces: you, Gianni, Geoff or whatever. In Winchford they're there every week for most players … and other halves and kids. Here the players obviously don't have that … You know? A lot of 'em haven't been here long so don't have that support. They're bound to slip up in their home life. Where have they learned that from?

JRT: So at Winchford your 'home life' is there watching?

Edward: It ain't as simple as that. But, like I said, I don't think he meant anything by it.

Like those of his club captain, Edward's words were spoken with an air of commiseration. Both individuals seemed to imply that having a virtuous 'home life' was wholly incompatible with the demands of inner-city life. Whereas players like Lawrence and Alex took pride in their survival and the ongoing feat of supporting their families, Edward baulked at the number of stimuli available within the city, the sheer weight of which made some form of moral transgression inevitable. Such a place could never be conducive to the stability of 'home life' and, by extension, could never rightfully be called 'home'.

However, Lawrence and others in the squad saw the issue of morality as more supple; in approaching the question of what was morally acceptable, the same standards of negotiability and understanding were applied as marked the players' personal relationships with one another. The resulting moral code wasn't riveted to absolute conceptions of right and wrong. Rather, players were bound by necessity to a set of moral values that permitted flux and uncertainty. And here lay the root of non-understanding between the ethical universe of Winchford's players and that occupied by OUFC's denizens.

These ethical orientations were integral to respective versions of human difference that were similarly at odds. Edward's assertions about the ethical vacuum at OUFC were informed by his short stint at the club, but left much to supposition. They were formed at a distance and dominated by a sense of passivity; Edward and his captain – as well as Lawrence's former patron – offered advice but admitted no engagement with the moral dilemmas that (they imagined) confronted the young city-dweller. I asked for clarification on this issue:

JRT: So what are the main problems for these guys do you think?
Edward: In what way?
JRT: Well, the moral problems they face.
Edward: Like I said, no real support. They're coming from other countries and living in bad areas. You see the amount of killings among the black youth and that in these places. People have nothing to lose. [I] couldn't live in there, it's bound to have an effect. Morally, well, they don't know whether they're coming or going. Best thing is to stick together with family and that, but I'm not sure that's an option here. I was the only English player in the team here most weeks!

Edward had clearly embellished the impressions he had of the club during his three- month stay with press reports and hearsay. As a consequence, the fixed set of ethical values he promoted was attached to differences asserted and sustained in an imaginary realm. The absence of immediate relatives in the crowd, coupled with a lack of an 'English' (read white, British) presence in the team, was taken to indicate a dicey moral grounding. Edward put this down to 'immigration' and a related paucity of stable family units, which then impacted upon the life chances of players resident in areas where immigrants are traditionally housed.

On the other hand, the malleable set of ethical values advocated by OUFC's players was attached to human differences asserted and sustained in terms of the immediately given. That is, the (im)morality of an individual's conduct was judged on the basis of an intimate relationship with him and a deep familiarity with his circumstances. Indeed, in many cases the plight of an individual whose conduct had been called into question was knotted together with the life histories of other squad members. I asked Alex about Lawrence's transgressions of the law:

JRT: Do you think Lawrence will stay out of trouble now that he's going to be playing professional football?

Alex: [I] think so, yeah. You talk to him now and he's serious about football for the first time, man. Talking 'bout giving up fags even … But he needs the money from some place that ain't going to ask about his record or school stuff. Same for me, man. If I could get a one-er [£100] for playing football I'd be all over it. But we have to get by somehow.

JRT: So it's difficult to talk in terms of what's right and wrong?

Alex: Even coming from where we do, we all have things we won't do, man. But I know when I have to pay for my kid or like Giro, if I have to do what I have to to protect my family, then I'll do it. He never hurt anyone. And like I said, where else would he get the money from? Look at the people here and on the Grove queuing up to buy the stuff from him and keep it or sell it on. We was shitting it when he got nicked! But they [the police] don't care about what's going on, only when a nice gaff gets robbed … You can do what you want on the estate, sell whatever you like and get away with it. They don't care. [If] I go up to Meadson and start dealing, then I'd be fucked!

Whereas the connotations of the label 'impulsive' or 'instinctive' ensured that a series of ethical questions were posed (and judgements made) in relation to the black male, with his being, his behaviour and (later) his family identified as morally depraved, many factors served to quicken Alex's judgement before he would pronounce upon the (im)morality of another player's actions. The shortcuts offered by raciology were of no use here.

Denizenship and human difference: knowledge, power and ethics

Now we must return to the study's three ontological axes of knowledge, power and ethics. Though I have chosen to divvy up ethnographic analyses according to thematic concerns, it is important to keep sight of the study's key theoretical pivot points – those that in earlier chapters oriented my historical analysis of impulse and instinct as raciological ideas. Of course, surveying historical materials with the benefit of hindsight and alongside a canon of existing academic interpretations is a very different task to the one undertaken here. The challenge is to provide a similar treatment of ethnographic material in analysing how configurations of knowledge, power and ethics work to define and legitimate certain 'truths' within the broad area of human variation, and, more specifically, how these truths factor in the constitution of self and others.

Knowledge, power, ethics and human difference
at Oldfield United FC

When considering how knowledge featured as an ontological axis of players' conceptions of human difference, the issues of space and spatiality are central. The players' blithe expectation that other squad members would be foreign was related to other assumptions about the marginal spaces of the inner city and the inhabitants of these areas. This space was essentially viewed as alien territory: a series of places where resident non-citizens lived together. It was the experience of living within alien space that framed the issue of human difference and variation.

Any assertion about human difference had to make sense in terms of the players' everyday ecology. Assumptions about bodily markers, performative cues, and any other morsels of information deemed relevant to the issue of human variation were legible because they issued from a reading of the local landscape. Having passed through the filter of day-to-day existence, these bits of information were layered and contradictory but gained purchase because they featured in the players' strategies of survival.

Their acceptance of other people's alterity made them comfortable amid uncertainty on matters relating to ethnicity. This was revealed in their playful approach to determining the ethnic background of other players. In these attempts players consulted their own subjective experiences and elements of their own subjectivity; as suggestions were sifted through an inventory of experiences they were appraised according to elements of the self. So although players shrunk social reality in novel and nuanced ways, at other times they showed respect for the individuality of self and others. For example, the ability to safely navigate the local network of estates was developed by the individual through lessons he had learned from everyday experience. In the same way that signs of danger were successfully identified because of an individual's nous and know-how, the ability to thrive within the local underground economy, spotting opportunities and managing the related risks, entailed mastering the qualitative uniqueness of those involved. This approach to human variation was hardly compatible with the totalising logic of 'race', where, as we saw in the case of the impulsive black male, even exceptions serve to underline the rule.

The players' retreat into the local underground economy and their rejection of the state and state-sanctioned forms of activity, engagement and consumption more generally, points to the issue of power. As the ethnographic material attests, and others have previously argued (Lefebvre 1991; Foucault 1984a; Soja 1989, 1996, 2000; Harvey 1990, 2006, 2009), space is fundamental in any exercise of power. The logic that informed the players' rejection of citizenship and its requirements involved a deep resentment of the power of the state – represented most immediately by local government and the police – to shape urban space; in the case of the Grove, by abandoning it. Players' attempts to comprehend and classify human differences in terms of the constitution of self and other were related to this sense of spatial exclusion.

The tendency of the state to create alien territory was all the more obvious in a city where the gap between rich and poor is the largest in the developed world (Dorling 2010). However, as in previous chapters, the tendency to cast issues of power through the simple metaphor of domination – comprising active agents and passive recipients – was resisted, it is important here to see power operating within a complex configuration of relay points. While it is impossible to deny the conditions imposed upon the nucleus of OUFC's players, we should also concentrate on their strategies of resistance as well as the way they reinscribed the relations of power within which they figured. As we have seen, notions of human difference featured prominently in such everyday behaviours of resistance and reinscription.

Though players recognised that they and their families had been deposited in estates typically home to the poor and 'foreign', they possessed little, if any, desire to travel outside the bounds of the local area. The local conditions which defined life on the estate(s) informed judgements on the sameness and difference of others. In this way players reinscribed the boundaries within which they lived, whether in terms of the limits of an urban estate or the M25 frontier. But having resigned themselves to life within areas of urban deprivation, the players had come up with various strategies of survival.

As staple members of the 'precariat', the majority of OUFC's players in current employment worked unstable, cash-in-hand jobs. Like the widening gap of wealth inequality – thrown into relief by the close juxtaposition of rich and poor in certain areas of inner-city London – this surge of precarious wage work has been a characteristic result of the neoliberal policies pursued in Britain since the late 1970s (Harvey 2005; Hall 2011). The resulting sense of durable expulsion drew players into the underground economy and strengthened the appeal of casual work. Both tactics of survival – by no means mutually exclusive – involved appraising an individual's character-istics and circumstances carefully, and in this way empowered the young man who had fostered such a measured sense of judgement. The same was true of a player's abilities on the pitch, which were explained by his suc-cessful negotiation of local circumstances. It was only where weaknesses were concerned that players called upon groups to dilute responsibility. As I have already noted, the players' delineation of these groups lay flush with their view of the local landscape, allowing them to shrink reality in ways that made sense while formulating nuanced moral judgements; judgements not possible within the deterministic regime of racio-logic.

These judgements relate to the study's third and final axis, ethics. The set of ethical values held by players were conditioned by an imperative of survival, itself a response to spatial constraints. The moral dimension of this imperative involved a wavering allegiance to home; this saw estates like the Grove cast as ethical borderlands: 'Living on borders and [in] margins, keeping intact one's shifting and multiple identity and integrity, is like trying to swim in a new element, an "alien" element that has become familiar – never comfortable ... but home' (Anzaldúa 1987: unpaged preface). To survive required a withdrawal from and/or refusal of citizenship and its demands, along with related notions of right and wrong, which together influenced the players' conceptions of human difference. Players called upon fluid conceptions of right and wrong, as well as an intimate knowledge of that individual's personal circumstances, when making moral judgements about the conduct of another young man. And because the areas that players lived in were seen as containers for alien elements – where 'everyone is foreign' and most likely, poor – the ethic of survival and the related underground economy necessitated an intimate, frequent interaction with these other aliens, with mutually dependent relationships being forged between them.

In this way the nuances of the immediately given shaped players' subjectivities and the way that notions of human difference figured therein. The fixed moral code applied to the behaviour of OUFC's players by suburban outsiders was infuriating because it promoted distance and passivity; such rigid moral standards courted the logic of 'race', a logic which forecloses engagement with personalism and qualitative uniqueness.

Having found little in the way of raciology when investigating the conceptions of human difference subscribed to at OUFC, in the study's final chapter I compare and contrast these conceptions with the stubborn raciological ideas examined in Part 1; in doing so I attempt to draw conclusions with regard to the form and function of raciology as well as reflect on the study's strengths, limitations and the central implications of its findings.

Chapter 7

Conclusion

In raising the stories told in foregoing chapters to the level of theoretical attention, in this final chapter I venture some tentative conclusions on the issue of raciology, its functions, and the habits which see raciological ideas reproduced in social life. More specifically, I contrast the raciological ideas examined in Part 1 with the schemas of human variation encountered in Part 2. The chapter ends with a discussion of the study's main strengths and limitations, as well as the key theoretical implications suggested by its findings.

To begin, let us take the emergence of the 'impulsive' black sportsman as an object of knowledge. What conclusions can be drawn from this history in terms of the form and function of raciological ideas? In this history one can trace the transformation of a bundle of thoughts, hopes, fears, dreams, memories, etc. into an empirically 'proven' raciological idea. Faced with a newly minted, mechanistic conception of the natural world, British explorers and plantation owners justified their actions in terms consonant with its principles. Others followed in their stead, with various experts, specialists and technocrats striving to prove that their immediate, short-term, professional and political tactics were qualified by a scientific grasp of the natural world. In revisiting the distinction between *connaissance* and *savoir*, these individuals translated the distinction between rationality and impulsiveness, contained in the orthodoxy of Descartes and Newton – elemental principles approaching the depth of *savoir* – into raciological forms of 'surface' knowledge. Even from the narrow standpoint of a specific raciological idea, here we have proof of Laski's (1997 [1936]) argument that the scientific revolution was popular because it lent powerful psychological aid to the rationalising force of capitalism.

More specifically, these 'experts' made impulsivity and the 'impulsive' black male into an epistemological artefact that could be individuated, measured and described within the Newtonian frame of absolute space and time; the cumulative effects of their efforts created new (or reinforced existing) possibilities for being. But besides strengthening the argument that raciological ideas are socially constructed and that these constructions serve certain political and economic ends, the history of the 'impulsive' black sportsman tells us more about the function of raciology.

The moves of reasoning endorsed by the idea, as well as serving the needs of trade and business, relieved its adherents of any obligation to engage openly with others. That is to say, the idea foreclosed the prospect of unconditional dialogue with or regarding particular 'types' of people, because 'experts' had already set the terms of any such engagement. Forms of discussion or investigation informed by the idea were shallow and nakedly instrumental; they served to harden the original set of assumptions and/or economise the 'impulsive' nature of the black male as given in advance. This underlines the circular logic of so-called empirical investigations ordered by racial distinctions and casts doubt upon their pretensions to scientific objectivity.

In broader terms, here we see the appeal of habitualising a racial optic. It allows devotees to remain ontologically secure, making instant and certain judgements rather than forming these judgments in an enduring, open interaction with the social world. That this appeal is sanctioned by certain institutional authorities only reinforces the manner in which advocates constitute themselves and others as objects of raciological knowledge.

OUFC's players framed the issue of human variation in an altogether different manner. The relational notions they held were forged during the course of deep and enduring engagement. Alex's ideas about why one player was fast or another was wily were informed by a detailed knowledge of that player's life and its distinctive urban setting. Nothing was given in advance bar the fact that his friends and associates would most likely be 'foreign', and this acceptance of alterity made him comfortable in the face of uncertainty regarding the ethnicity of others. The resulting approach to ethnicity was playful and open-ended. This was evident in Slemie's typology of flatulence. His way of classifying the foul aromas of the changing room meshed together ethno-national, religious and even neighbourhood referents. The result was confusion. But just as Reg joked with his players about the logic each of them employed in trying to guess at Slemie's ethno-national background, the guesses which corresponded to Slemie's typology were self-consciously frivolous and underdetermined.

The ethic of survival that players lived by required that a portrait of each friend and associate be created and sustained which showcased their individuality. These portraits were not fixed. Players had a keen eye for the contingencies that figured in the lives of friends/teammates; knowledge of people in their ambit was combined with a reading of the local landscape, but not reduced to it. Indeed, players accepted that the qualitative unique-ness of people could not be expressed according to exact measurement or calculation. It was the uniqueness of others that framed the players' encounters with them, while the impressions and thoughts that gave these encounters meaning were continually and necessarily renewed. Unlike those 'experts' and other interested parties, eager to prove that the chaos of nature could be reduced to law through the exercise of reason, players realised that the issue of human variation wasn't amenable to narrow categorisation.

For Alex or Lawrence to 'get by' within the local underground economy he had to nurture relationships of exchange capable of accommodating the totality of individual personality and individual agency. Alex knew that in order to receive free electricity from Lawrence he must provide him with lifts to training. To keep his end of the bargain he had to consider Lawrence's gambling habit, the requirements of signing on, the demands of fatherhood, and his love of a 'cheeky half'. This information, combined with a detailed knowledge of the local landscape, meant that Alex could sometimes locate Lawrence if he had not arrived at the appointed time and place. But he wasn't always right; the vicissitudes of Lawrence's life meant that predicting his behaviour was an unruly affair.

In this way the shortcuts offered by raciology did not square with the players' experience of the world. Their livelihood depended on a perpetual and intimate commerce with those who shared their plight. The impressions they garnered from relationships with friends and associates had to be rich, yet flexible and unfinished; to replace these impressions with the faded replicas of routinised detachment would not have done. It is this routine, this impoverishing of experience, which raciology gives structure to. To banish the virtual realities brought to life by raciological lore (Gilroy 2000) it will not be enough to uproot the feelings associated with 'race'; in addition, we must see a commitment to discard the experiential patterns ordered by raciology.

These feelings dwell in realm of thoughts and emotions, where attraction mingles with revulsion, and measurement and calculation are impossible. They are given shape in the 'real' world, where every thesis has its antithesis, and x can be identified, quantified and posited relative to y. This 'making real' warrants a failure to engage in the social realm, and passes off *a priori* judgements as genuine understanding. But OUFC's players relied on such understanding, recognising that their conception of human variation made any number of meanings possible and the lack of any final meaning more or less inevitable.

As well as providing a summary of the study's key findings and what they say about people's approaches to the issue of human variation, I should pause to reflect critically on the study's credentials. Here I provide a brief, critical examination of the study by identifying its strengths, limitations and the key implications of its findings for future research.

In terms of the study's strengths, I think the programme of study undertaken here is informed by a novel approach to the examination of 'racial' difference and conceptions of human variation more broadly. First, I hope to have demonstrated that it is more fruitful to excavate the logic which underpins particular assertions of racial difference rather than focus our attention on the point beyond which expressions of this so-called difference become 'racist' because they offend a generally accepted set of moral sensibilities. Second, I hope to have shown that it serves us better – as far as possible – to trace the historical emergence and development of a single raciological strain, rather than address our efforts to general, unspecified expressions of racism. The elements which contribute to the construction and sustenance of particular raciological ideas – as noted in the case of the 'impulsive' black male – have far-ranging institutional sources. It is these sources and the way they intersect with the utility of the idea, its methods of verification, and the short-term objectives of those peddling it, which are worthy of sociological attention.

While the juncture between the study's historical and ethnographic components may (despite my best efforts) be a little jarring – a point I will revisit shortly – I think the combination of these methods provides a richness which the study may have lacked had one method of inquiry been adopted at the exclusion of the other. I hope that my preoccupation with people's possibilities for being (proffered by Hacking), the relationship of these possibilities to conceptions of human variation, and the opportunities for action which attach thereto provide a sense of continuity which the study lacks in its deployment of methods.

The foregrounding of Hacking's ontological scheme provides, I think, another of the study's strengths. That is, Hacking's (2002a) generalisation of Foucault's 'permanent critique of ourselves' (1984b: 43) and the ways we are 'constituted as subjects of our own knowledge' (ibid: 49) to include 'all manner of constitutings' (Hacking 2002a: 4), provides a way out of the idealist vs. materialist bind which often dogs the study of 'race' and 'racial' difference. His focus on the provenance of ideas as well as the ways in which they are essentialised through use in institutions allows us to tack between the idealist and materialist poles, without relegating either the realm of ideas or that of institutional and/or structural phenomena to a subordinate role. Throughout the study we have seen how the interplay between ideas, material structures, and practices has shaped the formation of labels, types, names, etc. which help people to make sense of human variation. In this way possible self-understandings have both informed and been shaped by a range of practices – political, economic, religious, etc. It is therefore important that historical ontology legislates for the arrow of causation running in both directions (Taylor 1989).

However, discussing the virtues of Hacking's scheme also points to one of the study's limitations. Though I have paused wherever possible to take stock of the possibilities for being available to people in terms of conceptions of human variation, space constraints and other basic practicalities have prevented me from applying ontological analysis more evenly and continuously throughout the study. Doing so may have provided greater insight into the regularities laid down by depth knowledge – *savoir* – and how these shape the utterances, articles, reports, etc. – instances of *connaissance* – of those professing institutional expertise. This criticism also holds for the application of Foucault's three axes of knowledge, power and ethics; these might have ordered analysis more consistently throughout the course of the study, uncovering with greater specificity the manner in which Foucault's axes align and articulate in the production, verification and dissemination of 'truth'.

A further criticism also relates to the precepts of historical ontology. The study's findings suggest that these precepts may be underdeveloped with regard to space and, more specifically, with spatial possibilities for being. The methodological and philosophical scheme Hacking develops out of Foucault's 'historical ontology of ourselves' privileges the analysis of subjectivity and more general categories of knowledge – according to Foucault's axes of knowledge, power and ethics – over *time*. Though he hints at a spatial dimension in describing how the possibilities for being are 'woven around us', this allusion to the relationship between ontology and space is not followed up. It is important to examine the different ways in which time and space are conceived, and to explore how the possibilities for being are shaped as much by spatial circumstances as by the specificities of a given temporal setting. In doing so, we might remedy the privileging of time within historical ontology, broadening our scope to include an examination of the spatio-temporal possibilities for being, along with the choices or actions that attach to these possibilities.

A balance which might have been struck more effectively – particularly in Part 1 – is that which weighs expository against critical modes of commentary. While I have tried to restrict passages which deal exclusively and/or extensively with contextual or explanatory material to endnotes, at times it has been necessary to include some of this material in the main body of the text. Indeed, in many cases the critical commentary which subsequently appears is bound up with the context in which statements are made, reports released, etc. By the lights of the distinction between *savoir* and *connaissance*, the elemental rules laid down by the former, and the statements made within the institutional settings of the latter, at times require both expository and critical commentary in order to arrive at a level of understanding which is sufficient in terms of richness and depth. Nevertheless, the balance between these modes of commentary could have been struck more finely.

My next reflexive criticism concerns the juncture between the study's historical and ethnographic components. As already noted, though I endeavoured to gloss the terminal point of Part 1 as the point of departure for Part 2, the transition between modes of analysis may be sharper than I had intended. The task was more difficult given that the historical and ethnographic investigations operate on different scales. The historical examination seeks to chart the emergence and consolidation of the 'impulsive' black sportsman as an object of knowledge throughout the passage of British history. The argument and analysis contained in Part 1 therefore has a broader sweep than the ethnographic observations contained in Part 2, which are naturally confined to local horizons. This shift in scale begs the further question of replicability. It is possible to defend the conclusions of Part 1 in terms of their application within British society. However, elements of the argument put forward in Part 2 focus on the nuances of local conditions and their influence on people's conceptions of human difference, at the expense of taking discussion to a higher plane of generality.

Finally I should outline what I think are the study's main implications for subsequent research. The first of these echoes my earlier assertion regarding the importance of examinations of raciological ideas, as opposed to more broad and generic conceptions of racism. I have already underlined the virtues of work which takes strains of raciology as its object. We stand a better chance of challenging (and potentially banishing) assertions of racial difference if we reach a level of understanding where strands of raciology are unravelled, with the history and utility of these ideas laid bare. The study has tried to access this body of raciological ideas through sporting institutions and the forums they provide. As detailed in Part 1, the raciological idea of impulsivity manifests itself in numerous institutional settings with far-reaching effects in terms of the formation of subjects and the construction of categories, labels, etc. Ideas partaking of racio-logic can therefore be found within many institutions; the task is to excavate these ideas in terms of the possibilities they offer in the constitution of self and other as objects of knowledge. This brings me to the study's next implication for further research.

By examining the way in which possibilities for being can involve material of a raciological nature – as well as ideas, categories, etc. identified with other notions of human difference – and the impact on life choices should such material be incorporated in the constitution of self or other, the study has emphasised the need for further investigation into the processes whereby subjectivity and subjectivation become racialised. Many valuable studies have been undertaken which address either the history of subjectivity or the relationship between subjectivation and the workings of power (Elias 1968; Foucault 1977; Hacking 2002a; Rose 2000; Taylor 1989), a number of which I have drawn upon here. However, there appears to be a gap when it comes to the relationship between subject-formation and racio-logic, and, of course, the possibilities for action which are at stake in this connection.

The study also has implications for the sociological examination of urban settings and urban life. I have argued that the tradition of cosmopolitanism – no matter how many dimensions are added to its conceptual core – may not suffice in making sense of the contemporary city.

Indeed, we have seen how the traditions of liberalism and cosmopolitanism tend to create outsiders, figures such as the denizen. Further empirical work might test the category of denizenship, giving it greater depth and clarity, and continue to interrogate formulations structured by the principles of cosmopolitanism.

Notes

I Introduction

1 This definition appears as part of Gilroy's argument that 'race' and raciology are in crisis:

> It is impossible to deny that we are living through a profound transformation in the way the idea of 'race' is understood and acted upon. Underlying it there is another, possibly deeper, problem that arises from the changing mechanisms that govern how racial differences are seen, how they appear to us and prompt specific identities. Together, these historic conditions have disrupted the observance of 'race' and created a crisis for raciology, the lore that brings the virtual realities of 'race' to dismal and destructive life.
>
> (2000: 11)

2 Foucault's introduction to (and commentary on) Kant's *Anthropology*, presented in 1961 as his 'secondary' doctoral thesis, was published in 2008 by MIT Press (see Foucault 2008b).

3 In *The Order of Things* (1970) Foucault argued that all periods of history possess underlying conditions of truth (which together form an episteme) that constitute what is acceptable as, for example, scientific discourse. He wrote *Archaeology of Knowledge* (2002 [1972]) in order to deal with the reception of *The Order of Things*. This represented Foucault's main excursion into considerations of methodology, whereby he provided an anti-humanist excavation of the human sciences, particularly psychology and sociology.

4 The axes of knowledge, power and ethics are discussed in Hacking (2002a: 1–26) and Foucault (1984b).

5 I should situate Hacking's notion of 'historical ontology' in relation to other terms/devices in the Foucauldian lexicon, such as 'episteme', 'discursive formation' and 'archaeology'. Foucault's archaeological method dug up the 'historical *a priori*' of a time and place; this pointed towards the conditions of the possibilities of knowledge within a 'discursive formation' or 'episteme'. These conditions are, as Hacking states, 'as inexorable, there and then, as Kant's synthetic *a priori*. Yet they are at the same time conditioned and formed in history, and can be uprooted by later, radical, historical transformations' (2002a: 5). While historical ontology generalises Foucault's concern with how 'we' constitute ourselves to examine a range of constitutings, it scales down his ambition to unravel entire discursive formations and the 'depth' knowledge which comprises its unconscious underlying structure. The method of inquiry laid out

by Hacking allows us to identify the postulates which, in approaching the depth of *savoir*, allow *connaissance* to run its course.

2 Plato, property and humanity

1 Interestingly, in the aftermath of Ron Atkinson's rant about Marcel Desailly, Hansen (2004) wrote of the extenuations of live broadcasting:

> Television makes us say things we don't often mean. There is a part of every television pundit who fears that in some moment of madness they will be the victim of the 'open-mic'. That one stupid, ill-judged comment that does not represent their views at all will be picked out and used to define their character for ever more.

2 On this score we should also consider the implications of Elias's evolutionism. Elias – having trained initially as a medical student – argued that the biological and social dimensions of the organism–person were indivisible (Kilminster 1989; Quilley 2004). In his later works such as *Involvement and Detachment* and *The Symbol Theory*, Elias developed a Comtean theory of knowledge in which biological and social dimensions of the human condition were understood as emergent phenomena at different levels of integration. However, these lines of inquiry are implicit in his earlier works. In terms of the 'conditions of possibility' for Elias's evolutionism, the epistemological framework centring on integrative levels and emergent dynamics has a long history in biology. Quilley (2010) has reviewed the history of 'holism', 'vitalism' and 'organicism' in twentieth-century biology – and particularly the tradition of embryology and developmental biology identified with Waddingon, Needham and the Theoretical Biology Club. He subsequently argued that Elias was heavily influenced by an organicist zeitgeist that had become subtly paradigmatic in the 1940s, around the time of the elaboration of the 'modern synthesis' in genetic-evolutionary theory. As well as its possibilities for being in terms of knowledge, the hierarchy of organisational relations associated with the theory of integrative levels certainly has implications with regard to Foucault's other axes of power and ethics: what are the consequences for speakers and subjects of projecting the organicist theorisation of 'organisation' and whole/part relations in biology into the social world (dubbed as 'levels of integration')? What ethical values attend this hierarchy of organisational relations?

3 Menn (1998) has provided a thorough examination of the relationship between Augustinian and Cartesian philosophy.

4 For a fuller consideration of the dawning of modernity see Toulmin (1990).

5 The English Navigation Acts were a series of laws which restricted foreign shipping. The Acts were originally aimed at excluding the Dutch from the profits made by English trade. Resentment against the Navigation Acts was a cause of the Anglo-Dutch Wars (1652–4, 1665–7, 1672–4 and 1781–4) and the American Revolutionary War (1775–83).

6 This is not to say that Newton and Descartes agreed on every point. Though their names appear in juxtaposition throughout the chronology detailed here, as John Dewey noted in the Gifford lectures of 1929, Descartes was 'for a time the great rival of Newton for supremacy in the scientific world' (1930 [1929]: 111).

7 To compare notions of 'Negro' idleness with similar ideas regarding Malay, Filipino and Javanese 'natives', see Syed Hussein Alatas's *The Myth of the Lazy Native* (1977).

8 Scottish philosopher and economist David Hume was more candid, and as such did not require the figure of the child through which to refract his opinions on racial difference:

> I am apt to suspect the negroes, and in general all the other species of men (for there are four or five different kinds) to be naturally inferior to whites. There never was a civilized nation of any other complexion than white, nor even any individual eminent either in action or speculation ... there are NEGROE slaves dispersed all over Europe, of which none ever discovered any symptoms of ingenuity.
>
> (1964 [1753]: 252n)

So, though Hume granted 'Negroe slaves' a place at the table of humanity, this came at the price of innate inferiority. For him, they possessed no capacity for rational thought, no 'ingenuity'.

9 The form that capitalism took in Britain was called economic liberalism, a broad ideology consonant with the cosmopolitan ethic and its stance in relation to universalism. In political terms liberalism was identified with the philosophy of figures such as Locke, Hume and J. S. Mill. However, regimes of liberal government did not translate the formulations of these philosophers directly and exactly into government policy; though this is not to say, of course, that the touchstones of liberal philosophy evident in the work of Locke, Hume and Mill cannot be detected in regimes of liberal government, particularly where exclusionary practices are concerned. Here I seek to avoid, on one hand, an overly canonical view of liberalism, and on the other, one too occupied with instances where the practices of liberal government deviate from the philo-sophical tradition of liberalism or take their cue from less elevated sources. Following Rose (1999), I approach liberalism as an ethos of governing which endeavours to tack between governing too much, and thereby inhibiting the free operation of those institutions upon which sound government depends – families, personal autonomy and responsibility, and above all, the market – and governing too little, and thereby failing to establish the conditions of order, stability and civility which enable the strategies of liberal government (i.e. limited intervention) to operate effectively. In the economic realm, liberalism likewise entails little or no direct intervention in the operation of free markets and the attendant mechanisms of production and exchange. Free individuals become the subjects of a contractual agreement from which liberal institutions derive. By expressing their consent, subjects charge such institutions with creating and sustaining an environment in which the family, the market, notions of autonomy and respon-sibility, etc. can operate freely. More specifically, this means sustaining a free market in labour and removing any factors that might hamper the labourer when entering into production through the wage contract (ibid).

10 Here space is viewed as an already existing, immovable, unchanging and con-tinuous framework – initially understood as empty of matter – within which dis-tinctive objects can be identified (located on a grid, for example). Such space is amenable to Euclidean geometry and other standardised forms of calculation and measurement. Plots of private property, bounded by walls or fences, are a good example of such spaces, as are the urban grids that demarcate so many of the world's cities. In both cases space can be measured and calculated, and ultimately, controlled (Harvey 1973; 2009).

11 Kramer (1997) has chronicled the origins of private property as found in Locke's writings.

12 According to Kant, Burmese women wore indecent clothing and took pride in getting impregnated by Europeans, the Hottentots were lazy and gave off a nasty stench, and the Javanese were conniving thieves. For a fuller discussion of Kant's remarks in his *Geography* see Eze (1997; 2001).

13 'Hospitality means the right of a stranger not to be treated as an enemy when he arrives in the land of another. One may refuse to receive him when this can be done without causing his destruction' (Kant, cited in Benhabib 2004: 27).

14 As Azade Seyhan has argued:

> German Romanticism's real and symbolic links to the French Revolution inhere both in the passion generated by ideals of equality, fraternity and freedom that resounded beyond French borders in 1789 and in mourning an irretrievably lost world of unity and harmony. Thus, the French Revolution also came to represent a shift in the understanding of movement in history. The Judeo-Christian tradition has represented time as the agent of sacred history, whereas the Revolution became in the Romantic mind an allegory of disruption in time.
>
> (2009: 6)

15 Individuals such as Hölderlin, Hegel and the young Schelling saw their task as the reunification of reason and nature (Taylor 1989). Though they saw the initial breach as necessary for man to develop powers of reason and abstraction, the destiny of humankind was conceived as a return to nature in which reason and desire would be synthesised at an elevated level. As Hölderlin put it in *Hyperion Fragment*: 'Like lovers' quarrels are the dissonances of the world. Reconciliation is in the midst of strife and all things separated come together again. The veins separate and return in the heart and everything is one unified, eternal glowing Life' (quoted in Unger 1975: 21). The newly unified relation between reason and nature would manifest itself in a new politics and culture, the seat of which would be Germany.

16 Like Rousseau, Herder had an interest in the origins of language, an interest which stimulated the emergence of new attitudes towards music in the eighteenth century. Both Rousseau and Herder suggested that the first language was 'music'. This gave rise to the idea that something was lost in the move from instinctual expression to conventionalised social articulation (Bowie 2007; Thomas 1995), a loss connected to 'longing' in the work of Hoffmann and taken up by Friedrich Schlegel and Novalis. The notion of 'longing' expressed the feeling that humans were no longer at home in the modern world, and that music may restore something of the expressive immediacy sacrificed in the move from pre-semantic to semantic expression.

17 Unsurprisingly, the expressive view came to give art an exalted status in terms of self-exploration and-discovery. Artistic creation became the paradigm vehicle for giving full definition to imperfectly formed impulses. This entailed a change from the traditional view of art as mimesis, in which art imitated reality. In its stead emerged the idea of art as expression; here artistic endeavour made something manifest while also realising it, and making it complete. This empowered the artist and gave rise to the particular Romantic concept of the symbol. Unlike allegory, the symbol provides a form of language in which something otherwise beyond our reach becomes visible. It cannot therefore be separated from what it reveals, as a sign can be separated from its referent. This conception of the symbol was partly inspired by Kant's third critique and, more specifically, his notion of the aesthetic object as manifesting an order for which no adequate concept is available (Taylor 1989).

18 The centrality of territory and national difference within this view helps to explain its stance regarding 'outsiders' – people without a territory – and with them Herder's negative view of European Jews (1912: 702). Yet it also accounts for his anti-racism and anti-imperialism (Bhatt 1999).

19 He argued that his cures (which were predominantly applied to nervous complaints) were effected via the workings of ephemeral universal fluid which passed through the cosmos and human body alike, the blockage or lack of which explained all forms of illness. The cure involved the administering of magnetic strokes (using a magnetiser soaked in magnetic fluid) to re-establish the patient's relation to cosmic harmony.

20 Indeed, Freud's essay on the uncanny (2003) [1919] contains a psychoanalytical interpretation of Hoffmann's *The Sandman* (2008) [1816].

21 In fact, one of Long's sources – as pointed out by Peter Fryer – was the *Universal History* (published between 1736–65 and containing entries by George Sale, George Psalmanazar, Archibald Bower among numerous others) which plumped for the view that Africans were 'lazy, thievish, and addicted to all kinds of lust ... If we look into those few manufactures and handicrafts that are amongst them, we shall find them carried on with the same rude and tedious stupidity' (cited in Fryer 1984: 153–54).

22 Consider the following account which appeared in the *English Review* (1788: 277):

> Black is a colour which nature abhors. The eye startles and shrinks from it when it is first presented; nothing inanimate wears this horrid gloom; and, in the living world, a black skin is peculiar to animals of the most odious and loathsome kind.

23 For a fuller description of the economic imperatives of the slave trade and anti-slavery, see Williams (1964) and Drescher (1987).

24 This conception of rational acquisitive man, acting in his own interests, had been gathering momentum ever since Adam Smith wrote of the butcher, brewer and baker acting not from benevolence, 'but from their regard to their own interest' in *The Wealth of Nations* (1986 [1776]: 119). And while 'economic man' was not explicitly formulated until John Kells Ingram's *History of Political Economy* in 1888 (and eventually in *homo economicus* by Pareto in 1908), this current of thought was very much in evidence in Britain throughout the nineteenth century.

25 Hyde Park was the scene of rioting in 1866 following the defeat of the Reform Bill put forward by the Reform League, an organisation created in 1865 to campaign for manhood suffrage rights and the ballot in Great Britain (Nym Mayhall 2003). The British government's suspension of Habeas Corpus in Ireland, precipitated by a call made by the Irish Republican Brotherhood's Council of War for an immediate uprising, also triggered disturbances that year (McGee 2007).

26 Tarde's notion of the group mind – central to which were the forces of imitation and innovation (see Tarde 2005 [1890]) – was taken up and developed by the French sociologist and social psychologist Gustav Le Bon, influencing his theories of crowd psychology and herd behaviour. 'A crowd is at the mercy of all external exciting causes, and reflects their incessant variations. It is the slave of the impulses which it receives', wrote Le Bon. 'Like a savage, it is not prepared to admit that anything can come between its desire and the realisation of its desire' (2008 [1895]: 18–20).

3 Darwin, Freud and 'good instincts'

1 For example, we can see the influence of Plato's oppositions between higher and lower life, and Lyell's re-figuring of geological time, in the conception of evolution, as well as Malthus's notion of competition in Darwin's scheme of natural selection (Toulmin 1982).

2 This abiding masculinity can be explained by the changing imperatives of Britain's colonial project. As these shifted from the conquest of the African landscape to the conquest of African people, so the dominant metaphors of conquest became masculine rather than feminine. While images of the African continent as a (female) body whose landscape and cavities warranted (male) exploration had dominated in the past, the focus was now on the conquest of its (male) inhabitants and the dual imagery of the savage (McClintock 1995).

3 The poem was originally published in the popular magazine *McClure's*, with the subtitle 'The United States and the Philippine Islands', and has been the subject of competing interpretations. Some readers thought it supported the view that white people had an obligation to rule over and encourage the cultural development of people from other ethno-cultural backgrounds until Western ways had been fully adopted by subject populations. Others focused on its philanthropic implications, i.e. that the rich had a moral duty to help 'the poor' to progress, whether the poor invited such intervention or not (Chapman 2002).

4

> The misunderstanding of passion and reason, as if the latter existed as an entity by itself, and not rather as a state of the relations between different passions and desires; and as if every passion did not contain in itself its own quantum of reason.
>
> (Nietzsche 1973 [1901]: 387)

5 Here he called upon an outlook enshrined during the last few decades of the nineteenth century. This saw time imbued with a spatial dimension (Fabian 1983). McClintock has described this shift: 'Time became a geography of social power, a map from which to read a global allegory of "natural" social difference. Most importantly, history took on the character of a spectacle' (1995: 23).

6 *The Golden Bough: A Study in Magic and Religion* was a comparative study of mythology and religion. Frazer argued that ancient religions were fertility cults revolving around the worship (and sacrifice) of a sacred king. Frazer cited evidence garnered during his time with the Australian 'savages' as part of his wider attempt to define the common elements of religious belief (Fraser 1990).

7 These refer to the ideas, beliefs and values elaborated by a collectivity, but which are not reducible to individual constituents. Collective Representations were central to Durkheim's search for the sources of social solidarity (see Durkheim 1990 [1912]), being created through the intense interaction of religious rituals. However, being richer than individual activities they come to be autonomous of the group from which they emerged.

8 The discourses of 'culture contact' which sought to pathologise the African mind echoed earlier concerns over the fitness of Jews for the rigours of urbanisation and modernity. These emerged around the end of the nineteenth century and identified the Jewish mind as the site of supposed fragility. As Sander Gilman (1993: 130) has argued, these claims leant on fudged statistics about levels of mental illness (more precisely madness and hysteria), citing the 'resultant inability of the Jew to deal with the complexities of the modern world'. The fact that Britain's colonial subjects were being beaten with the same stick says a lot about the dominance of psychological discourse in the twentieth century.

9 With one eye on the longevity of his career, he shamelessly endorsed the value of these findings: 'Educational authorities dealing with the backward native races cannot afford to neglect the teachings of anthropology and psychology. If it is proved that the physical basis of "mind" in the East African differs from that of the European, it seems quite possible that efforts to educate these backward races on European lines will prove ineffective and potentially disastrous' (Sequeira 1932: 581).

10 In America similar concerns had been aired following emancipation, where the national census reported that of the 17,000 insane and feeble-minded in the United States, almost 3,000 were black. If these staggering statistics were correct, the incidence of mental illness among free blacks was eleven times that of slaves and six times that of whites (Gilman 1985). The intimation was that blacks were not fit to be autonomous subjects and independent citizens. For them freedom was debilitating and only heightened risks of ill health.

11 'Mau Mau' is a disputed term. According to Fred Majdalany (1962), it derives from a coded-language game played by Kikuyu boys and came to be used by British authorities as a shorthand label for the Kikuyu ethnic community. Former 'Mau Mau' detainee, J. M. Kariuki (1975), claims it was ascribed by the British to rebelling Kikuyu in an attempt to deny legitimacy to their cause. Kariuki insists that the resistance movement initially referred to itself as the Kenya Land and Freedom Army (KLFA), and only adopted 'Mau Mau' in response to the term's use in British propaganda.

12 By 1953 this influx from the 'New Commonwealth' had become a concern. The Home Office appointed a working party on 'Coloured People seeking Employment in the United Kingdom', inviting contributions from policemen, immigration officials, etc. over the character of the new arrivals. The subsequent report contained the following excerpts on the character of West Africans: 'Arrogant and violent … and have little regard for law and order and other people's property'; 'work-shy and content to live on national assistance'; 'little more than savages' (cited in Aspden 2007).

13 As we have seen, Foucault understood power as a productive force:

> What gives power its hold, what makes it accepted, is quite simply the fact that it does not weigh like a force, which says no, but that it runs through, and produces, things, it induces pleasures, it forms knowledge, it produces discourses; it must be considered as a productive network which runs through the entire social body much more than as a negative instance whose function is repression.
>
> (1980: 61)

14 While Nietzsche was destroying age-old oppositions in developing his monism and Freud was furthering the cause of psychoanalysis by underscoring the universal importance of emotion and the unconscious, the 'hard' scientific certainties enshrined by Descartes and Newton were slowly being undermined. In 1893 C. S. Peirce fired a broadside against the Age of Reason, and more specifically, its repudiation of chance:

> Chance itself pours in at every avenue of sense: it is of all things the most obtrusive. That it is absolute is the most manifest of all intellectual perceptions … chance does play a part in the real world, apart from what we may know or be ignorant of.
>
> (Quoted in Hacking 1990: 200)

What this amounted to was a rejection of determinism, the doctrine that every fact in the universe is determined by law. The vulgarity of chance was being challenged and the world becoming probabilistic (Hacking 1990). Furthermore, a revival of epistemology occurred in the early twentieth century, particularly in the work of Bertrand Russell and Ernst Mach, which took the inertia of matter as a conceptual given. But as quantum physics attained legitimacy after 1900, with key contributions in Schrödinger's wave mechanics and Heisenberg's quantum mechanics, such assertions became more precarious (Toulmin 1990). Newtonian orthodoxy was also being undercut. Between 1890 and 1910 J. J. Thomson, Albert Einstein, and Max Planck, with their researches in physics, showed that physical theory now relied less on Newton's postulations than was the case in previous eras. Their physical theory was predicated on tiny particles, space and time with no sharp-edged distinctness, and the interchangeable nature of matter and energy. This meant that Newtonian mechanics were no longer indispensable in gaining a rational understanding of Nature (ibid).

15 The thinly-veiled intimations kept on coming, as the authors explained the shortfall of blacks who were subjected to psychometric analysis: 'The requirement that the prisoner be able to read at least at the sixth grade level before taking the Minnesota Multiphasic Personality Inventory resulted in a restricted number of available psychometric indices of impulsivity. This restriction was especially apparent for black prisoners where only 16 test protocols were available from the 54 prisoners' (Dahlstrom et al. 1972: 374).

16 'Truth', said Foucault, 'is to be understood as a system of ordered procedures for the production, regulation, distribution and operation of statements. "Truth" is linked in a circular relation with systems of power which produce and sustain it' (1980: 133).

4 Setting the scene

1 I have changed the names of places (besides London), clubs and people to ensure anonymity.

5 Ways to be urban: people out of place

1 Ong (2006) has provided an account of citizenship and sovereignty under neoliberal regimes.

2 See Benhabib (2004) and Harvey (2005) for discussion of the relationship between territory, capital and individual rights.

3 The Rwandan Genocide occurred in 1994 and saw the murder of an estimated 800,000 people. From early April until mid-July, over 500,000 people were killed (Des Forges 1999). Tutsis and moderate Hutus were targeted by Hutu extremists under the Hutu Power ideology, which alleged that the Tutsi intended to enslave the Hutu and must therefore be resisted at all costs. It was the culmination of longstanding ethnic tension between the minority Tutsi, who had enjoyed power for centuries until the revolution of 1959, and the majority Hutu peoples, who had come to power during the rebellion of 1959–62 by overthrowing the Tutsi monarchy (Melvern 2006).

4 The term Kosovo War denotes two armed conflicts which took place in Kosovo in 1998–99. From early 1998 the war was fought by the army and police of the Federal Republic of Yugoslavia against the Kosovo Liberation Army. From 24 March 1999 to 11 June 1999, NATO attacked Yugoslavia, while ethnic Albanian militants continued battles with Yugoslav forces amid a massive displacement of the Kosovan population estimated to be close to one million people (Judah 2000).

5 On the back of pioneering work by Manuel Castells (1972) and David Harvey (1973) in the area of urbanisation, a number of 'world cities' have been identified (Abrahamson 2004; Akler and Hood 2003; Berelowitz 2010; Brenner and Keil 2006; Knox and Taylor 1995; Marotta 2007; Massey 2007; Sassen 2001). These cities, it is argued, stand apart from other metropolitan centres because of the nodal points they occupy within the global economic system and their related economic, political, infrastructural and cultural qualities. Sassen (2001) compares London, New York and Tokyo in the context of her argument that a 're-scaling' of the strategic territories that articulate the new system has occurred; a system in which the national as a spatial unit has been weakened by privatisation, deregulation, and the associated strengthening of globalisation. For London's role as a 'world city' up to the end of the 1980s, see King (1990). On London's changing industrial structure, namely its shift from an industrial to a service-based city, see Hamnett (2003).

6 Ever since Simmel (1950) [1903] wrote of the impersonality and isolation of the big city in the early twentieth century, a series of authors have speculated on how best to dwell within the metropolis. Members of the Chicago School were quick to take up Simmel's analysis, with Robert Park (1925:43) commenting on the social and cultural heterogeneity of the city and how it 'encourages the fascinating but dangerous experiment of living at the same time in several different contiguous, but otherwise widely separated worlds'. Figures such as Louis Wirth (1938) and Harvey Zorbaugh (1926) – who both worked in and on Chicago – the generalist Lewis Mumford (1938) and, more recently, Richard Sennett (1970, 1977) and Ulf Hannerz (1980), all stand in this tradition of offering interpretations of city life. While, for example, Mumford stressed the dark side of urban life, Sennett argued that the disorder of the city could be harnessed as part of a meaningful communal life.

7 The task of getting to grips with this worldview was a challenging one. However, it also went a long way to foreclosing the possibility of 'going native' and writing an account that emanates 'from the inside', with all the methodological implications that this would entail (Bryman 1988; Fuller 1999; Kanuha 2000; Miles and Huberman 1984).

6 Denizenship, ontology and human difference

1 The M25 motorway, or London Orbital, is a 117-mile orbital motorway that almost encircles Greater London. Some sections, based on the now abandoned London Ringways plan, were constructed in the early 1970s. It was completed in 1986. The M25 is one of the world's longest orbital roads and one of the busiest and most congested parts of Britain's motorway network (Phippen 2004).

2 A Giro or giro transfer is a payment transfer from one bank account to another bank account instigated by the payer, not the payee. Before the use of electronic transfers of payments became the norm in the United Kingdom, the bi-weekly 'giro' payment was the normal way of distributing benefit payments. When unemployment peaked in the 1980s large numbers of people would receive their benefit payment on the same day, with 'Giro Day' being marked by the settlement of small debts and a noticeable increase in binge drinking.

3 Here we see elements of what Nestor Garcia Canclini (2005) has called 'hybrid culture' and, more specifically, his concern with a distinctive urban youth culture shaped by migratory patterns, the novel patterns of adolescents, as well as those 'employed' in informal markets.

4 In his 1903 essay *The Metropolis and Mental Life*, Simmel examined the effects of city living on the mind of the individual. He argued that the metropolis is a location wherein individuality and individual freedom are greatly expanded, with subjective life acting as a defence mechanism (see Simmel 1950 [1903]; Frisby 2002).

5 The Cheltenham Festival takes place annually at Cheltenham Racecourse in Gloucestershire, and is one of the most prestigious meetings in the National Hunt racing calendar in the United Kingdom (with amounts of prize money second only to the Grand National). Large sums of money are gambled during festival week, with hundreds of millions of pounds being staked over the four-day event (Oakley 2011).

References

Abrahamson, M. (2004) *Global Cities*. Oxford: Oxford University Press.

Ackroyd, P. (2000) *London: A Biography*. London: Vintage.

Agamben, G. (2000) *Means without End: Notes on Politics*. Minneapolis: University of Minnesota Press.

Akler, H. and Hood, S. (2003) *Toronto: The Unknown City*. Vancouver, BC: Arsenal Pulp Press.

Alatas, S. H. (1977) *The Myth of the Lazy Native: A Study of the Image of the Malays, Filipinos and Javanese from the 16th to the 20th Century and Its Function in the Ideology of Colonial Capitalism*. London: Routledge.

Allen, A. (2003) 'Foucault and Enlightenment: A Critical Reappraisal'. *Constellations*, **10**(2): 180–98.

Anderson, D. (2006) *Histories of the Hanged: Testimonies from the Mau Mau Rebellion in Kenya*. Gaithersberg, MD: Phoenix Press.

Anstey, R. (1975) *Atlantic Slave Trade and British Abolition, 1760–1810*. Basingstoke, UK: Palgrave Macmillan.

Anzaldúa, G. (1987) *Borderlands/La Frontera: The New Mestiza*. San Francisco, CA: Aunt Lute Books.

Appiah, K. (1992) *In My Father's House: Africa in the Philosophy of Culture*. London: Methuen.

—— (2007) *Cosmopolitanism: Ethics in a World of Strangers*. London: Penguin.

Arnot, C. (2007) 'Peter Squires: Straight Shooter'. *The Guardian*, 16 October.

Aspden, K. (2007) *Nationality – Wog: The Hounding of David Oluwale*. London: Jonathan Cape.

Asuni, T. (1961) 'Suicide in Western Nigeria', in T. Lambo (ed.) *First Pan-African Psychiatric Conference*. Ibadan, Nigeria: Government Printer.

Bacon, F. (1868) [1622] 'An Advertisement Touching an Holy War', in J. Spedding, R. L. Ellis, and D. D. Heath (eds) *The Works of Francis Bacon*. London: Longman.

Baker, S. W. (1870) *The Albert N'Yanza, Great Basin of the Nile and Explorations of the Nile Sources*. London: Macmillan and Co.

Banaji, M. R. (2002) 'Social Psychology of Stereotypes', in N. J. Smelser and P. B. Baltes (eds) *International Encyclopedia of the Social and Behavioral Sciences*. Oxford: Elsevier Science Limited.

Banton, M. (1987) *Racial Theories*. Cambridge, UK: Cambridge University Press.

Barkhoff, J. (2009) 'Romantic Science and Philosophy', in N. Saul (ed.) *The Cambridge Companion to German Romanticism*. New York, NY: Cambridge University Press.

Barnes, J. (1999) *John Barnes: The Autobiography*. London: Headline Book Publishing.

Barrows, S. (1981) *Distorting Mirrors: Visions of the Crowd in Late Nineteenth Century France*. New Haven: Yale University Press.

Bashford, A. and Levine, P. (eds) (2010) *The Oxford Handbook of the History of Eugenics*. New York, NY: Oxford University Press.

Bauböck, R. (2010) 'Studying Citizenship Constellations'. *Journal of Ethnic and Migration Studies*, **36**(5): 847–59.

Bean, R. B. (1906) 'Some Racial Peculiarities of the Negro Brain'. *American Journal of Anthropology*, **V**: 353–432.

Beck, U. (2004) 'Cosmopolitan Realism: On the Distinction between Cosmopolitanism in Philosophy and the Social Sciences', *Global Networks*, **4**: 131–56.

Belton, B. (2004) *Johnnie the One: The John Charles Story*. London: The History Press Ltd.

Benhabib, S. (2004) *The Rights of Others: Aliens, Residents and Citizens*. Cambridge, UK: Cambridge University Press.

Berelowitz, L. (2010) *Dream City: Vancouver and the Global Imagination*. Vancouver, BC: Douglas & McIntyre Ltd.

Berger, J. (1974) *The Look of Things*. New York: The Viking Press.

Bhatt, C. (1999) 'Ethnic Absolutism and the Authoritarian Spirit'. *Theory, Culture & Society*, **16**(2): 65–85.

Biesheuvel, S. (1943) *African Intelligence*. Johannesburg: South African Institute of Race Relations.

Birtley, J. (1975) *The Tragedy of Randolph Turpin*. London: New English Library.

Blalock, H. M. (1962) 'Occupational Discrimination: Some Theoretical Propositions'. *Social Problems*, **9**: 240–7.

Bobo, L. (2001) 'Racial Attitudes and Relations at the Close of the Twentieth Century', in N. J. Smelser, W. J. Wilson and F. Mitchell (eds) *America Becoming: Racial Trends and Their Consequences*. Washington, DC: National Academy Press.

Böhme, H. (1981) 'Romantische Adoleszenzkrisen: Zur Psychodynamik der Venus-kult-Novellen von Tieck, Eichendorff und E. T. A. Hoffmann', in K. Bohnen, S. A. Jârgensen and F. Schmoë (eds) *Literatur und Psychoanalyse. Vorträge des Kolloqiums am 6. und 7. Oktober 1980*. Copenhagen and Munich: Fink.

Bowcott, O. (2011) 'Facebook Riot Calls Earn Men Four-year Jail Terms amid Sentencing Outcry'. *The Guardian*, 16 August.

Bowie, A. (2007) *Music, Philosophy and Modernity*. Cambridge, UK: Cambridge University Press.

Brenner, N. and Keil, R. (2006) *The Global Cities Reader*. London: Routledge.

Brower, J. (1972) 'The Racial Basis of the Division of Labor among Players in the NFL as a Function of Racial Stereotypes'. Paper presented at the Pacific Sociological Association meetings, Portland, OR.

Bryman, A. (1988) *Quantity and Quality in Social Research*. London: Unwin Hyman.

Cabinet Office (2010) 'PM Launches National Citizen Service Pilots'. Cabinet Office, 23 July.

Calhoun, C. (2002) 'The Class Consciousness of Frequent Travellers: Towards a Critique of Actually Existing Cosmopolitanism', in S. Vertovec and R. Cohen (eds) *Conceiving Cosmopolitanism: Theory, Context, and Practice*. Oxford: Oxford University Press.

Canclini, N. G. (2005) *Hybrid Cultures: Strategies for Entering and Leaving Modernity*. Minneapolis: University of Minnesota Press.

Carlyle, T. (1853) *Occasional Discourse on the Nigger Question*. London: Thomas Bosworth.

Carothers, J. C. (1953) *The African Mind in Health and Diseases: A Study in Ethnopsychiatry*. Geneva: WHO Monograph Series.

—— (1954) *The Psychology of the Mau Mau*. Nairobi: Government Printer.

—— (1972) *The Mind of Man in Africa*. London: Tom Stacey.

Cashmore, E. (1988) *Black Sportsmen*. London: Routledge.

Castells, M. (1972) *La Question urbaine*. Paris: Maspero.

Chadwick, H. (2008) *Augustine of Hippo: A Life*. Oxford, UK: Oxford University Press.

Chandrasekhar, S. (1995) *Newton's Principia for the Common Reader*. Alderley, UK: Clarendon Press.

Chapman, A. (2002) *A Companion to Victorian Poetry*. Oxford, UK: Blackwell.

Coleman, K., Hird, C. and Povey, D. (2006) *Violent Crime Overview, Homicide and Gun Crime 2004/2005*. London: Home Office Statistical Bulletin.

Colley, L. (2003) *Britons: Forging the Nation, 1707–1837*. London: Pimlico Books.

Combe, G. (1825) *A System of Phrenology*. Edinburgh: John Anderson.

Communication with the Colonial Office (1866) 'Papers Relating to the Disturbances in Jamaica'. *Parliamentary Papers*, Part 1. Eyre to Cardwell, 8/12/1865, no. 321.

Conservatives.com (2010) 'David Cameron Launches Plan for a National Citizen Service'. 8 April.

Cooper, B. (2007) *Family Fictions and Family Facts: Harriet Martineau, Adolphe Quetelet and the Population Question in England 1798–1859*. London: Routledge.

Critical Eye (1991) *Great Britain United*. 12 September. London: Channel Four.

Dahlstrom, W. G., Welsh, G. S. and Dahlstrom, L. E. (1972). *An MMPI Handbook: Volume I: Clinical Interpretation*. Minneapolis: University of Minnesota Press.

Daily Mail Reporter (2011) 'Rioters May Have "Lower Levels" of Brain Chemical that Keeps Impulsive Behaviour under Control'. *Daily Mail*, 9 August.

Darwin, C. (1859) *The Origin of Species by Means of Natural Selection*. London: J. Murray.

Delanty, G. (2009) *The Cosmopolitan Imagination: The Renewal of Critical Social Theory*. Cambridge, UK: Cambridge University Press.

Dennett, D. C. (1996) *Darwin's Dangerous Idea: Evolution and the Meanings of Life*. London: Penguin.

Derzon, J. (2001) 'Antisocial Behavior and the Prediction of Violence: A Meta-analysis'. *Psychology in the Schools*, **38**(2): 93–106.

Des Forges, A. (1999) *Leave No One to Tell the Story: Genocide in Rwanda*. New York, NY: Human Rights Watch.

Desmond, A. D. and Moore, J. R. (1992) *Darwin*. London: Penguin.

Devine, P. G. (1989) 'Stereotypes and Prejudice: Their Automatic and Controlled Components'. *Journal of Personality and Social Psychology*, **56**(1): 5–18.

Dewey, J. (1930) *The Quest for Certainty: A Study of the Relation of Knowledge and Action*. London: Gifford Lectures.

Dorling, D. (2010) *Injustice: Why Social Inequality Persists*. London: Policy Press.

Drescher, S. (1987) *Capitalism and Antislavery: British Mobilization in Comparative Perspective*. New York, NY: Oxford University Press.

Du Bois, W. E. B. (1897) 'The Conservation of the Races', *American Negro Academy Occasional Papers*, No. 2.

Du Bois, W. E. B. (1983) [1940] *Dusk of Dawn: An Essay Toward an Autobiography of a Race Concept*. Piscataway, NJ: Transaction Publishers.

Duhem, P. (1956) [1906] *La Théorie physique: son objet et sa structure*. Paris: Chevalier & Rivière.

Durkheim, E. (1990) [1912] *Elementary Forms of the Religious Life*. Oxford, UK: Oxford University Press.

Editorial (1788a) ' Halifax Petition'. *Leeds Intelligencer*, 26 February.

—— (1788b) ' Petition'. *Sherborne Mercury*, 24 March.

—— (1792a) 'Halifax Meeting'. *Leeds Intelligencer*, 19 February.

—— (1792b) 'Birmingham Petition'. *Aris's Birmingham Gazette*, 27 February.

—— (1792c) 'Petition'. *Leeds Intelligencer*, 27 February.

—— (1859) 'The Negro'. *John Bull*, 24 December.

—— (1866) 'On the Negro Revolt in Jamaica'. *Saturday Review*, 13 October.

—— (2006) 'Knife UK: The Rise of Knife Culture'. *The Independent*, 04 November.

Edwards, B. (1793) *History of the British West Indies*. Dublin: Luke White.

—— (1796) *The History, Civil, and Commercial, of the British Colonies in the West Indies*. Dublin: Luke White.

Edwards, H. (1973) *Sociology of Sport*. Chicago: Dorsey.

Egan, P. (1823) *Boxiana; or Sketches of Ancient and Modern Pugilism*. London: Sherwood, Jones and Co.

Eitzen, S. and Tessendorf, I. (1978) 'Racial Segregation by Position in Sports: The Special Case of Basketball'. *Review of Sport and Leisure*, 2: 109–28.

Elden, S. and Mendieta, E. (eds) (2011) *Reading Kant's Geography*. New York, NY: State University of New York (SUNY) Press.

Elias, N. (1969) *The Civilizing Process*. Oxford: Blackwell.

—— (1987) *The Society of Individuals*. Oxford: Basil Blackwell.

Elias, N. and Dunning, E. (1986). *The Quest for Excitement: Sport and Leisure in the Civilizing Process*. Oxford: Basil Blackwell.

Elkins, C. (2005) *Britain's Gulag: The Brutal End of Empire in Kenya*. London: Pimlico.

Ellis, H. (1860) *The Criminal*. London: Scott.

England (2009) [1772] *Letters Concerning the Current State of England*. London: General Books LLC.

English Review XI (1788) '"Slavery: A Poem" by Hannah More: A Review'. London.

EstConnexions (2007) *Information, Advice and Guidance Services for Young People in Essex, Southend and Thurrock Needs Assessment 2007/08*. London: EstConnexions.

Evans, J. (2005) *Edward Eyre: Race and Colonial Governance*. North Dunedin, New Zealand: Otago University Press.

Eze, E. C. (ed.) (1997) *Race and Enlightenment: A Reader*. London: Wiley-Blackwell.
—— (2001) *Achieving Our Humanity: The Idea of a Postracial Future*. London: Routledge.
Fabian, J. (1983) *Time and the Other: How Anthropology Makes Its Object*. New York: Columbia University Press.
Ferrara, A. (2007) 'Political Cosmopolitanism and Judgement', *European Journal of Social Theory*, **10**(1): 53–66.
Finlason, W. F. (1869) *Justice to a Colonial Governor; or, Some Considerations on the Case of Mr Eyre*. London: Eyre Defence Committee.
Fiske, S. T. (1998) 'Stereotyping, Prejudice, and Discrimination', in D. T. Gilbert, S. T. Fiske and G. Lindzey (eds) *Handbook of Social Psychology*. New York: McGraw-Hill.
Fleischer, N. (1938) *Black Dynamite: The Story of the Negro in the Prize Ring from 1782 to 1938*. New York: C.J. O'Brien.
Foucault, M. (1970) *The Order of Things: An Archaeology of the Human Sciences*. London: Tavistock Publications.
—— (1977) [1975] *Discipline and Punish*. New York, NY: T Vintage Books USA.
—— (1978) *The History of Sexuality – Volume One: The Will to Knowledge*. London: Penguin.
—— (1980) 'Truth and Power', in C. Gordon (ed.) *Power/Knowledge: Selected Interviews and Other Writings, 1972–1977*. New York: Pantheon.
——(1984a) 'Space, Knowledge, and Power', in P. Rainbow (ed.) *The Foucault Reader*. New York: Pantheon.
—— (1984b) 'What Is Enlightenment?' In P. Rainbow (ed.) *The Foucault Reader*. New York: Pantheon.
—— (2000) [1961] *Madness and Civilization*. London: Routledge.
—— (2001) [1963] *The Birth of the Clinic*. London: Routledge.
—— (2002) [1972] *Archaeology of Knowledge*. London: Routledge.
—— (2007) *Security, Territory, Population: Lectures at the Collège de France, 1977–78*. Basingstoke, UK: Palgrave Macmillan.
—— (2008a) *The Birth of Biopolitics: Lectures at the Collège de France, 1978–1979*. Basingstoke, UK: Palgrave Macmillan.
—— (2008b) *Introduction to Kant's Anthropology*. Cambridge, Mass: MIT Press.
Francis, M. (2007) *Herbert Spencer and the Invention of Modern Life*. Durham, UK: Acumen Publishing.
Fraser, G. M. (1997) *Black Ajax*. London: Harper Collins.
Fraser, R. (1990) *The Making of The Golden Bough: The Origins and Growth of an Argument*. London: Macmillan.
Frazer, J. G. (1890) *The Golden Bough: A Study in Magic and Religion*. London: Macmillan and Co.
Freud, S. (1918) *Totem and Taboo: Some Points of Agreement between the Mental Lives of Savages and Neurotics*. London: Keegan Paul.
—— (2003) [1919] *The Uncanny*. London: Penguin.
Frisby, D. (2002) *Georg Simmel (Key Sociologists)*. London: Routledge.
Fryer, P. (1984) *Staying Power*. London: Pluto.
Fuller, D. (1999) 'Part of the Action, or "Going Native?" Learning to Cope with the "Politics of Integration"'. *Area*, **31**(3): 221–7.
Furst, L. R. (1979) *Romanticism in Perspective*. London: Palgrave Macmillan.

Galton, F. (1869) *Hereditary Genius: An Inquiry into its Laws and Consequences.* London: Macmillan and Co.

Garber, D. (2000) *Descartes Embodied: Reading Cartesian Philosophy through Cartesian Science.* Cambridge, UK: Cambridge University Press.

Geertz, C. (1988) *Works and Lives: The Anthropologist as Author.* Stanford, CA: Stanford University Press.

Geggus, D. P. (1982) *Slavery, War and Revolution: The British Occupation of Saint Domingue 1793–1798.* Oxford: Clarendon.

Gibson, M. (2002) *Born to Crime: Cesare Lombroso and the Origins of Biological Criminology.* Westport, CT: Greenwood Publishing.

Gibson Wilson, E. (1996) *Thomas Clarkson: A Biography.* London: William Sessions Limited.

Giddens, A. (1974) *Positivism and Sociology.* London: Ashgate.

—— (1991) *Modernity and Self-Identity: Self and Society in the Late Modern Age.* Stanford, CA: Stanford University Press.

Gillam, N. W. (2002) *A Life of Sir Francis Galton: From African Exploration to the Birth of Eugenics.* New York, NY: Oxford University Press.

Gilman, S. (1985) *Difference and Pathology: Stereotypes of Sexuality, Race and Madness.* Ithaca, NY: Cornell University Press.

—— (1993) *Freud, Race, and Gender.* Princeton, NJ: Princeton University Press.

Gilroy, P. (2000) *Between Camps: Nations, Cultures and the Allure of Race.* London: Routledge.

—— (2004) *After Empire: Melancholia or Convivial Culture?* London: Routledge.

—— (2009) 'A Response', *British Journal of Sociology*, **60**(1): 33–8.

Glover, J. and Travis, A. (2007) 'Teenage Gang Shootings Blamed on Family Breakdown, Poll Reveals'. *The Guardian*, 23 February.

Godwin, G. (1972) [1859] *Town Swamps and Social Bridges.* New York: Humanities Press.

Gordon, H. L. (1935) 'The Mental Capacity of the African'. *Journal of the African Society*, **33**(132): 226–42.

Green, J. P. (1988) 'Boxing and the "Colour Question"'. *International Journal of the History of Sport*, **5** (1): 115–19.

Grusky, O. (1963) 'The Effects of Formal Structure on Managerial Recruitment: A Study of Baseball Organization'. *Sociometry*, **26**: 345–53.

Hacking, I. (1990) *The Taming of Chance.* Cambridge, UK: Cambridge University Press.

—— (2002a) *Historical Ontology.* Cambridge, Mass: Harvard University Press.

—— (2002b) 'Inaugural Lecture: Chair of Philosophy and History of Scientific Concepts at the Collège de France, 16 January 2001'. *Economy and Society*, **31**(1): 1–14.

Hakluyt, R. (1914) [1589] *The Principal Navigations, Voyages, Traffiques and Discoveries of the English Nation, Made by Sea or Overland to the Remote and Farthest Distant Quarters of the Earth at Any Time within the Compasse of these 1600 Yeares.* London.

Hall, S. (2011) 'The Neoliberal Revolution: Thatcher, Blair, Cameron – the Long March of Neoliberalism Continues'. *Soundings*, 1 July: 9–27.

Hall, S., Critcher, C., Jefferson, T., Clarke, J. and Roberts, B. (1978) *Policing the Crisis: Mugging, the State, and Law and Order.* London: Macmillan.

Hammar, T. (1990) *Democracy and the Nation State: Aliens, Denizens and Citizens in a World of International Migration*. Aldershot, UK: Avesbury.

Hammersley, M. and Atkinson, P. (2004) *Ethnography: Principles in Practice*. London: Routledge.

Hamnett, C. (2003) *Unequal City: London in the Global Arena*. London: Routledge.

Hancock, L. (2008) 'Gun Crime 60% Higher than Government Figures'. (http://bnp. org.uk/2008/10/gun-crime-60-higher-than-government-figures/)

Hannaford, I. (1996) *Race: The History of an Idea in the West*. Washington, DC: Woodrow Wilson Center Press.

Hannerz, U. (1980) *Exploring the City. Inquiries Toward an Urban Anthropology*. New York, NY: Columbia University Press.

Hansard (1805) 'Commons Sitting: The Slave Trade'. *The Official Report*, 28 February.

Hansen, A. (2004) 'Ron's Gone, but Not Forgotten'. *Daily Telegraph*, 26 April.

Haraway, D. (1990) *Primate Visions: Gender, Race, and Nature in the World of Modern Science*. London: Routledge.

—— (1995) 'Universal Donors in a Vampire Culture: It's All in the Family: Biological Kinship Categories in the Twentieth Century United States', in W. Cronon (ed.), *Uncommon Ground: Toward Reinventing Nature*. New York: W. W. Norton.

Harding, J. (2007) 'London Calling'. *The Times*, 13 March.

Haringey Community and Police Consultative Group (2005) (http://www. haringeycpcg.org.uk/documents/Minutes_25_May_2005.doc)

Harvey, D. (1973) *Social Justice and the City*. London: Edward Arnold.

—— (1990) *The Condition of Postmodernity: An Enquiry into the Origins of Cultural Change*. Oxford, UK: Blackwell Publishers.

—— (2005) *A Brief History of Neoliberalism*. Oxford: Oxford University Press.

—— (2006) *Paris, Capital of Modernity*. London and New York: Routledge.

—— (2009) *Cosmopolitanism and the Geographies of Freedom*. New York: Columbia University Press.

—— (2010) *The Enigma of Capital and the Crises of Capitalism*. London: Profile Books.

Healy, J. (1991) 'Introduction', in Pliny the Elder *Natural History: A Selection*. London: Penguin.

Heilbrun, A. B. and Heilbrun, K. S. (1977) 'The Black Minority Criminal and Violent Crime: The Role of Self-Control'. *British Journal of Criminology*, **17**: 370–7.

Heilbrun, A. B., Knopf, I. J. and Bruner, P. (1976) 'Criminal Impulsivity and Violence'. *British Journal of Criminology*, **16**: 376–7.

Held, D. (2010) *Cosmopolitanism: Ideals and Realities*. London: Polity Press.

Henderson, M. (1982) 'An Empirical Classification of Convicted Violent Offenders'. *British Journal of Criminology*, **22**: 1–20.

Herder, G. H. (1912) *Sämtliche Werke, VIII*. Berlin: Weidmann.

Hern, E., Glazebrook, W. and Beckett, M. (2005) 'Reducing Knife Crime'. *British Medical Journal*, **330**: 1221–2.

Highfield, R., Berry, A. and Harnden, T. (1995) 'Get Set for the 3–1/2 Minute Mile'. *The Guardian*, 14 September.

Higman, B. W. (2010) *A Concise History of the Caribbean*. Cambridge, UK: Cambridge University Press.

Hill, D. (2001) *Out of His Skin: The John Barnes Phenomenon*. London: WSC Books Limited.

HM Government (2008) *Home Affairs Select Committee Inquiry: Young Black People and the Criminal Justice System*. London: HM Government.

Hoberman, J. (1997) *Darwin's Athletes: How Sport Has Damaged Black America*. Boston, MA: Houghton Mifflin.

Hoffmann, E. T. A. (2008) [1816] *Der Sandmann* [The Sandman]. Berlin: Deutscher Taschenbuch Verlag.

Home Office (2004) *Black and Asian Offenders on Probation*. London: Home Office Research, Development and Statistics Directorate.

Hooks, B. (1984) *Feminist Theory: From Margin to Center*. Boston: South End Press.

House of Commons Committee of Public Accounts (2011) *The Youth Justice System in England and Wales: Reducing Offending by Young People*. London: The Stationery Office.

Huard, R. L. (2006) *Plato's Political Philosophy: The Cave*. Washington, DC: Algora Publishing.

Hume, D. (1964) [1753] *Essays Moral, Political, and Literary*. Darmstadt: Scientia Verlag Aalen.

Hunt, J. (1864) *Negro's Place in Nature: A Paper Read Before the London Anthropological Society*. New York: Van Evrie, Horton & Co.

Ingram, J. K. (1888) *A History of Political Economy*. Edinburgh.

Isin, E. (1992) *Cities Without Citizens: Modernity of the City as a Corporation*. Montreal and New York: Black Rose Books.

James, C. L. R. (2001) [1938] *The Black Jacobins: Toussaint l'Ouverture and the San Domingo Revolution*. London: Penguin.

Johnson, B. (2006) 'Lefty Thinking'. (http://www.boris-johnson.com/2006/02/09/lefty-thinking/).

Jones, E. (1953) *The Life and Work of Sigmund Freud*. Harmondsworth: Penguin Books in association with Hogarth Press.

Jones, N. J. (1970) 'Difficult Boys in Approved Schools'. *British Journal of Criminology*, **10**: 136–46.

Joppke, C. (2010) 'The Inevitable Lightening of Citizenship'. *European Journal of Sociology* 51: 9–32.

Jordan, M. (2005) *The Great Abolition Sham: The True Story of the End of the British Slave Trade*. Stroud, Gloucestershire: The History Press.

Josephus, F. (1851) *Complete Works of Flavius Josephus*. London: Attic Books.

Judah, T. (2000) *Kosovo: War and Revenge*. New Haven, CT: Yale University Press.

Judowitz, D. (1988) *Subjectivity and Representation in Descartes: The Origins of Modernity*. Cambridge, UK: Cambridge University Press.

Jung, C. G. (1930) *Modern Man in Search of a Soul*. London: Mariner Books.

—— (1970) 'Archaic Man', in H. Read (ed.) *The Collected Works of C. G. Jung*. London: Routledge and Kegan Paul.

Juhasz, A. (2004) 'Ambitions of Empire: The Bush Administration Economic Plan for Iraq (and Beyond)'. *Left Turn Magazine*, **12**: 27–32.

Kant, I. (1974) [c.1772] *Anthropology from a Pragmatic Point of View*. The Hague: Martinus Nijhoff.

—— (1999) [c.1756] *Geographie (Physische Geographie)*. Paris: Bibliothèque Philisophique.

Kanuha, V. K. (2000) '"Being" Native versus "Going Native": Conducting Social Work Research as an Insider'. *Social Work*, **5**(1): 439–47.

Kariuki, J. M. (1975) *'Mau Mau' Detainee: The Account by a Kenya African of His Experiences in Detention Camps 1953–1960.* New York and London: Oxford University Press.

Kaufmann, W. (1974) *Nietzsche: Philosopher, Psychologist, Antichrist.* Princeton, NJ: Princeton University Press.

Keith, M. (2005) *After the Cosmopolitan? Multicultural Cities and the Future of Racism.* London: Routledge.

Kelner, M. (2010) 'Why Alan Shearer Could Find Plum Job as a Behavioural Geneticist'. *The Guardian*, 30 August.

Khan, S. M. (2000) *The Shallow Graves of Rwanda.* London and New York: I. B. Tauris.

Kiernan, V. G. (1969) *The Lords of Human Kind: European Attitudes towards the Outside World in the Imperial Age.* London: Weidenfeld & Nicolson.

Kilminster, R. (1989) 'Editor's Introduction', in N. Elias. *The Symbol Theory.* London: Sage.

King, A. D. (1990) *Global Cities: Post-Imperialism and the Internationalization of London.* London: Routledge.

Kluckhohn, P. (1941) *Das Ideengut der deutschen Romantik.* Tübingen: Niemeyer.

Knox, P. L. and Taylor, P. J. (1995) *World Cities in a World System.* Cambridge, UK: Cambridge University Press.

Knox, R. (1850) *The Races of Men: A Fragment.* Philadelphia: Lea & Blanchard.

Kramer, M. H. (1997) *John Locke and the Origins of Private Property: Philosophical Explorations of Individualism, Community, and Equality.* Cambridge, UK: Cambridge University Press.

Ladyman, I. (2007) 'Sad Shaun Fails to Take His Chance'. *Daily Mail*, 8 February.

Lagden, G. Y. (1924) *The Native Races of the Empire.* London.

Lashley, H. (1989) 'Black Participation in British Sport: Opportunity or Control?' *Coaching Focus*, **7**: 41–53.

Laski, H. (1997) [1936] *The Rise of European Liberalism.* New Brunswick, NJ: Transaction Publishers.

—— (2007) [1920] *Political Thought in England from Locke to Bentham.* Fairford, UK: Echo Library.

Laubscher, B. J. F. (1937) *Sex, Custom and Psychopathology: A Study of South African Pagan Natives.* London: Routledge and Kegan Paul.

Lawrence, W. (1819) *Lectures on Physiology, Zoology and the Natural History of Man.* London: J. Callow.

Lawson, T. T. (2007) *Carl Jung, Darwin of the Mind.* London: Karnac Books.

Le Bon, G. (2008) [1895] *The Crowd: A Study of the Popular Mind.* Minneapolis, MA: Filiquarian Publishing.

Lefebvre, H. (1991) *The Production of Space.* Oxford: Blackwell Publishers.

Levy-Bruhl, L. (1923) *Primitive Mentality.* London: Allen & Unwin.

—— (1926) *How Natives Think.* London: Allen & Unwin.

Linebaugh, P. and Rediker, M. (2000) *The Many-headed Hydra: Sailors, Slaves, Commoners, and the Hidden History of the Revolutionary Atlantic.* London: Verso.

Linnaeus, C. (1792) *The Animal Kingdom, or Zoological System of the Celebrated Sir Charles Linnaeus.* Translated by R. Kerr, J. Murray and R. Faulder. London: J. Murray.

Lipsey, M. W. and Derzon, J. H. (1998) 'Predictors of Violent or Serious Delinquency in Adolescence and Early Adulthood: A Synthesis of Longitudinal Research', in R. Loeber and D. P. Farrington (eds) *Serious and Violent Juvenile Offenders: Risk Factors and Successful Interventions*. Thousand Oaks CA: Sage.

Locke, J. (1880) [1693] *Thoughts Concerning Education*. London: Spottiswood.

—— (1960) [1662] *Second Treatise on Government*. New York: Mentor Books.

—— (1975) [1690]. *An Essay Concerning Human Understanding*. Oxford: Clarendon Press.

Lombroso, C. (2006) [1876] *Criminal Man*. Translated and with a new introduction by M. Gibson and N.H. Rafter. Durham, NC: Duke University Press.

Lombroso, C. and Lombroso-Ferrero, G. (1911) *Criminal Man, According to the Classification of Cesare Lombroso*. New York: Putnam.

Long, E. (2002) [1774] *The History of Jamaica: Reflections on Its Situation, Settlements, Inhabitants, Climate, Products, Commerce, Laws, and Government*. Montreal: McGill-Queen's University Press.

Longmore, A. (1988) *Viv Anderson*. Suffolk: Richard Clay Ltd.

Lorimer, D. A. (1978) *Colour, Class and the Victorians: English Attitudes to the Negro in the Mid-nineteenth Century*. Leicester: Leicester University Press.

Lovejoy, A. O. (1976) *The Great Chain of Being: A Study of the History of an Idea*. New York: Harper & Row.

Lovell, N. (1998) 'Introduction', in N. Lovell (ed.) *Locality and Belonging*. London: Routledge.

Loy, J. and McElvogue, J. (1970) 'Racial Segregation in American Sport'. *International Review of Sport Sociology*, 5: 5–23.

Maguire, J. (1988) 'Race and Position Assignment in English Soccer: A Preliminary Analysis of Ethnicity and Sport in Britain'. *Sociology of Sport Journal*, 5: 257–69.

Mahone, S. and Vaughan, M. (2007) *Psychiatry and Empire*. Basingstoke and New York: Palgrave Macmillan.

Majdalany, F. (1963) *State of Emergency: The Full Story of Mau Mau*. Boston, MA: Houghton Mifflin.

Manuel, F. E. (1971) *French Utopias: An Anthology of Ideal Societies*. New York: Free Press.

Marotta, V. (2007) 'Multicultural and Multiethnic Cities in Australia', in R. Hutchison and J. Krase (eds) *Ethnic Landscapes in an Urban World*. Oxford: JAI/Elsevier.

Marrin, M. (2008) 'Britain is Creating Youths Who Have Nothing to Lose by Crime'. *The Times*, 13 July.

Marx, K. and Engels, F. (2005) [1848] *The Communist Manifesto*. London: Penguin Classics.

Massey, D. B. (2007) *World City*. London: Polity Press.

Mayhew, H. (1851) *London Labour and the London Poor: A Cyclopaedia of the Condition and Earnings of Those that Will Work, Those that Cannot Work, and Those that Will Not Work*. New York: Harper.

McClintock, A. (1995). *Imperial Leather: Race, Gender, and Sexuality in the Colonial Contest*. New York: Routledge.

McCulloch, J. (1995) *Colonial Psychiatry and 'the African Mind'*. Cambridge, UK: Cambridge University Press.

McGee, O. (2007) *The IRB: The Irish Republican Brotherhood, from the Land League to Sinn Fein*. Dublin: Four Courts Press.

McGurk, B. (1978) 'Personality Types among "Normal" Homicides'. *British Journal of Criminology*, **18**: 146–61.

Megargee, E. I. (1966) 'Undercontrolled and Overcontrolled Personality Types in Extreme Anti-social Aggression'. *Psychological Monographs, 80*: 611–28.

Mehta, U. S. (1999) *Liberalism and Empire: A Study in Nineteenth-Century British Liberal Thought*. Chicago: University of Chicago Press.

Melvern, L. (2006) *Conspiracy to Murder: The Rwandan Genocide*. London: Verso Books.

Menn, S. (1998) *Descartes and Augustine*. Cambridge, UK: Cambridge University Press.

Merleau-Ponty, M. (1973) 'Phenomenology and the Science of Man', in M.A. Natanson (ed.) *Phenomenology and the Social Sciences*. Evanston, Ill: Northwestern University Press.

Mignolo, W. D. (2000a) *Local Histories/Global Designs: Coloniality, Subaltern Knowledges, and Border Thinking*. Princeton, NJ: Princeton University Press.

—— (2000b) 'The Many Faces of Cosmo-polis: Border Thinking and Critical Cosmopolitanism'. *Public Culture*, **12**(3): 721–48.

Miles, M. B. and Huberman, A. M. (1984) *Qualitative Data Analysis: A Sourcebook of New Methods*. London: Sage.

Mill, J. S. (1859) *On Liberty*. London: J.W. Parker and Son.

Monbiot, G. (2012) 'Deny the British Empire's Crimes? No, We Ignore Them'. *The Guardian*, 23 April.

Montesquieu, C.S. (1959) [1748] *De l'esprit des Lois*. Paris: Larousse Kingfisher Chambers.

Moynihan, I. (2012) '18-year-old Jailed for Attack on Ashraf Rossli'. *The Independent*, 9 March.

Muckenhoupt, M. (1997) *Sigmund Freud: Explorer of the Unconscious*. Oxford, UK: Oxford University Press.

Mumford, L. (1938) *The Culture of Cities*. New York: Secker & Warburg.

Murphy, T. (2004) *Pliny the Elder's Natural History: The Empire in the Encyclopaedia*. Oxford, UK: Oxford University Press.

National Audit Office (2008) *Violent Crime: Risk models, Effective Interventions, and Risk Management*. London: NAO.

Newton, I. (1991) [1687] *The Principia: Mathematical Principles of Natural Philosophy*. Berkeley: University of California Press.

Niekerk, C. (2009) 'The Romantics and Other Cultures', in N. Saul (ed.) *The Cambridge Companion to German Romanticism*. New York, NY: Cambridge University Press.

Nietzsche, F. (1969) [1887] *Thus Spoke Zarathustra: A Book for Everyone and No One*. Harmondsworth, England: Penguin Books.

—— (1973) [1895] *The Anti-Christ*. London, UK: Filiquarian Publishing.

—— (1973) [1901] *The Will to Power: In Science, Nature, Society and Art*. NY: Random House USA Inc.

—— (1983) [1874] *Untimely Meditations*. Cambridge, UK: Cambridge University Press.

Nkrumah, K. (1973) *Revolutionary Path*. London: Panaf Books Ltd.

Nordau, M. S. and Mosse, G. L. (1993) *Degeneration*. Lincoln, NE: University of Nebraska Press.

Nym Mayhall, L. E. (2003) *The Militant Suffrage Movement: Citizenship and Resistance in Britain, 1860–1930*. New York, NY: Oxford University Press, USA.

Oakley, R. (2011) *The Cheltenham Festival: A Centenary History*. London: Aurum Press.

Oglaza, G. (2011). 'Clegg Vows Lib Dems Will Have Stronger Voice'. *Sky News*, 11 May.

Oldfield, J. R. (1998) *Popular Politics and British Anti-Slavery: The Mobilisation of Public Opinion against the Slave Trade, 1787–1807*. London: Routledge.

Ong, A. (2006) *Neoliberalism as Exception: Mutations in Citizenship and Sovereignty*. Durham, NC: Duke University Press.

Ornstein, R. E. (1992) *Evolution of Consciousness: Darwin, Freud and the Cranial Fire – The Origins of the Way We Think*. Upper Saddle River, NJ: Prentice Hall.

Pareto, V. F. D. (1971) [1908] *Manual of Political Economy*. Fairfield, NJ: Augustus M. Kelley.

Park, R. E. (1925) 'The City: Suggestions for the Investigation of Human Behavior in the Urban Environment', in R. E. Park, E. W. Burgess and R. D. McKenzie (eds) *The City*. Chicago: University of Chicago Press.

Phillips, C. (2007) *Foreigners – Three English Lives*. London: Harvill Secker.

Phippen, R. (2004) *The M25: Travelling Clockwise*. London: Pallas Athene Arts.

Pitt Rivers, A. H. (1891) 'Typological Museums, as Exemplified by the Pitt Rivers Museum at Oxford, and His Provincial Museum at Farnham, Dorset'. *Journal for the Society of Arts*, **40**: 15–22.

Pitts, J. (2006) *A Turn to Empire: The Rise of Imperial Liberalism in Britain and France*. Princeton, NJ: Princeton University Press.

Plato (1987) [c. 380BC] *The Republic*. London: Penguin.

Pliny the Elder (1991) [77AD] *Natural History: A Selection*. London: Penguin.

Poe, D. Z. (2003) *Kwame Nkrumah's Contribution to Pan-Africanism: An Afrocentric Analysis*. New York and London: Routledge.

Pollock, J. (2007) *Wilberforce*. London: Kingsway.

Porter, R. (2001) *The Penguin Social History of Britain: English Society in the Eighteenth Century*. London, UK: Penguin.

Porteus, S. and Babcock, M. (1926) *Temperament and Race*. Boston: Richard G. Badger.

Prime Minister's Office (2011) 'PM's Speech at Munich Security Conference'. (http://www.number10.gov.uk)

Prins, H. A. (1969) 'Some Thoughts on the Unstable Offender'. *British Journal of Criminology*, **9**: 51–61.

Prior, I. (2004) 'TV Pundit Ron Atkinson Sacked for Racist Remark'. *The Guardian*, 22 April.

Pugh, M. (1986) *Women's Suffrage in Britain, 1867–1928*. London: The Historical Association.

Quetelet, A. (1835) *A Treatise on Man and the Development of His Faculties*. Edinburgh: W. & R. Chambers.

Quigley, R. (2010). 'Your Country Needs You: Cameron Launches National Service Summer Camp for Teens'. *Daily Mail*, 22 July.

Quilley, S. (2004) 'Ecology, "Human Nature" and Civilising Processes: Biology and Sociology in the Work of Norbert Elias', in S. Loyal and S. Quilley (eds) *The Sociology of Norbert Elias*. Cambridge: Cambridge University Press.

—— (2010) 'Integrative Levels and "the Great Evolution": Organicist Biology and the Sociology of Norbert Elias'. *Journal of Classic Sociology*, **10**(4): 391–419.

Richter, J. P. F. (Jean Paul) (1970) *Sämtliche Werke*. Munich: Hanser.

Ritchie, J. F. (1943) *The African as Suckling and as Adult: A Psychological Study*. Manchester: Rhodes-Livingston Institute.

Rose, N. (1999) *Powers of Freedom: Reframing Political Thought*. Cambridge, UK: Cambridge University Press.

—— (2000) *Governing the Self*. London: Free Association Books.

—— (2006) *The Politics of Life Itself: Biomedicine, Power, and Subjectivity in the Twenty-First Century*. Princeton, NJ: Princeton University Press.

Rosen, F. (2003) *Classical Utilitarianism from Hume to Mill*. London: Routledge.

Rousseau, J. J. (1761) *La nouvelle He?loi?se*. Paris: Firmin-Didot.

—— (1964) [1762] *Emile*. London: Basic Books.

Russett, C. (1989) *Sexual Science: The Victorian Construction of Womanhood*. Cambridge, Mass: Harvard University Press.

Said, E. (1978) *Orientalism*. London: Routledge & Kegan Paul Ltd.

Saint Augustine of Hippo (1991) [c.390AD] *On True Religion*. Washington, DC: Regnery Publishing.

Sampson, R. J. (2009) 'Disparity and Diversity in the Contemporary City: Social (Dis)Order Revisited'. *British Journal of Sociology*, **60**(1): 1–31.

Sampson, R. J. and Raudenbush, S. W. (2004) 'Seeing Disorder: Neighborhood Stigma and the Social Construction of Broken Windows'. *Social Psychology Quarterly*, **67**(4): 319–42.

Sassen, S. (2001) *The Global City: New York, London, Tokyo*. Princeton, NJ: Princeton University Press.

—— (2006) *Territory, Authority, Rights: From Medieval to Global Assemblages*. Princeton, NJ: Princeton University Press.

Schelling, F. W. J. (2004) [1799] *First Outline of a System of a Philosophy of Nature*. New York, NY: State University of New York Press.

—— (2011) [1798] *Von der Weltseele* [On the World-Soul]. Charleston, SC: Nabu Press.

Schlutz, A. M. (2009) *Mind's World: Imagination and Subjectivity from Descartes to Romanticism*. Washington, DC: University of Washington Press.

Schmidt, R. (2009) 'From Early to Late Romanticism', in N. Saul (ed.) *The Cambridge Companion to German Romanticism*. New York, NY: Cambridge University Press.

Seller, J. (1685) *A New Systeme: Of Geography*. London: John Seller.

Semmel, B. (1962) *The Governor Eyre Controversy*. London: MacGibbon and Kee.

Sennett, R. (1970) *The Uses of Disorder: Personal Identity and City Life*. London: Penguin Books.

—— (1977) *The Fall of Public Man*. London: Penguin Books.

Sequeira, J. H. (1932) 'The Brain of the East African Native'. *The British Medical Journal*, **1**(3715): 580–1.

Sewell, M. (2008) 'Race'. (http://race.martinsewell.com)

Seyhan, A. (2009) 'What is Romanticism, and Where Did It Come from?', in N. Saul (ed.) *The Cambridge Companion to German Romanticism*. New York, NY: Cambridge University Press.

Shachar, A. (2009) *The Birthright Lottery*. Cambridge, MA: Harvard University Press.

Shelley, H. and Watson, W. (1936) 'An Investigation Concerning Mental Disorder in the Nyasaland Natives'. *Journal of Mental Science*, **82**: 701–30.

Silvestri, A., Oldfield, M., Squires, P. and Grimshaw, R. (2009) *Young People, Knives and Guns: A comprehensive Review, Analysis and Critique of Gun and Knife Crime Strategies*. London: Centre for Crime and Justice Studies.

Simmel, G. (1950) [1903] 'The Metropolis and Mental Life', in K. H. Wolff (ed.) *The Sociology of Georg Simmel*. New York: The Free Press.

—— (1969) 'Faithfulness and Gratitude', in K. H. Wolff (ed.) *The Sociology of Georg Simmel*. New York: The Free Press.

Speke, J. H. (1864) 'Captain Speke's Journal: The Journal of the Discovery of the Nile' *Blackwood's Edinburgh Magazine* No. DLXXIX, VOl. XCV. January 1864: 1–24.

Skeat, W. W. (1924) *An Etymological Dictionary of the English Language*. Oxford: Clarendon Press.

Smith, A. (1986) [1776] *The Wealth of Nations*. London: Penguin.

Soanes, C. (ed.) (2002) *Oxford English Dictionary*. Oxford: Oxford University Press.

Soja, E. (1989) *Postmodern Geographies: The Reassertion of Space in Critical Social Theory*. London and New York: Verso.

—— (1996) *Thirdspace: Journeys to Los Angeles and Other Real-and-Imagined Places*. Cambridge, Mass: Blackwell Publishers.

—— (2000) *Postmetropolis: Critical Studies of Cities and Regions*. Cambridge, Mass: Blackwell Publishers.

Southey, R. (1829) *Colloquies on the Progress and Prospects of Society*. London: Longman and Roberts.

Spadafora, D. (1990) *The Idea of Progress in Eighteenth-Century Britain*. New Haven: Yale University Press.

Spencer, H. (1876) *The Principles of Sociology*. London: Macmillan.

Spencer, I. R. G. (1997) *British Immigration Policy Since 1939: The Making of Multi-racial Britain*. London: Routledge.

Spivak, G. C. (1988) 'Can the Subaltern Speak? Speculations on Widow Sacrifice', in C. Nelson and L. Grossberg (eds) *Marxism and the Interpretation of Culture*. London: Macmillan.

Steele, J. (2002) 'Police Fear Crime Explosion as School-age Muggers Graduate to Guns'. *The Telegraph*, 2 January.

Stepan, N. (1982) *The Idea of Race in Science: Great Britain 1800–1960*. Hamden, Conn: Archon Books.

Stocking, G.W. (1968) *Race, Culture and Evolution: Essays in the History of Anthropology*. Chicago: University of Chicago Press.

—— (1987) *Victorian Anthropology*. London: Collier Macmillan.

—— (1996) *Romantic Motives: Essays on Anthropological Sensibility*. Madison, WI: University of Wisconsin Press.

Storkey, M., Maguire, J. and Lewis, R. (1997) *Cosmopolitan London: Past, Present and Future*. London: London Research Centre.

Stump, E. and Kretzmann, N. (2001) *The Cambridge Companion to Augustine*. Cambridge, UK: Cambridge University Press.

Sullivan, E. P. (1983) 'Liberalism and Imperialism: J. S. Mill's Defense of the British Empire'. *Journal of the History of Ideas*, 44(4): 599–617.

Sumner, P., Boy, F., and Chambers, C. (2011) 'Riot Control: How Can We Stop Newspapers Distorting Science?'. *The Guardian*, 22 August.

Tarde, G. (2005) [1890] *The Laws of Imitation*. New York, NY: Bibliolife.

Taylor, C. (1989) *Sources of the Self: The Making of the Modern Identity*. Cambridge, UK: Cambridge University Press.

Thomas, D. A. (1995) *Music and the Origins of Language: Theories from the French Enlightenment*. Cambridge, UK: Cambridge University Press.

Thomson, I. (2009) *The Dead Yard: Tales of Modern Jamaica*. London: Faber and Faber.

Tilley, C. (1994) *A Phenomenology of Landscape: Places, Paths and Monuments*. Oxford and Providence, RI: Berg.

Tomlinson, S. (2005) *Head Masters: Phrenology, Secular Education, and Nineteenth-century Social Thought*. Tuscaloosa, AL: The University of Alabama Press.

Toulmin, S. (1982) *The Discovery of Time*. London: Hutchinson.

—— (1990) *Cosmopolis: The Hidden Agenda of Modernity*. Chicago: University of Chicago Press.

Travis, A. and Stratton, A. (2011) 'David Cameron's Solution for Broken Britain: Tough Love and Tougher Policing'. *The Guardian*, 16 August.

Tyndall, J. [to J. D. Hooker] (1867) Copies of Letters in Huxley Papers. Nov 1866, 10: 318.

UNESCO (1950) *Unesco and Its Programme: The Race Question*. Paris: UNESCO.

Unger, R. (1975) *Hölderlin's Major Poetry*. Bloomington, IA: Indiana University Press.

Vasili, P. (1998) *The First Black Footballer: Arthur Wharton 1865–1930*. London: Frank Cass.

—— (2000) *Colouring over the White Line: The History of Black Footballers in Britain*. Edinburgh: Mainstream Publishing.

Vieira, P. and Beckerman, D. (2005) *Vieira: My Autobiography*. London: Orion.

von Hardenberg, G. P. F. (Novalis) (1953) *Sämtliche Werke*. Heidelberg: Verlag Lambert Schneider.

Wacquant, L. (2008) *Urban Outcasts: A Comparative Sociology of Advanced Marginality*. Cambridge, UK: Polity Press.

—— (2009) *Punishing the Poor: The Neoliberal Government of Social Insecurity*. Durham, NC and London: Duke University Press.

Waldron, J. (2002) *God, Locke, and Equality: Christian Foundations in Locke's Political Thought*. Cambridge, UK: Cambridge University Press.

Walvin, J. (1973) *Black and White: The Negro and English Society, 1555–1945*. London: Allen Lane.

Warnek, P. (2006) *Descent of Socrates: Self-Knowledge and Cryptic Nature in the Platonic Dialogues*. Indianapolis, IA: Indiana University Press.

Weakly, K. (2011). 'Cameron Launches National Citizen Service Recruitment Drive'. *Civil Society*, 17 February.

West, D.J. (1988) *The Delinquent Way of Life*. London: Heinemann Educational.

White, M. (2011). 'Muscular Liberalism: Nick Clegg Finds New Use for an Old Phrase'. *The Guardian*, 11 May.

Williams, E. (1964) *Capitalism and Slavery*. London: Andre Deutsch.

Williams, L. L. (2000) *Nietzsche's Mirror: The World as Will to Power*. Lanham, MD: Rowman & Littlefield.

Williams, R. and Youssef, Z. (1979) 'Race and Position Assignment in High School, College and Professional Football'. *International Journal of Sport Psychology*, **10**: 252–8.

Williams, Z. (2011) 'The UK Riots: The Psychology of Looting'. *The Guardian*, 9 August.

Wirth, L. (1938) 'Urbanism as a Way of Life'. *American Journal of Sociology*, **44**: 1–24.

Wolpoff, M. and Caspari, R. (2007) *Race and Human Evolution: A Fatal Attraction*. New York, NY: Simon & Schuster.

Woodcock, A., Bentley, D. and Churcher, J. (2010) 'David Cameron Launches National Citizen Service Scheme'. *The Independent*, 8 April.

Wright, I. (1997) *Mr Wright: The Explosive Autobiography of Ian Wright*. London: Harper Collins.

—— (2010) 'Hansen's Theo Blast So Wrong'. *The Sun*, 24 August.

Young, R. J. C. (1995) 'Foucault on Race and Colonialism'. *New Formations*, **25**: 57–65.

Zorbaugh, H. W. (1926) *The Natural Areas of the City*. Chicago: University of Chicago Press.

Index

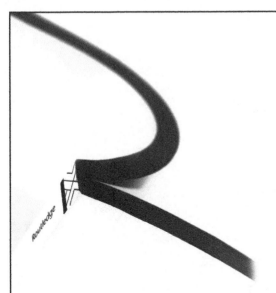